Learie Constantine and Race Relations in Britain and the Empire

Learie Constantine and Race Relations in Britain and the Empire

Jeffrey Hill

BLOOMSBURY ACADEMIC
LONDON • NEW YORK • OXFORD • NEW DELHI • SYDNEY

BLOOMSBURY ACADEMIC
Bloomsbury Publishing Plc
50 Bedford Square, London, WC1B 3DP, UK
1385 Broadway, New York, NY 10018, USA

BLOOMSBURY, BLOOMSBURY ACADEMIC and the Diana logo are trademarks of
Bloomsbury Publishing Plc

First published in Great Britain 2019
Paperback edition published 2020

Cover image: Trinidadian-British cricketer Learie Constantine (1901–1971), 28 June 1944.
(© Keystone/Hulton Archive/Getty Images)

A catalogue record for this book is available from the British Library.

A catalog record for this book is available from the Library of Congress.

ISBN: HB: 978-1-3500-6983-1
PB: 978-1-3501-6874-9
ePDF: 978-1-3500-6984-8
eBook: 978-1-3500-6985-5

Typeset by Newgen KnowledgeWorks Pvt. Ltd., Chennai, India

To find out more about our authors and books visit www.bloomsbury.com
and sign up for our newsletters.

Contents

Figures

Acknowledgements

As with everything I have ever written, little could have been accomplished without someone else's help. For this project, then, my special thanks are owed to the archivists and librarians of the following organizations for granting me access to material in their keeping:

National Library and Information System (NALIS) Port of Spain, Trinidad, with special thanks to librarians Donna Hall-Commissiong, Jasmin Simmons, Elizabeth Sorzano, Marguerite Anne Moore and all at the Heritage Library

British Library, London

Institute of Commonwealth Studies, Senate House, London

Manuscripts and Rare Book Library, Columbia University, New York

BBC Written Archives, Caversham Park, Reading

National Archives, Kew, London

Church of England Archives, Lambeth Palace, London

MCC Archives, Lord's Cricket Ground, London

Cadbury Research Library, Birmingham University

Nelson Cricket Club

Borough of Lambeth Archives, London

I am grateful to Learie Constantine's daughter, Mrs Gloria Valere, for allowing me to use photographic images from the Lord Constantine Collection at NALIS, and for very kindly taking the time to talk to me about her father on 23 September 2016; to the *Evening Standard* for permission to include the cartoon 'Imperial Welcome' by David Low; to the National Portrait Gallery, London, for permission to use the portrait of Constantine by Godfrey Argent; and to the BBC for allowing me to quote from material in its Written Archives. Some material in Chapter 4 previously appeared in ' "Connie" – Local Hero, National Icon: Cricket, Race and Politics in the Life of Learie Constantine', *Sports Historian*, 22 (i), 2002, 70–99; I am grateful to Professor Dave Day, editor-in-chief of *Sport in History*, for giving permission for me to draw upon it.

For their advice and inspiration, I owe a deep gratitude to Jack Williams, John Bale, Richard Holt and Neil Carter; as I do also to Beatriz Lopez of Bloomsbury Academic for her help in steering the book through publication, and to the publisher's two anonymous reviewers for their very helpful comments on my manuscript.

Mary has put up with my absences, and the expense of them, involved in all those research visits; and, together with Katharine, Tim and Richard, has cast a benevolent eye and a calming influence over the whole process.

Preface

It was my father who first introduced me to Learie Constantine – not in the flesh, that is, but through some of the many stories that did the rounds in Lancashire seventy and more years ago. He had watched 'Connie' at Seedhill in the 1930s and had himself played a few games for Nelson in the early years of the 1939–45 War. I recall his showing me a wristwatch he had bought himself from the proceeds of a collection for taking three catches from fierce drives in a Lancashire League match. One of them might have dismissed Winston Place, but my Dad was something of a romancer, so it might not. By this time Constantine had left Nelson Cricket Club, and the cricketer who my father most admired was not Constantine but his successor at Nelson, Lala Amarnath. Lala was a fine player, and a bit of a rebel who had fallen foul of his team's management during the Indians' tour of England in 1936. But he never acquired the legendary status of Constantine. No one did. Connie had after all been at Nelson for nine seasons. He was an institution in the League. Like all cricket geniuses he was fallible. He could disappoint, but there were times he did things nobody else could match. Though a fearsome fast bowler and a punishing hitter as a batsman, Constantine was best remembered for his skills as a fielder. In his youth, in the Caribbean of the mid-1920s, he had reached heights at cover point that were scaled in later years only by such marvels in that position as Colin Bland, Clive Lloyd and Derek Randall. He was that good – 'electric heels' they called him in his early days at Nelson. By his mid-thirties his preference was for close fielding. His shrewd anticipation and lightning hand-eye reflexes were responsible for some extraordinary catches and run outs. It was around this particular attribute that the Constantine stories were fashioned. The basic one is that Constantine would catch a ball close to the wicket when everyone else on the ground, players and spectators alike, were looking to the boundary to see where the ball had crossed the rope: but all the time it was in Constantine's pocket, from which after a brief hiatus he would produce it, as the conjurer produces the rabbit from a hat.

For the first five or six years of my life, my family lived no more than a short bus ride from Constantine's house in Nelson. He kept his home there until 1949, when he moved to London. At that point my contact with him became distant. His book *Colour Bar* was too serious for me in 1954, though I was aware of it.

Trinidad politics, in which Constantine was immersed for the next eight years, were likewise too arcane a subject in my teenage years. But I became reacquainted with him on his return to England in 1962, and as an undergraduate was pleased to read in my *New Statesman* that he had been at the Old Trafford test in 1963, when Frank Worrell's West Indians defeated England by a considerable margin.[1] Just before this, he had appeared on the television as the subject of 'This Is Your Life', a show that upset Nelsonians by giving too little attention to Constantine's association with the town. The neglect seemed wrong. For many, Nelson *was* Constantine, just as Constantine owed so much personally to the town. He died in 1971, but that was not the end of his story. For me it continued when I started doing research on the politics and popular culture of north-west England; Constantine kept cropping up in one guise or another in my reading. Some people suggested that I might write about him, and I did produce various bits and pieces; but there was a fine biography by Gerald Howat that came out in the mid-1970s, and later on an equally good one by Peter Mason, and these seemed to say most that needed to be said. But, perhaps, not quite all. There was a mass of detail in various archives that had not yet been quarried. Much of it related to Constantine's non-cricketing life. It told not just of the man but of the circumstances in which he lived; of Constantine as a marker of historical change, especially in matters of race. It seemed worth a shot.

1

Constantine

This is a book about what was arguably the foremost social problem of the twentieth century, and which continues to challenge twenty-first-century minds: race and race relations. The focus of the book falls upon a man whose entire life was shaped by race, and who, in part because of his championing of race equality, achieved an eminence that few men or women of colour were able to experience during his time in history.

Learie Nicholas Constantine was born in colonial Trinidad in 1901.[1] He died in London in 1971. The contrast between these two dates is startling, in both personal and historical terms. Constantine was the first-born son of black parents who, though by no means well off, might just have been regarded as part of an indigenous lower middle class. His paternal great-grandfather, however, had been a slave, while Constantine's mother, Anaise Pascall, was the daughter of slaves. By the time of his own death, their eldest son Learie was a highly respected member of the British establishment. The historian Anne Spry Rush has placed him as 'upper middle-class', a status that might flatter his financial position but suitably captures his social standing.[2] Having made his name as a cricketer, and been honoured as a Member of the British Empire (MBE) for his work as a British civil servant during the Second World War, by the early 1960s he had received a knighthood, and from 1969 sat in the House of Lords. He was a member of the Inns of Court and served on the Race Relations Board, the Sports Council and the Board of Governors of the British Broadcasting Corporation (BBC). In recognition of the part he fulfilled in the independence movement of the country of his birth, he had been appointed High Commissioner in London of Trinidad and Tobago. In addition he might even be regarded as a 'public intellectual', at least in matters of race and race relations. Alongside various pieces of journalism and broadcasting that Constantine had contributed over the years, there were nine books, mostly on cricket but in one case a publication that added significantly to the British post-war discourse on race – *Colour Bar*, published in 1954. All of this qualified him for that exclusive, if informal, club of 'the great and the good'. He had acquired an international celebrity. If perhaps not a household name he was certainly very well known. In his lifetime Constantine bridged several worlds: colonial and metropolitan, local and national, working class and middle class, black and white. Constantine's success in a climate of racial prejudice and hostility appears both exceptional and praiseworthy. In contrast to most black people of his era, some of them well-loved sportsmen, his is a history of impressive mobility, crossing geographical, social, cultural and racial boundaries.[3]

I

From the late 1940s onwards the migration of black people to Britain exercised what was probably the most profound effect on British identity of the later twentieth century. Those West Indians who arrived in the mother country just after the Second World War did not see themselves as 'migrants'; they were simply British subjects, switching from one imperial territory to another. As the Trinidadian writer and broadcaster Trevor McDonald has pointed out, going to England was seen as 'going to the *centre*.'[4] Yet while the West Indies migrants with their British passports saw themselves as genuinely British subjects, the reception they experienced from white residents on arrival in Britain suggested something quite different. To many they were not welcome; they were not 'British'. The newcomers were seen as 'strangers', their dark skins and supposed cultural otherness marking them out from what were assumed to be the norms of British life. These norms, it was thought, were to be found in a sense of Britain as a country distinguished essentially by its 'whiteness'.[5] Although the numbers of immigrants were not particularly high initially, around 2,000 from the Caribbean in 1953, they had quickly come to be seen as presenting a 'problem'.[6] Communities of black people had long existed in certain towns, notably Cardiff and Liverpool, but it was with the concentration of the post-war migrants in London, the capital city – in Brixton and Notting Hill especially – that the question of race really came into national prominence. From this emerged a new problematic: how to define and, if possible, cohere the 'races'. Thus the idea of 'race relations' entered the vocabulary of public life and produced a succession of investigations into the problem.[7]

Learie Constantine was present at the birth of this enterprise. Relatively little attention had been directed in the past to scrutinizing the black communities. The perceived problems posed by the immigrant had been focused chiefly on

Irish and Jewish groups, against both of which there was ample and deep-rooted animosity; but for both groups there had over time been a degree of assimilation with indigenous peoples. In his work as a welfare officer in Liverpool during the Second World War, Constantine became immersed in the experiences of a small contingent of West Indian voluntary workers, mostly Jamaican, who provided an almost laboratory case study of race relations in a large city. It was for Constantine a quite new experience of racial division, different in tone and situation from his colonial days. While in Liverpool, as in Trinidad, race relations were part of an existing class structure of rich and poor, in Liverpool race also figured far more actively *within* classes: that is to say, there was no equivalent in Trinidad to a working class divided between black and white. Although no detailed academic analysis of race relations on Merseyside appeared until Anthony Richmond's study of 1954,[8] Constantine had imbibed much from his own dealings with white people, and also from what he observed in the treatment of other people of colour in areas such as employment, housing and leisure. He was among the first to direct the public's mind to the 'colour bar',[9] the term he used as the title of the book he brought out in 1954.[10] Its appearance was doubly remarkable. It was exceptional not only in its authorship – a former professional cricketer, and a black one at that, but also in making a statement, in a direct and readable form, about race problems in Britain and other parts of the world. Constantine did not hold back. Though the book had many failings, it did not shrink from delivering some harsh criticisms of contemporary attitudes and practices on race prejudice and discrimination. Unlike the academic studies of race that appeared around this time, *Colour Bar* had a populist tone that rendered it accessible to a general readership. It was well suited to expanding its readership and message through the serialization it underwent in sections of the tabloid press.

Constantine was, then, among the first in the field on the topic of race relations. Given his public status in the early 1950s, he might have risen to a position of some influence in this area, but for two things: shortly after the publication of *Colour Bar* he left England to work in Trinidad and was absent from British debate on race questions for some eight years; further, his early initiatives were overtaken by a cadre of academic sociologists and anthropologists who consolidated their position as experts on race questions during the 1950s. Anthony Richmond, Ruth Glass, Michael Banton, Sheila Patterson and especially Kenneth Little, who had spearheaded academic studies of race in Britain in the late 1940s, took the lead.[11] As Chris Waters has it, 'these experts secured their status as an authoritative voice on matters of race in Britain, monopolizing control over a relatively new domain of knowledge.'[12]

What their monopoly resulted in was a discourse on race distinguished by a new methodology in which two notions stood out. First, in an attempt to understand race, analysts tended to work with a model of separate and fixed groups, indigenous (white) and newcomer (black) or as they were often described, 'hosts and strangers'. It had the effect of ascribing singular characteristics to each group and of giving to the 'hosts' the normative standards from which the 'strangers' were deemed to depart. From this followed a second notion, with important implications for public policy: that of 'assimilation' – the absorption of the strangers into the lifestyle of the hosts. The more flexible 'multiculturalism' – which for all its practical flaws nonetheless moved away from the assumption that to assimilate meant becoming more like 'us' – was still some way in the future. But at least the race relations project of the 1950s was an attempt to seek answers to 'race' that were not confined simply to limiting immigration. Constantine himself was profoundly influenced at the time, and in the years to come, by this new science of race relations and its idea of assimilation. And it was not only Constantine who was influenced by it; assimilation for a while was the conceptual framework in which many people in Britain thought about race relations. Assimilation melted away from the 1970s onwards when challenged by new formulations of black identity and by the enduring power of whiteness.

Few of those who in the twenty-first century study race conceive of it any longer in biological terms. Some indeed have sought to dispense with the term 'race' altogether, although this is perhaps an unhelpful move to the extent that it loosens a grasp on identities and relationships that are actually perceived, rightly or wrongly, by many people.[13] There is, as Karl Spracklen has pointed out, a 'taken-for-grantedness' about racial difference.[14] Most commentators on race now apply the term to social and cultural constructions of identity, but this is not to say that the value of race as an explanatory tool in social analysis has been overtaken by 'class', 'ethnicity', 'nation' or whatever else. In the later work of the cultural theorist Stuart Hall, we find race very much to the fore as a marker of identity, a 'discursive construct', a 'sliding signifier', 'the centrepiece of a hierarchical system that produces differences'.[15] Hall perceives a residual presence of race: 'The physical or biological trace, having been shown out of the front door, tends to sidle around the edge of the verandah and climb back in through the pantry window!'[16] One body of recent writings on race typifies this persistent presence very clearly. It is what I might call the 'whiteness turn' in race studies that has flourished in the United States, particularly since the 1990s. It does not, as the term whiteness might suggest, attempt to champion white supremacy, though it can deal with the sentiments and anxieties of those who do. The slogans articulated at Donald Trump rallies during the 2016 American presidential election campaign – the constant refrain of 'Make America Great Again' and the less noticed but more sinister 'Make Race Great Again' – are a vivid example of such thinking. They draw upon a still common American belief in white superiority, an ingrained collective refusal to acknowledge that the Civil War and subsequent campaigns to establish civil rights and to pass into a 'post-racial age' have erased the 'fact' of white supremacy.[17] Whiteness studies encompass a variety of academic disciplines and seek to explain the phenomenon of whiteness as it is manifested in people's thought and behaviour and even in the configuration of the built environment.

Whiteness is not an easy idea to grapple with and can become a rather slippery conceptual pathway. For this reason it has been criticized for what have been seen as methodological and definitional weaknesses inherent to the idea.[18] But what it has importantly achieved is a switch of emphasis in race studies away from a focus on simply black or brown groups and opened up a wider spectrum of study, including the intriguing notion of degrees of whiteness. It therefore takes something that has previously seemed self-evident and makes it problematical. It dispenses with a plain black and white 'racial' opposition and delves into the issue of how at different times immigrants of various kinds – Jews, Irish, Italians, East Europeans, African Caribbeans – have come to be seen as worthy, or not, of white status.[19] The central concern of whiteness studies appears to be the process by which 'white' has become established in many societies as the pre-eminent ideology. Katharine Tyler's work on British Asians amplifies this point profoundly. She argues that British Asians are represented in the 'white hegemonic imagination' as 'racialised immigrants' standing betwixt and between, neither 'us' nor 'them'.[20] Similarly, in his work on the American academic and black civil rights activist W. E. B. Du Bois, Kwame Anthony Appiah has remarked that, in the early twentieth century, Du Bois had never been in a place where what it meant to be black wasn't defined by whites.[21] While the concept of whiteness as it is presently articulated was unknown to Constantine, and to others in his time, the power to define and construct racial and ethnic inequality was not. His life history therefore helps to unravel some of that whiteness knot.

II

Constantine's life also connects aptly with another new and burgeoning academic field – Atlantic Studies. It aims to plot the cross currents of ideas and movements that make up an Atlantic network. 'Transatlantic history (re-)evaluates the flow and circulation of people, goods, and ideas, within and across the continents surrounding the Atlantic basin between the fifteenth century and the present.'[22] Such a focus represents a convergence of previous forms of thematic and area studies – Caribbean, North American, European and postcolonial. Its broad multidisciplinary range includes economic, political, social and cultural forces. An important concern in this book, then, is to examine through the experiences of Learie Constantine the formation and development of relationships in these various contexts.

Among a number of important writers on this subject the influence of one, Paul Gilroy, is particularly noteworthy.[23] Gilroy's understanding of the 'Black Atlantic' brings together the various influences that have affected people, especially black people, across the Atlantic basin. For Gilroy the concept of a Black Atlantic does not denote simply a geographical area, though that in itself would be a useful framework of analysis. By employing the concept Gilroy's purpose seems more complex and ambitious: to challenge both a dominant Eurocentrism that had become established in academic sociology, and an Anglocentric nationalism that was evident in the newer forms of cultural studies emerging towards the close of the twentieth century; further, to interrogate the ways in which the concept of race has been used as an analytical tool; to cast doubt on notions of 'nationalism' and 'ethnicity' as fixed, essentialized categories; and to emphasize the element of flux in all things bearing on ideas and identity – 'the instability and mutability of identities which are always unfinished, always being remade'.[24] Cultures, for Gilroy, are the product of an inter-mixing of historical traditions and contacts. It is in the region of the Atlantic, Gilroy insists, where we should seek to understand what we might describe as a black experience.

A recurring motif, then, in my discussion of Constantine is the geographical and cultural framework of Constantine's life and work: the constant movement within countries and between continents with which he became so familiar. From a twenty-first century perspective we might see Constantine as an early version of 'globalized' man. In a conversation with his daughter, Gloria Valere, in which I suggested that this book would be a 'transatlantic history', she reminded me that her father spent at least half of his life in England. The point is well made. Constantine himself was apt to describe Nelson in Lancashire, where he and his family lived for twenty years, as 'home', and a good case can be made for him, purely in the sense of residence, as a 'black Englishman'. Constantine often used this term in relation not only to his own position but to that of West Indians generally, especially those who had come to live in England after the

Second World War The phrase suggests that the longevity of his time in England might have erased at least some of his Caribbean inheritance. I argue, however, that enough of it remained, and that it did so because he himself perpetuated it in various ways – through his writings, his stance on cricket, his work in race relations and through the contacts he maintained with Trinidad. As a cricketer he spent most of his career in England, but made frequent journeys back and forth across the Atlantic as a player and later a reporter on cricket. His political and diplomatic roles amplified this world presence, intellectually if not always physically. His daughter has told the story that when Constantine accompanied the prime minster of Trinidad, Eric Williams, to meet Jawaharlal Nehru on a goodwill tour to India in the late 1950s, thousands lined the streets: it was Constantine, the great cricketer, the people had turned up to see – few, if any, had heard of Williams.[25] As a wartime civil servant, Constantine was positioned at a key point in an Atlantic nexus, serving West Indian technicians who had volunteered to work in war production in England, and who were regarded by the British authorities as temporary residents destined to return to the Caribbean with new skills that would be put to the service of their country's own post-war development. In fact, many of them stayed put, becoming immigrants who brought new cultures to the mother country. They (and Constantine too, for he was not an exception to this) carried with them throughout their lives ideas that were the product of *Atlantic*, not simply English, experiences. The idea of the Black Atlantic provides therefore a transnational framework for a black culture formed of movements and ideas circulating across continents – to produce what Gilroy calls a 'double consciousness', a term borrowed from W. E. B. Du Bois.[26] Stuart Hall has placed this concept in his own 'diasporic experience' as a Jamaican academic in Britain attempting to come to terms with the juxtaposition of a black Caribbean heritage and an English lived culture – 'belonging to more than one world, of being both "here" and "there", of thinking about "there" from "here" and vice versa; of being "at home" – but never wholly – in both places; neither fundamentally the same, nor totally different.'[27]

This perspective provides a particularly appropriate way of thinking about the life's journey of Learie Constantine. Connecting with it is the life of another figure, the Trinidadian radical C. L. R. James (1901–1989), an exact contemporary of Constantine, born but a few miles from him, and who also spent much of his life away from his native land, in the United States and Britain, interspersed with visits to West Africa and back again to Trinidad. He became a leading figure in the transatlantic Left, a man of multiple talents and astonishing intellectual energy who contributed in so many ways to Marxism, Caribbean history, the study of literature, Pan-Africanism and the understanding of the role of sport in society. If we are seeking an embodiment of the Black Atlantic, there could be few finer examples than James. His influence in politics and political ideas was certainly greater than that of Constantine, especially if measured in literary output, though curiously it was to Constantine that James attributed the awakening of his own radicalism in the early 1930s. The two men knew each other from childhood. James had been a cricketer of some quality as a young man in Trinidad, and remained among the keenest followers and observers of the game throughout his life. In his famous book *Beyond a Boundary*[28] he credited Constantine, through his cricket, with a seminal role in the creation of a nationalist consciousness in the West Indies. Indeed, it is through the pages of *Beyond a Boundary* that we have become most familiar with the impact of Constantine in his early Trinidad days.

Constantine and James were not, of course, alone in experiencing this movement across an ocean. Hundreds of thousands of people had been doing so since the sixteenth century, most of them as slaves. The creation of an Atlantic trading empire from the sixteenth century onwards was the work of several European nations, with Spain, Portugal, Britain and France taking the lead. It was fundamental to the prosperity enjoyed by these nations, which later shared in the intellectual movements often described as the 'Enlightenment'. Slavery and Reason were the two sides of the coin of Western development at this time. By the eighteenth century the British occupied the primary position in the Atlantic economy and had, as James Walvin points out, shipped vast numbers of black Africans as slaves to the Caribbean and North America.[29] And, Walvin further and crucially reminds us, this was a movement of peoples that continued to affect Britain economically, socially and culturally long after the ending of the institution of slavery, especially when in the middle years of the twentieth century the direction of the migration swung towards Britain itself, creating a significant minority population of black people in many British cities. The slave trade and the complex Atlantic diaspora it created must therefore be seen as part of the fabric – 'the warp and the weft' in Walvin's term[30] – of British history itself, not simply an offshore event. It left many legacies. The overriding one was racism. Long after slavery itself had disappeared in British dominions, black people were left to contend with the status of racial inferiority that past economic servitude and a continuing psychology of 'white superiority' had dealt them. Learie Constantine shouldered such burdens with some success, but his life also helps to illustrate why many did not.

III

Accounts of Constantine's life are numerous. There are several short descriptions,[31] and Constantine himself frequently introduced biographical fragments in his own books.[32] Greater depth is offered by Udine Giuseppe's useful overview of Constantine's achievements.[33] More especially there are two biographies of fuller length. Gerald Howat's study, published shortly after the subject's death, deals with all the main points of Constantine's life.[34] It is an undeniably respectful work, distinguished by the deployment of a wide range of oral testimonies from a number of people who knew and in many cases worked with Constantine in a variety of contexts. Peter Mason similarly offers a perceptive story, rather more critical than Howat, set out around the principal phases of Constantine's life, very much in the manner of Howat's life history.[35] Both take an approach to Constantine that can only be described in the final analysis as complimentary. In this they comply with other accounts that have Constantine as a 'good man'. While such an interpretation is not necessarily invalid, it is not one that should either escape critical scrutiny or prohibit alternatives.

My approach is differentiated from previous writings in various ways. First, it is not biographical in the accepted sense, though in highlighting the life and work of a single individual it inevitably has a biographical turn. Second, what emerges with greater emphasis than that found in previous writings is the historical context that shaped Constantine's thinking and circumscribed his actions. In this respect I take my cue from Marx's dictum about men [sic] making their own history, but not in circumstances of their own choosing.[36] Third, I employ a fuller use of primary sources, public and private, to analyse these historical circumstances. The sources, ranging from government papers to private memos and correspondence, have not previously been employed in any depth to explore Constantine's activities. However, in spite of his prominence in many fields, his life is not as well documented as might be supposed. This is seen in the extensive and recently compiled collection of material in the Lord Learie Constantine archive at the National Library of Trinidad and Tobago (NALIS) in Port of Spain. The collection is not yet fully catalogued and digitized, so that working through it can be a somewhat hit and miss procedure. It is rewarding on some aspects of Constantine's activities, disappointingly thin on others.[37] Nonetheless, these gaps can to a degree be compensated for by reference to other sources not before consulted on Constantine-related topics. They are to be found in, among others, the papers of the Colonial Office, the Ministry of Labour, the

Race Relations Board, and the BBC. Fourth, I attempt to move away from a congratulatory mode and seek a more critical stance on Constantine; this should not imply an absence of respect for a figure who was clearly admired by many, and deservedly so, but as a wish to bring out failings as well as successes in a career that offered many opportunities for influencing the lives of others.

To set the scene on Constantine, his life might be divided chronologically into three portions. Until his early twenties it was confined largely to Trinidad, where his race and status encouraged aspirations of upward mobility associated with his background as a member of what I call a 'Western educated elite'. They were to motivate him throughout his life. He became a promising cricketer. He earned a living in a variety of clerical jobs, there being only a very limited and poorly remunerated form of professional cricket in the West Indies at that time. However, by making a mark at cricket, particularly during tours of England in 1923 and 1928, it became possible for Constantine to exploit his sporting skills for a very different kind of livelihood. Thus, the second part of his life began in 1929, when he joined Nelson Cricket Club in Lancashire as its professional. He was the first black person to achieve this kind of position.[38] He remained in Lancashire as a cricket 'pro' throughout the 1930s, intermittently leaving Nelson to play international cricket in the Caribbean, Australia and India. At this point, though, nothing had been mapped out by way of a career when his playing days came to an end. He had long nourished an ambition to become a lawyer, but possessed no qualifications for it beyond work experience as a clerk in solicitors' offices in Trinidad. Fortuitously, the war provided new opportunities that chimed with his life in cricket. We might say that, for Constantine, the 1939–45 conflict was a 'good war'. The gentlemanly yet combative demeanour he had displayed on the cricket field, allied to the respect he earned as a player, singled him out for the diplomatic tact needed as a welfare officer handling the problems posed in integrating wartime volunteer workers from the West Indies into the British workforce. This pitched him squarely into the problems of race and race relations with which his name was to be associated for the remainder of his life. Up to that point Constantine had operated largely in a regional context: cricket pro in Nelson and wartime civil servant on Merseyside. Early in the war, however, he had begun, in a small way at first, an association with the BBC. It grew over the next decade into a broadcasting presence that gave him a national profile. It culminated eventually in a seat on the Corporation's Board of Governors. He was also briefly Chairman of the League of Coloured Peoples (LCP) in Britain until its dissolution in 1951, and then between 1956 and 1962 he joined the independence struggle in Trinidad. Here he became Chairman of the People's

National Movement (PNM), was elected a member of the Legislative Council, and served as a minister in Eric Williams's pre-independence administration. Thus from the early 1940s until his death he entered, so to speak, his third age, one of public service on both sides of the Atlantic. In England, this took him into an area of influence and prestige reserved for very few.

Constantine's earliest and strongest impact was felt in sport. As a cricketer he undoubtedly set new standards – pioneering a path that others followed to give Caribbean cricketers greater employment opportunities, and establishing a style of cricket performance that sooner or later others would seek to emulate. The art of fielding, for example, for long an undervalued aspect of cricket, owed a great deal to Constantine's example. He was an all-round cricketer – batsman, bowler and fieldsman – worthy of selection at the highest level for any one of these positions. He was in fact the very prototype of the dynamic player now valued in that most commercial of cricket competitions, the Indian Premier League. But an equally important contribution to the game was felt not so much on the field as beyond the boundary, where he lent his voice to attempts to change the form of play, the social relations and the power structure of cricket. This process assumed many forms over many years. It resulted in the insertion of a new kind of shortened form of play in first-class cricket, a type with which Constantine had originally become familiar as a club professional in the North of England during the 1930s. This in turn introduced a bolder style of attacking cricket that Constantine had always encouraged and which he regarded as having a West Indian provenance. The change wrought in cricket by such innovations was closely related to other developments that carried a more political weight; namely, a challenge to the control of cricket that had been exercised since the nineteenth century by an upper-class elite. The chief wielder of this control was the Marylebone Cricket Club (MCC). Its agent on the field of play was the gentleman amateur. By the 1960s the status quo it had long maintained was disintegrating. In its place developed, among other things, an increased status for the place of the professional, something that Constantine had also advocated over many years. For black West Indians, however, more important than either of these was the struggle to end white supremacy in their own cricket structure, symbolized not only by the white gentleman amateur but also by the tradition, itself a product of the racial hierarchy of club cricket in the Caribbean, of a white man captaining what, by the 1940s, was a predominantly black national team. Alongside his friend C. L. R. James, Constantine helped to promote this campaign, which resulted in the appointment of the first black captain of the West Indies in 1960.

Constantine's experiences in sport, all of which had political implications in one form or another, seeped through into the wider world. They shaped the later part of Constantine's life. In contrast with the lives of many black sportsmen in the twentieth century Constantine's post-cricket years were ones of relative prosperity and, perhaps more important, public esteem. Boxing, the sport in which black men most frequently found celebrity in the first half of the twentieth century, provides several examples of financial, social and even mental decline once the sporting life has ended: Joe Louis, the great American heavyweight champion of the 1930s and 1940s, is perhaps the chief example.[39] Far less famous, though no less sorrowful, is the footballing case of Leeds United's South African winger Albert Johannson, who lived neglected in poverty after his playing days had ended in the 1960s.[40] Indeed, few professional sportsmen and women, whether black or white, could have expected to attain the position achieved by Constantine after he had finished playing cricket. Fellow black West Indians Arthur Wint and E. McDonald Bailey enjoyed success in athletics just after the Second World War, though neither had anything like the sustained eminence of Constantine in his life after sport.[41] Constantine himself could scarcely have expected it either. As in all personal success stories he enjoyed an element of good fortune (luck, to put it more bluntly) – unplanned opportunities came his way that he then exploited to his advantage. He worked hard in his various endeavours, and managed his career adroitly, with quiet though persistent help from his wife, Norma. Almost everything flowed from his achievements on the cricket field, from which he created a public persona that exactly suited the aspirations of a man of his race and background in a country – England – still largely unenlightened in matters of race relations.

IV

It is almost half a century since Constantine's death. His name is now less familiar than it once was and there is a sense in which Constantine, once probably the most famous black person in Britain and the Caribbean, has become something of a 'forgotten man'. There are, for example, only scant references to him in the literature on modern race relations and, even more noticeable, little mention of him in the studies of Trinidadian politics that deal with the period when he was a leading figure in the PNM. He is not, though, completely removed from the public gaze. There is an English Heritage blue plaque on a house in Earl's Court, London where the Constantines lived from 1949 until 1954, when they returned to Trinidad. In Nelson there is now (since 2011) a blue plaque (not endorsed by English Heritage) on his house in Meredith Street where the family lived for almost twenty years. Strangely, it seems to many, there is no statue in Nelson honouring his contribution to the town, where he was a Freeman of the Borough.[42] There is a Learie Constantine Centre in North London, not far from Dollis Hill tube station, run by the Learie Constantine West Indian Association, providing youth, community, and mental health services. Also in London the National Portrait Gallery has a bronze bust of Constantine, made just before his death, by Karin Jonzen. In Trinidad, the land of his birth, the old Concrete Stand at the Queen's Park Oval in Port of Spain has been renamed after him. The memorial is, however, somewhat overshadowed by newer buildings commemorating other Trinidad cricketers, notably Jeffrey Stollmeyer and Gerry Gomez. Both were white players and, later in life, leading cricket administrators. The main stand at the ground is named after Brian Lara, the country's most recent cricket hero, for whom there is also a statue at the head of Independence Avenue in the centre of Port of Spain. Constantine has no such prominent monument, but there is a sports ground in the suburb of Tunapuna bearing his name.

Do these memorials merely hark back to a previous era, suggesting that Constantine is now a distant memory, a figure with little relevance to the twenty-first century? Many people, even those who remember his name, might be hard pressed to say why his life might still be worth remembering for us today. In one sense this is a way of posing the old question: 'what is the use of history?' And, perhaps, supplementing it with a further, more quarrelsome one: 'must history *always* be shown to have a contemporary relevance?' There is nowadays a strong impulse in both popular and academic writing to answer 'yes' to that second question, and by so doing to provide an answer to the first; that is, 'there is no use in history *unless* it can be shown to have relevance to our lives today.' Were this test to be applied to Constantine (though I am not suggesting that it necessarily should be) two aspects of his life would demand close scrutiny for their twenty-first century relevance: cricket and race. In cricket, a game that has evolved in a variety of forms since Constantine began playing in the 1920s, his ideas about it and his own on-field performances connect readily with the formats in which the game is played today. Race problems are as important today as they were when Constantine first became seriously involved in trying to deal with them in the 1940s. His work in this field illustrates if nothing else the perdurability of racial attitudes and conflict, and provides us with examples of approaches that might, or might not, serve in shaping contemporary solutions to a still important social problem.

Finally, over and above these precise topics, the third phase of his life – from about 1940 until the early 1970s – presents us with one man's experiences of a significant period in the history of Britain and the Caribbean. It is a period of distinctive public policies, social relationships, and notions of statehood often collectively referred to as the 'social-democratic consensus.' The ideas inherent in it – of the welfare state, full employment, progressive direct taxation, a managed and planned economy with its key sectors in public ownership and a striving for some degree of social equality – were ones that Constantine sought to implement, to secure for people of colour on both sides of the Atlantic a share in the benefits they brought. Not all these ambitions were realized. But since Constantine's death a great deal has changed. The social-democratic ideology has, during the past thirty years, lost out in political life and thought to a neo-liberal body of ideas. 'Neo' it might be called but in many ways it represents a return to the 1930s. By the second decade of the twenty-first century, however, this experiment in political economy is itself appearing threadbare and demanding of reconsideration. Constantine's life therefore reminds us of what we have lost, what we should not forget and what might one day be restored.[43] Above all, notably on the question of race, it reminds us of what is still to be done.

2

Trinidad

The experience of race and race relations permeated the entire life of Learie Constantine. He grew up on the island of Trinidad, one of a group of Anglophone territories in the Caribbean and South American mainland governed as colonies of Britain. Each been acquired at different times. Of the economically more important islands, Jamaica and Barbados had been English colonies since the middle of the seventeenth century. Trinidad, on the other hand, was in the possession of Spain until forcibly taken by the British in 1797. By the end of the nineteenth century each colony experienced different forms of government under British rule. Jamaica and Barbados, for example, had a degree of autonomy in the form of elected local assemblies. Trinidad, as a Crown Colony, was ruled directly by the British crown through an appointed governor – a system whose purpose was laconically defined by Trinidad's first black prime minister, Eric Williams, as being 'to make sure that the Crown could govern without the impediment of local elected assemblies'.[1] Over and above these differences, however, colonies had at least one thing in common: they experienced only a limited capacity for independent action. In economic, political and social life white (mainly British) interests determined the form of the economy, the degree and kind of any local political autonomy and organization, the nature of social relations, and even some aspects of cultural life. This subordination was most evident in politics and governance, where only a few local people were granted a consultative influence, and also in the structure of society, which was rigidly stratified according to race and status. White Creole and black populations – and in Trinidad a large number of Asians – coexisted according to subtle (and often not-so-subtle) conventions of power and deference that applied both between and within the populations. Through such controls the way of life of local people was shaped by British power. There was little in the way of an alternative. Some native traditions persisted but as C. L. R. James, and Constantine himself, was always quick to point out, for those who sought an intellectual advancement there was no indigenous culture available to counter the hegemony of Western values.[2] The inhabitants of the islands tended to think of themselves essentially as British, and of Britain as the 'mother country'.[3]

I

Social relations were largely determined by the islands' economic functions. The local economies were based on primary production, with sugar traditionally the staple export crop. The area had long had a role in a wider Atlantic economy in which economic relations were divided between a 'core' and a 'periphery'. Since the seventeenth century the Caribbean[4] had fulfilled an agricultural function in an imperial trading economy that at various times encompassed Western Europe (the core) together with large areas of west Africa, the eastern and southern part of north America, the Caribbean and South Asia (the periphery). As colonies, the islands were structured into a trading partnership in which they exported primary products in exchange for manufactured goods from Britain, and, given the predominance of cash crop cultivation in the islands, some foodstuffs. This tendency towards monoculture made the local economies susceptible to changing policy and demand in the core. Slavery had a big part in these arrangements. Large estates owned by white (Creole)[5] planters were given over to the commercial cultivation of the staple crop of sugar using the labour of slaves. The de facto ending of slavery in 1838, and the subsequent development of a free peasantry, removed this supply of cheap labour, while at almost the same time traditional tariff protection for the British sugar-producing islands was removed by the Sugar Duties Act of 1846, which favoured British domestic consumers. Sugar producers in the British Caribbean territories were exposed to competition from Cuba and Brazil. When sugar prices declined there was little else to fall back on. For example, competition from European beet sugar affected Caribbean cane exports to Britain, and the introduction after 1898 by the United States of preferential tariffs in relation to Cuba, the region's largest producer, reduced further export opportunities for the British islands. The last twenty years of the nineteenth century saw a decline in sugar prices and an economic downturn that has been described by one commentator as 'disastrous'.[6] Although the market picked up again in the years until the end of the First World War, from 1920 there was a steady decline. The British colonial authorities had recognized these fundamental economic problems as early as the 1830s, when a policy of making grants of cheap land for small farmers had been enunciated. The most vigorous application of the principle had been given by Governor A. H. Gordon of Trinidad in the 1860s by selling Crown land for small-scale cocoa production, an initiative that greatly assisted the development of a crop, which during the next fifty years became Trinidad's leading export staple in value. In the other islands, although sugar's former dominance declined in comparison to other products, the crop nonetheless continued to be a leading export commodity, its position maintained by the adoption by British governments of imperial preference policies in the 1920s. But the successive crises affecting sugar bred a sense of uncertainty in economic life that in turn aroused grievances the British authorities were never able to fully resolve.

Trinidad was in some respects shielded from the full force of these general trends. By the standards of the eastern Caribbean it was a large island, about the same size as the pre-1974 English county of Lancashire. Trinidad was a colony with a history of immigration from a variety of sources. Its hybrid, multicultural population imprinted itself on the island's economic life. While not without its problems, Trinidad was developing in a more economically and socially diversified form than most of its Caribbean neighbours. Sugar was initially the most important crop, and was to remain so for much of the nineteenth century, but the opening up of new lands permitted the cultivation of cocoa,[7] notably by French Creole planters who had migrated there in the 1780s before the island had become a British possession. Together with coconuts and rice these crops contributed to Trinidad becoming 'relatively prosperous' by this time.[8] Oil production, which had begun in the 1850s and 1860s but then lapsed because of technical problems in drilling, resumed in far greater quantities in the early twentieth century. It quickly became Trinidad's leading resource, accounting for two thirds of the country's exports over the first half of the twentieth century.[9] By the time of the Second World War, Trinidad's oil exports to Britain were critical in sustaining the war effort. In agriculture, the policy by successive governors of selling Crown lands to create small holdings helped to stimulate domestic food production for the market, and thus make Trinidad less reliant than most Caribbean islands upon imported foodstuffs.[10]

These developments brought the various immigrant groups into the labour market. Trinidad was a place of multiple identities. Spanish, French and Portuguese had early on established a position in the community. Once the island became a British colony the population was augmented by English settlers who formed a powerful planter and merchant class. In addition, of course, a large proportion of the population was made up of black slaves. There were fears throughout the Caribbean islands that the ending of slavery would result in a labour shortage in those sectors of the economy, notably the sugar plantations, dependent on large numbers of unskilled workers. It was anticipated that former slaves would take advantage of the opportunity to set up as small tenant farmers. Some did, but the fears of planters were dispelled in Trinidad at least by the recruiting of new workers from a wide geographical area: the eastern Caribbean itself, Venezuela, and further afield from Madeira, Africa, China and chiefly the Indian subcontinent. In the years between the 1850s and the end of the First World War approximately 135,000 indentured labourers from the Indian subcontinent had arrived in Trinidad, making up a large community with a distinct ethnic identity.

When Learie Constantine moved school in 1908 upon his father's changing jobs, the boy came face to face with some of this racial mix: his fellow pupils were 'Negroes mostly, East Indians, and some Chinese, poor boys most of us'.[11] East Indians were regarded for a long time as something of an 'outsider' group, marginal and not expected to be a permanent feature in society. Creoles – people of European or African descent who saw themselves as 'native' Trinidadians – made up the core of society but were highly stratified in terms of race, class and culture. As Brereton has shown white Creoles (both English and French) dominated through wealth and political power, attempting as far as possible to impose their cultural norms on those below. Below them were the black masses, composed of free peasants and manual workers in estate or service trades. They often spoke a patois rather than English, and their cultural life displayed many features of an African heritage. Attitudes to such things as marriage, the place of women in society and leisure activities were markedly different from those of the English. In religion, Roman Catholicism rather than Protestantism was often the preferred attachment among this group in society (as the Constantine family illustrates). This is not surprising given the religious traditions of the pre-British period in Trinidad.

II

Between these upper and lower strata was a very interesting group that is often described as a 'black middle class'. Sociologists of colonialism have identified this group as playing a key part in the forming of an oppositional stance towards the colonial authority in various parts of the world. In places as different as India and the various African colonies the middle class (sometimes referred to as a 'Western educated elite') has been associated with nationalist independence movements, of which the Indian National Congress was the exemplar. Such a group was fluid; it could contain widely diverging social types – in India, for example, there was a large social distance between a figure like the British-educated Jawaharlal Nehru, from a wealthy family, and other people in the Congress movement who came from much humbler backgrounds – M. K. Gandhi himself even. What bound such people together, in spite of their differences, were two unifying characteristics: they were not white, and they were not part of a native aristocracy with which the colonial power collaborated. As such, they were the group in society that, while they had benefited from colonialism through the creation of Western-style jobs, felt their social isolation keenly. They were simultaneously distanced from the poorest sections of the black population by their education, but barred from the highest reaches of colonial society on account of their colour. The notion of a 'colour bar' affected them deeply.

The experience of colonialism for this middle class was therefore problematical. As far as Trinidad was concerned the black middle class was itself a diverse group. Better-off sections were close to the white planters and merchants. Educated at elite schools they were capable (especially if lighter skinned) of forming, to an extent, a union with white Creoles. But there was also a large and relatively poor middle class in terms of possessions – its defining characteristic, as with C. L. R. James, was an intellectual one: 'command of European culture'.[12] In other words, they were people who, for reasons to do with their employment (as, e.g., clerks, teachers, or other forms of public service), had acquired a European education, spoke English and were involved in some form or another with the colonial administration. Their European education had given them a glimpse of a social advancement that the racialism of the colonial system then denied them. They were the people who most of all in colonial society were likely to feel its injustices. Learie Constantine's mind was, throughout his life, constantly attuned to this feeling, which was later reflected in his book *Colour Bar*, published when he was in his fifties.

In Trinidad one of the intellectually most distinguish members to emerge from the black middle class was C. L. R. James, a man of many parts: in the words of Stephen Howe James was 'revolutionary and aesthete, novelist, historian, literary critic, philosopher, political analyst, and in many eyes the foremost of all writers on cricket'[13] In the late 1920s he was an important member of an indigenous literary and cultural movement, which included the figures of Albert Gomes, Alfred Mendes and R. A. C. de Boissiere. They sought, through their journal *The Beacon*, set up by Gomes in 1930, to develop a distinctive black West Indian voice in the arts. James's early life reveals very clearly the aspirations and anxieties that prevailed among black Trinidadians of this kind in the early years of the twentieth century. One characteristic stands out: hard work in pursuit of an education. By applying himself to this principal James's father had qualified as a schoolteacher and was to rise to the position of headmaster. He instilled in his son the same qualities. James undoubtedly possessed both determination and ability, winning a highly prized free exhibition to the elite Queen's Royal College in Port of Spain for his secondary education. His passion for cricket and literature meant that on eventually leaving school he chose not to translate his educational advantage into the expected professional post, preferring instead to make his way as a writer. It was a decision in some ways untypical of middle class behaviour, though it reflected a burning desire for knowledge and the transmission of it. In this James, as much as anyone, fulfilled the imperative for the 'command of European culture' that marked out the black middle class. It came through very forcefully in one of his later writings, the semi-autobiographical *Beyond a Boundary* (1963)[14] – perhaps his best known book as far as the general reader is concerned, and certainly the one most devoted to his great love of cricket. In the early parts of the book James reflects on his Trinidad childhood, recalling formative events and personalities. European culture is pervasive – in reading, and in the imbibing through school cricket of an English ethos for 'playing the game'. In a letter written probably in the early 1960s to the Barbadian politician Grantley Adams, later prime minister of the short-lived West Indies Federation, James reveals the school links that both maintained a sense of solidarity among the black middle class and ensured the durability of a British inheritance in people of the West Indies. 'Do you remember the first time that we met, it was when you came to QRC Trinidad with the Harrison College team [Barbados], I think it was 1919. Neither of us played.' He goes on to tell Adams about the book he is writing (which became *Beyond a Boundary*):

> The book is West Indian through and through, particularly in the early chapters on my family, my education, and the portraits of West Indian cricketers of the previous generation, some of them unknown ... But the book is very British. Not only the language but on page after page the (often unconscious) literary references, the turn of phrase, the mental and moral outlook. That is what we are ... and we shall never know ourselves until we recognise that fully and freely and without strain.[15]

This striving for learning and correct behaviour was accompanied by a certain social hauteur on the part of his family.[16] The Jameses were not native Trinidadians; they hailed from Barbados ('one of the smaller islands' as James put it) whence C. L. R.'s grandfather had arrived 'probably with nothing'.[17] They were intent on 'getting on'. James's mother was dismissive of the young James's interest in the one authentic Trinidadian art form, calypso – 'a matter for ne'er do wells',[18] while his father insisted that his son keep an eye firmly on the path to success. Respectability was the watchword. It was defined in contrast to its opposite, the wayward lifestyle of the rough indigenous working class, typified in neighbour Matthew Bondman: 'an awful character, dirty, lazy, loud'. Whether Matthew, whose family rented a property from the Jameses, was a real person or a figment of the older James's memory is not clear, and probably matters not. What is important is the 'otherness' he embodied. The Bondman family was the antithesis of the earnest, improving middle class, a social type to be avoided, to be talked about disdainfully, to be despised. For the young C. L. R., however, there was one rather troubling aspect to this duality: Matthew Bondman, for all his violence and loutishness, was a very good cricketer – 'Matthew could bat'.[19] Cricket was the one thing that connected the two young men. That a relationship could be formed in cricket points up the importance of the game in Caribbean society. In all other respects, though, James was enclosed in the world of the Western educated elite. Cut off from the Bondmans and his fellow blacks below him – 'an alien in my own environment among my own people'[20] – and shut out of those higher reaches of social life that was the preserve of the white plantocracy and merchant class.

The Constantine family was in a similar position. Less academically endowed and probably less affluent than the James family, the Constantines nonetheless experienced the same mixture of hope and anxiety. Learie's father was in fact more intimately associated with the colonial economy than was James's. It is striking that Learie frequently referred to his (maternal) grandfather having been a slave, freed in the 1830s. His mother, Anaise, was only, so to speak, one step away from servile status. Unlike C. L. R.'s father, who had moved, as a teacher, into the 'free professions' Lebrun Constantine, the grandson of slaves, worked in the frontline of the new and expanding cocoa industry.[21] We know relatively little about Lebrun's working life. Learie tells us that he was an 'overseer' on a cocoa estate, responsible for making sure that the labourers did their job.[22] He was in other words a foreman, probably effective enough to have been promoted when Learie was seven or eight years old, because at this point the family moved house. Learie remembers it as being on a plot large enough to accommodate a cricket pitch where all the family played – Lebrun and Anaise, with daughter Leonora, and boys Learie, Elias, Oswald and Rodney (often joined by Uncle Toy, Victor Pascall, a leading slow bowler in the islands) – and which became a venue for most of the kids in the neighbourhood. Lebrun, methodical in most things, prepared a good wicket on which to play some proper cricket. This is a not untypical story in the sportsperson's autobiography: the willing parents encouraging an early interest in the sport in which s/he was to become famous. Looking back on his upbringing, Learie was always inclined to praise his parents' discipline: 'If more parents today' he said in an interview in the early 1960s 'were as strict – and at the same time as straight – as mine were, I am convinced there would not be the difficulties there are with young people.'[23] With Learie, however, there is one important difference. His father was already famous – probably the most distinguished black cricketer in Trinidad, if not the entire Caribbean. By the time the family moved house, Lebrun had already played with success in inter-island matches for Trinidad. He toured England with all-West Indies teams in 1900 and 1906. He was a batsman who could also bowl and, at need, keep wicket. On the 1900 tour Lebrun became the first West Indian to score a century in England: and he made it not just anywhere, but against the Marylebone Cricket Club (MCC) at Lord's. Learie, then, had a famous father. It is usually a helpful asset, and can be crucial as the foundation of a career.

Lebrun's success gave the family a distinctive social position. It owed something to patronage from the better-off section of the black middle class. His place on the 1906 tour to England was assured by the financial support he received from Michael Maillard, the owner of a large department store in Port of Spain. It enabled Lebrun to play as an amateur. This was important socially. It was possible for black cricketers to earn a living as professionals in the islands, working at the elite clubs by bowling at members in the nets, cleaning kit and preparing the ground. They were not permitted to play in inter-island cricket, but in one or two cases supplemented their earnings during the Caribbean close season by travelling to New York and playing in the leagues there. Their status, however, was a low one. They were especially looked down upon in Barbados, where racial and social discrimination was stronger than in other islands. The case of the black professional Fitz Hinds demonstrates the problem. In endeavouring to make his mark as a player, rather than simply as a servant professional, Hinds was rejected by his original employer, the Pickwick club, a white-only set up. He moved to a black club, Spartan. Even there his social position (he was a house painter by trade) was considered too lowly; his application to join the club was initially opposed, but when later accepted he still found himself snubbed by certain members. In Spartan's matches against Pickwick, moreover, some players of the opposition refused to turn out against a team that included their former black employee. Poor Hinds, then, suffered both racially and socially.[24] A similar experience befell Tommie Burton, Lebrun's teammate from British Guiana ('Demerara' as it was often then known) who had batted in a big stand with Lebrun Constantine against the MCC in 1900 when Lebrun scored his hundred. Playing as a professional on the 1906 tour to England Burton, by this time one of the senior members of the team in playing terms, was sent home early following a dispute with the tour management over pocket money. Burton, moreover, was sternly criticized for his stance by his local newspaper. Lebrun, with Maillard's sponsorship, had an independence that enabled him to sit above this kind of treatment. He played as an amateur and therefore enjoyed a social position that was further elevated by his cricketing prowess. His son benefited from the father's status, which placed the family among the Western educated elite, not through education but through cricket.

The similarities between the James and Constantine families are exemplified in the bonds between the two sons. Their social backgrounds, together with a love of cricket, ensured a lifelong adult friendship between Learie and 'Nello' (as C. L. R. James was known to his friends). Their relationship was sometimes close, sometimes distant – because of either physical or political separation – but it endured, always capable of being revived. In the early 1930s James lodged for some eight months with Learie, his wife Norma and young daughter Gloria, in their house in Nelson. There, joint work was done on Constantine's first book, *Cricket and I*.[25] James then left for the United States, where he lived until the early 1950s, campaigning on the far left reaches of the American socialist movement. Constantine never explored those areas of politics. The two men met up again in the later 1950s in Trinidad, to where Constantine had returned with his family in 1954, after qualifying in England as a barrister. Constantine and James were both involved in the push for Independence in Trinidad with the People's National Movement (PNM), Constantine as chairman of the party, James as editor of the party journal *The Nation*. It was a tempestuous journey from which neither escaped unscathed. It certainly confirmed the clear distance between them politically, though it did not prevent them from working together again on a new publishing venture in England in the mid-1960s. In their different ways both men had fulfilled a black middle-class ambition: Constantine as the respected professional, James lionized on the Left as a writer and agitator. Of the two, James reputation has lived on the stronger. His is an intellectual influence to be grappled with in the academic world of postcolonial studies.

III

In the Caribbean, questions of race, class, status and power are nowhere better illustrated than in the organization of the cricket clubs. They were an essential mechanism in the ordering of colonial society. In a celebrated passage in *Beyond a Boundary* James described the process plainly. In Trinidad there was a social and racial hierarchy of clubs playing cricket at the top level: Queen's Park – the principal club, with its own ground just off the Savannah, a membership of wealthy whites, and occasionally coloured men of 'old well-established mulatto families'.[26] In the same bracket was Shamrock – 'almost exclusively' white and Catholic. Of Queen's Park and Shamrock James says: 'I would have been more easily elected to the MCC than to either.' Constabulary was for the police: teams were mixed in race but captains were always chosen from the rank of inspector, or above. Stingo was plebeian, 'the butcher, the baker, the candlestick maker, the casual labourer, with a sprinkling of unemployed': 'totally black and no social status whatever'. Maple was composed of the 'brown-skinned middle class'; colour of skin was the overriding principle here – 'they didn't want any dark people in their club.' Shannon was 'the club of the black lower middle class: the teacher, the law clerk, the worker in the printing office … the clerk in a department store'. The captain in James's youth (when the club was known as Victoria) was Lebrun Constantine; Learie played, as did the enigmatic batting genius Wilton St Hill ('the clerk in a department store').[27]

A young man with local knowledge, wanting simply to play cricket, would know intuitively which was the 'right' club to join. Sometimes the rules could be bent, at least slightly. James was black but ended up playing for Maple; he had friends there who smoothed his path, though James later regretted that his decision delayed his getting to know Learie Constantine better. Constantine had joined Shannon just after the First World War. It was the leading club in playing strength. Shannon provided many of the West Indian test players of the interwar period, and possessed above all a powerful esprit de corps, which fostered a tough form of cricket: 'They played as if they knew that their club represented the great mass of black people in the island.'[28] For such people, no matter how good at cricket they were, membership of the white clubs was out of the question. To be sure, white and black clubs did play against each other, but when the match was over the two sets of players went their separate ways. There was no socializing.

Such was Trinidad. The situation in the other islands was not vastly different. Brian Stoddart has matched James's close observations of the cricket hierarchy in his own analysis of the club structure in Barbados. He points to the 'feeder' role of leading schools in inducting players into various clubs. Just as James had left Queen's Royal College and gone to play at Maple so in Barbados it was Harrison College that supplied white sons of the plantocracy or the mercantile elite to Wanderers, the club of the magisterial batsman George Challenor.[29] Another elite school, the Lodge, often sent its pupils out to the slightly lower-status Pickwick, where the great Tim Tarilton played. As Stoddart notes, Challenor and Tarilton, the two leading white players of the 1910s and 1920s, were 'clearly great friends' but inhabited subtly different social worlds that prevented their being in the same club. Wanderers was a club for the highest echelon of Barbadian society, of which Tarilton was not a member. Roy Marshall, born in 1930, was the son of a long-established planter family. He was educated at the Lodge and played for Wanderers before graduating to the West Indies team for the 1950 tour of England. Marshall had benefited from his family's planter wealth, which enabled them to have a cricket pitch at the rear of their house (doubtless a rather grander affair than that of the Constantines). The men of the Marshall family had jobs that allowed plenty of time off for cricket.[30] In Trinidad Jeffrey Stollmeyer was the scion of another wealthy planter family, cocoa rather than sugar in this case; Jeffrey and his brother Victor came into the West Indies team just before the Second World War, and Jeffrey later became captain. The family's Port of Spain home, an architectural monstrosity on the edge of the Queen's Park Savannah known locally as Stollmeyer Castle, symbolized the family's economic, social and political standing. Jeffrey himself served as a cricket administrator for many years after his playing days ended, unusually joined the PNM (a predominantly black party) and later, after Independence, became a senator. In British Guiana and Jamaica similar hierarchies existed with the same fusion of white economic and social power evident in both politics and cricket.[31] The organization of cricket secured a kind of stability in Caribbean society. 'Until 1914 at least,' says Stoddart, 'the colonial elites established a cultural primacy through cricket as much as through economic and political position.'[32]

'Until 1914 at least': but colonialism was changing, as was cricket. The old white dominance was slowly being challenged. Trinidad provides an example. Prior to the First World War politics in the island had been relatively quiescent. There had been little in the way of representative government. Since the early 1830s the governor ruled through two bodies. A small executive council comprised of leading public officials together with an even smaller group of local persons specially selected by the governor himself. This body deliberated in secret. Then there was the Legislative Council. It was composed of 'official' members – who were the leading officers of the colonial government – and 'unofficial' members, a slightly larger group of local planters and merchants partly nominated by the governor himself. There were twelve official members and thirteen 'unofficials' at the end of the 1920s.[33] While the apologists of Crown Colony rule might claim that such people 'represented' the whole of local society they, in practice, represented the dominant economic and commercial interests in the island. The idea of there being in any sense a 'working-class' presence in politics was unrealistic for most of the nineteenth century. Movements to change the status quo – in effect, to widen the social and economic basis of the legislative council – were relatively rare and weak, and when they did arise they were spearheaded by educated, middle-class men like the journalist Philip Rostant, who used his newspaper *Public Opinion* in the 1880s to lead a campaign for elections to the council.[34] Most historians have seen the origins of a more populist (and radical) movement for change as coming in the Water Riots of 1903, when government attempts to impose water restrictions, and to bar the public from a meeting of the legislative council where these measures were to be debated, triggered a mass demonstration. It spilled over into an ugly confrontation between protesters and the police in which sixteen people were killed and many more wounded.[35] This event took place against a background of recent authoritarian interventions by the colonial secretary in London, Joseph Chamberlain, to reinforce Crown Colony government. That which most incensed local opinion was the abolition of the Port of Spain municipal council in 1898. The council, while limited in its franchise and membership, had been at least an elected assembly that had some semblance of a 'democratic' presence in the political arena. Its removal not only contributed to the Water Riots, but also gave an impetus to more permanent movements of protest such as the Ratepayers' Association and the Trinidad Workingmen's Association (TWA), founded around the turn of the century. The authorities were able to resist demands for popular participation in colonial government during the period up to 1914, but thereafter, with wartime changes helping greatly to consolidate and expand the base of popular opinion, it became much more difficult to withstand the pressure building up on the streets. By the early 1930s it was possible for C. L. R. James to write, with some justification, that 'For a community such as ours … the Crown Colony system of government has no place … It was useful in its day, but that day is now over. It is a fraud, because it is based on assumptions of superiority which have no foundation in fact.'[36]

During the entire interwar period popular discontent was being voiced in various forms. The days when Constantine was establishing his place as one of

Trinidad's leading cricketers was also a time when the political and economic status quo of the pre-War years was under question. From being a preserve of the white plantocracy and merchant class, with an increasing involvement by the black middle class – an exclusivity that mirrored, in fact, the limitations in organized cricket of the pre-1914 period – the politics of the post-First World War years was vastly different. Direct participation in the war prompted new mentalities about participation in politics. Black men had been involved in military service in Europe and the Middle East with the British West Indies Regiment (BWIR). Colour prejudice had prevented the regiment being deployed in a front-line role, and its troops experienced various forms of racial discrimination and humiliation: digging latrines was frequently their lot. The experience sent them home angry and looking for changes in the island's polity. A white Creole, Captain A. A. Cipriani, had acquired a political standing and admiration as an army officer defending the cause of black soldiers of the BWIR, and back in Trinidad it was Cipriani who emerged as the spearhead of a new movement.

By 1919 Cipriani had taken a lead in organizing protests for constitutional reform in Trinidad. At the same time local workers' groups, with the dockworkers of Port of Spain prominent, were taking action to demand wage increases and improvements in their working conditions. It has been estimated that prices in Trinidad had risen by 145 per cent between 1914 and 1919, with no accompanying increase in money wages.[37] The early 1920s thus saw the emergence for the first time of mass protest movements and strikes, which converged under the leadership of the TWA, its membership and influence immeasurably boosted by working-class discontent. Cipriani became its president in 1923 and during the following decade exercised an unquestioned political and moral authority over the protest movements in Trinidad. It was nowhere better illustrated than in C. L. R. James's tribute to his work, *The Life of Captain Cipriani*, published in England in 1932. Ironically, however, by the time of its publication Cipriani's influence was weakening. His strategy of political reform had run into the buffers of white resistance in the island's Legislative Council.

The effects of the world depression, notably the fall in prices of agricultural products, were severe in the Caribbean. Economic and social conditions, already bad, worsened during the course of the 1930s. Between 1934 and 1939, in an endeavour to prevent wage reductions and to do something about worsening housing conditions, strikes, hunger marches and mass demonstrations were organized by working men and women throughout the area. They were, in Howard Johnson's words, 'unprecedented in their scope and scale.'[38] They posed the most serious challenge to colonial hegemony yet witnessed in the region. Brereton has noted further that by this time Cipriani's influence in workers' movement had passed to far more radical figures who linked material discontent to race consciousness and the idea of black nationalism.[39] There was thus a political, as well as an economic, dimension to the protests. Uriah Butler was the most conspicuous of these new leaders, and it was his presence at demonstrations in Trinidad in 1937, and the attempt by the authorities to arrest him, that sparked riots in which several people were killed. These incidents, exacerbated by a reactionary response from the Trinidad authorities, forced the British government to intervene in 1938 with a move that promised some form of palliative action. A Royal Commission (the Moyne Commission) was set up to make recommendations about tackling the various unresolved political, economic and social problems that had been developing in Caribbean since the late-nineteenth century. The Commission, whose members included Walter Citrine, the secretary of the British TUC, offered for the first time a sympathetic hearing to the discontents of the working class. Citrine urged in particular immediate action on housing conditions. The Commission's recommendations were published in February 1940 (although the full report was not disclosed until 1945) and included a proposal to create a West Indian Welfare Fund, to be administered outside the confines of the local colonial administrations. It was embodied in the Colonial Development and Welfare Act of that year, which made available injections of cash for such things as subsidies to the sugar industry and the provision of basic social and welfare services. Little was spent, however, before the end of the Second World War, and what is more none of the schemes resulting from the unrest of the 1930s presented any solutions to the deeper structural problems that had beset the Caribbean economies during the past century.[40] When local people from the Caribbean islands who served in Britain during the 1939–45 war either as factory workers or in the armed services returned home afterwards many of them found work very difficult to come by. The answer seemed to be in going back to the mother country to look for jobs there. Here lay the roots of the mass migrations across the Atlantic in the second half of the century.

IV

'Getting on' in this world, where challenges to white authority seemed simply to stiffen the plantocracy's conservatism, was not easy without the necessary credentials. Where a secondary education of the kind James had enjoyed would usually assure a man of a respectable post, Constantine had received no such training. He was saved from a life of relative obscurity by cricket. It helped that his father was a renowned player, though Lebrun seems, judging from his son's writings, to have been rather pessimistic, and rightly so, about his son's prospects in cricket. There seemed very few avenues leading to a career in which a black player might sustain himself and his family through earnings in cricket. Learie was at pains to point out that Lebrun insisted he should not expect any favours and preferred that he concentrate on obtaining a clerical job.[41] In fact, for the first three years after leaving school Constantine played very little cricket. When he did resume he had to fend for himself. 'I started to play second-class cricket for Victoria, my father being strangely reluctant that I should play. He would not help me in any way and I had to save a shilling or two week by week out of my scanty pay to provide myself with a pair of regulation flannel trousers.'[42] When he scored six not out in his first game, batting for almost an hour, he was, he claims, strongly rebuked by Lebrun: 'You wasted your time ... You have a bat in your hands to score runs with, instead of which you stayed there trying not to get out.'[43] Nonetheless, Lebrun's influence was probably responsible, at least indirectly, for Learie ('Young Constantine') becoming noticed and making valuable connections in the game. Lebrun stood down in important trial matches to give Learie a chance of selection to the 1921 Trinidad team, and his father's financial support helped Learie through a difficult patch of unemployment in 1924–25.[44] After a modest beginning Learie made the most of opportunities that came his way on the cricket field, and natural ability began to show.[45] Playing in the hard regime of Shannon cricket he attracted the attention of influential figures. Major Harragin, for example, a former white West Indies player who captained Trinidad, recommended Learie for consideration for the island team.[46] Yet more important, the doyen of Caribbean cricket, H. B. G. Austin, who had led the 1906 tour in England when Lebrun was a member of the party, was the prime mover in the still relatively inexperienced Learie being selected for the 1923 tour to England. Learie had played in only a few big matches by this time. Austin liked Constantine's fielding, though on the basis of his achievements so far with bat and ball his selection was something of a gamble. But the 1923 tour was a good one to go on. Challenor impressed mightily with his batting, while Constantine, as *Wisden* later recalled, 'earned widespread praise for his fielding at cover point'.[47] From then on his progress in West Indies cricket was uninterrupted, and rapid. He added slip fielding to his repertoire, developed into a genuinely fast bowler, and showed that he could produce from time to time (often when it mattered) an attacking innings with the bat. By 1926 he was impressing for the West Indies team against a strong MCC touring party, and in the following season, though now playing his club cricket in the oilfields on account of a new job there, his stature was assured: as the *Port of Spain Gazette* reported of his performances for Trinidad against Barbados – 'All worked hard – Constantine, as usual, was the outstanding figure.'[48] When the West Indies, now with full test match status, visited England in 1928, Constantine was at the peak of his powers.

Cricket, however, while it brought him admiration as a sportsman, earned him no money. Outside the game his prospects were limited. His future was certainly not assured, but neither was it entirely without promise. It was here that Constantine experienced the real world of colonialism. He needed to earn a living and there was no guaranteed advancement in the labour market for a black man. Leaving school during the First World War he originally nourished the ambition of going into the law, though the training required was surely beyond the means of a large family with four other children. He took on clerical jobs in solicitors' offices largely because it would allow him, after ten years' service, to take the solicitor's exams. But, to concentrate on cricket, these posts, which increased in responsibility over the course of some five years, fell by the wayside, to be followed by a series of temporary posts with few prospects. Yet, as Constantine himself said, 'Cricketers, like other people, must live', especially when, in 1927, they are married with a newly born child the following year.[49] Constantine, as the local Trinidad paper noted, 'is in no affluent circumstances'.[50]

In the absence of a fully professionalized system in West Indies cricket, some form of patronage, similar to the one his father had benefited from, was one way forward. It was not out of the question for Learie. The prospect of such a position arose in a recent growth-sector of Trinidad's economy: oil. As Brereton points out, oil production had taken off as a result of the development of the internal combustion engine at the turn of the century.[51] Oil overtook sugar and cocoa as the island's main export by the early 1930s, and was even more to determine Trinidad's economic future as a fundamental resource for the British war economy in the Second World War. Trinidad oil came to account for some 80 per cent of the island's export. The industry attracted labour from a wide area of the Caribbean and beyond, and among the leading recruiters in this early phase of development was the British-owned company Trinidad Leaseholds Ltd (TLL), which had the island's largest refinery at Pointe-a-Pierre. Yet race antagonisms were as deeply embedded here as elsewhere. For black people the jobs available at the oil companies were invariably menial ones. The industry was notorious for racial discrimination when it came to applying for anything above the level of unskilled manual labour. Black workers were 'debarred from staff positions'[52] and excluded from the social and sports clubs in the oil installations. The oil drillers were white, often from the southern states of the United States or South Africa, and arrived with intransigent segregationist ideas. These people were, as viewed by the left-wing observer Arthur Calder-Marshall, 'despised' by the black people for the discriminatory attitude they adopted.[53] It contrasted markedly with the rather milder and more paternalist attitudes of the white Creoles. As may be imagined, the harsh discipline in the oilfields' industrial relations became an important factor contributing to the outbreak of industrial unrest on the island in the later 1930s.

For Constantine, however, the industry was a possible source of security. In 1927 his celebrity as a cricketer brought an opportunity that promised to take him through the oilfields colour bar. He was offered employment at TLL.[54] Being based in the oilfields meant that, as far as cricket was concerned, he was unable to play for Shannon during the 1927 season. But the company granted him leave of absence to go to England with the 1928 West Indies team. According to some accounts Constantine was determined to seize the opportunity while on tour to stake a claim for employment as a professional in England.[55] It would be his personal revolt against colonialism. But it came about (as did many other things in his later life) because his celebrity in cricket allowed him to evade the normal oppressions of colonial racism. His eventual success in finding a job at Nelson Cricket Club in the Lancashire League is often regarded as Constantine's escaping the constraining and humiliating circumstances of the system in which he had been brought up.[56] But at the same time Nelson presented an immense gamble, in both cricketing and racial senses. Would he succeed in the cricket of the northern English leagues? Would he be accepted by the local people? If he were not, what would be his reception when he returned to Trinidad? Might he have preferred to stay in Trinidad and seek to prosper in a relationship of patronage?

Another point to consider was a significant local 'pull' factor. It manifested itself in the form of a groundswell of local opinion to keep Constantine in the West Indies. The motive seems not to have sprung from a desire to do Constantine a personal favour so much as to assuage national cricketing pride. The *Port of Spain Gazette*, one of the two leading papers in Trinidad, had a prominent voice in this opinion. The *Gazette* had never been a particular friend of the black community. It spoke to a white English readership, exemplified in its reports of cricket, which usually gave more prominence to English county matches than to local competitions. But when it became clear during July 1928 that an English league club had made Constantine an offer, which the *Gazette* described as 'a very good one', the paper launched a campaign to keep the player in Trinidad. The *Gazette* recognized Constantine's value to the West Indies team, and that without him the test match status recently granted by the Imperial Cricket Conference might be jeopardized. It was a matter of some concern in Caribbean cricket circles that the team should fulfil international expectations. The *Gazette's* line was, in effect, if we in Trinidad want to keep Constantine, we must find the financial resources to back him. Constantine himself had held off accepting Nelson's terms and expected to return to the West Indies after the tour before making a decision. Perhaps he wanted to see if the newspaper's campaign produced results. He had earlier said that he could do nothing until the advice of his family had been sought. His father and mother had both indicated that they hoped he would not leave Trinidad, but much depended on the view of his wife.[57] Many people, however, appeared already to have assumed that the Nelson offer was a done deal. This probably explains why a fund, started in the islands in mid-June 1928 with the aim of raising money to keep Constantine in the West Indies, received initially only a lukewarm response.[58] In the light of this the *Gazette* hinted at measures of a more forceful nature being taken: 'It is unfortunate that any effort should be made to rob West Indies cricket of its best player and it is probable that influences will be brought to bear with the object of preventing this.'[59] Quite what these 'influences' might have been, and whether they would have produced the desired effect, was not made clear, and as it worked out the means to keep Constantine in the Caribbean did not materialize. The *Gazette* had always understood that the scheme might not work: 'Love of one's birthplace may be very strong', it commented reluctantly, 'but when one sees that nothing is being done in the land of one's birth, goodbye to Home Sweet Home is the only alternative.'[60]

'Goodbye' it was. When the Nelson club came up with its offer the sums proved too tempting to refuse. It was carefully scrutinized by two senior figures: Lebrun Constantine himself, and Fred Grant, the president of the recently formed West Indies Cricket Board. Both agreed that the proposed contract was sound: 'The opportunity', as Grant put it, 'should not be missed.' It gave Learie an appointment for three years, with an option of renewing for a further two, at a salary of £500; that is, £25 a week for a season of twenty weeks between April and August. In addition there was talent money at £1 for fifty runs and the same for five wickets.

A return passage to Trinidad was provided for Learie and Norma, allowing them to spend the winter in the Caribbean.[61] Constantine accepted the deal for the financial rewards it offered. It was also a possible exit route from the colour bar of the West Indies. But at the same time there was doubt: that a colour bar set even higher would confront him in England.

3

Cricket

Cricket's development has always been shaped in a process of global exchange. Initially the geographical extent was demarcated by the limits of the British Empire.[1] Ideas about how the game should be played were created, transmitted and contested within this framework. Imperial power relations and imperial racial mentalities were therefore instrumental in shaping the form the game adopted. These forces were most evident in the fashioning of an 'aesthetic' of cricket.

Cricket has long been a game bound by a concern with 'correct' play – a notion of performance that combines physical technique, mental attitude, moral behaviour and bodily style. It has been ingrained in its players over the years through countless coaches and coaching manuals. Such literature has, in many cases, been informed by rules that had their origin in English private schools. Adherence to approved methods, it might be claimed, has ensured efficient technique which in turn has created and reproduced the 'beauty' of the game – an aesthetic sensibility celebrated and reproduced in the game's extensive literature.[2] The harmonizing of 'correct' techniques in batting and bowling with a gentlemanly demeanour in the conduct of the game created cricket's distinctive art form. Cricket was regarded as a sporting manifestation of civilized behaviour. In the game, as in life generally, what was not civilized was said simply to be 'not cricket'. The dominance in the game of the 'amateur' – a person not *paid* to play – and of the social class to which he invariably belonged, ensured that this spirit was maintained in cricket. It is, to a certain extent, a class-based aesthetic. It is also compounded of racial ideology – it is a white aesthetic.

How might the precepts be applied to the development of cricket in the Caribbean? Can we see cricket enveloped in a controlling colonial discourse, an extension of the racial power relations that prevailed in the British Empire? And if so, when and how might such a cultural hegemony have been challenged and changed? One legend that requires careful attention in considering these questions is the notion that black West Indian cricketers have brought an especial 'carefree-ness' into cricket. Their game, it has often been asserted, manifests a 'natural' approach to sport, embodying a lissome grace, in contrast to the more studied methods adopted by white English players.[3] This notion was present most vividly in the writings of Neville (later Sir Neville) Cardus, who for some fifty years following the Great War served as the influential cricket and music correspondent of the *Manchester Guardian* newspaper. Here, for example, is Cardus describing Learie Constantine soon after encountering him on his second tour of England, in 1928: 'The movements of Constantine in the field are strange, almost primitive, in their pouncing voracity and unconscious beauty, a dynamic beauty, not one of smooth curves and relaxations.'[4] Constantine, the 'thick set rather slow boy' encountered by fellow Trinidadian C. L. R. James aged 11[5] had developed into the striking athlete who toured England with H. B. G. Austin's team of 1923 and who astonished everyone by his speed and brilliance at cover point. Fascination with his predatory presence in the field was established at this time and never waned, from the day 'Cricketer' (Cardus again) watched him at Old Trafford in 1928 and wrote in the *Manchester Guardian* of his animal-like power:

> His action as he hurled the ball at the stumps was thrilling because of its vehemence and poise. Constantine is a graceful cricketer: his aggressiveness – nay ferocity – is expressed in beautiful curves. Strength comes out of his body so easily and swiftly that coarseness is expelled by manhood's own rhythm.[6]

Cardus, a writer ever alert to the mythic dimension of sport, created of Constantine the 'representative' (as he termed it) West Indian cricketer. His superbly athletic, apparently spontaneous play expressed, claimed Cardus, the West Indian 'temperament':

> When we see Constantine bat, bowl or field we know at once that he is not an English player ... we know that his cuts and drives, his whirling fast balls, his leapings and clutching and dartings in the slips, are racial; we know they are the consequences of impulses born in the blood, heated by sun, and influenced by an environment and a way of life much more natural than ours – impulses not common to the psychology of the over-civilized quarters of the world.[7]

In celebrating what he saw as Constantine's uninhibited style of cricket, Cardus was implicitly contrasting it with a 'safety first' dullness that seemed to have seeped into the English game by the 1930s. There is a hint in all this of D. H. Lawrence's notion of a post-1918 'decline' of a West in need of revitalization through the primitivism of more elemental cultures. It saw in black people a capacity for spontaneous energy that stemmed from their assumed closeness to nature. Their very 'underdevelopment', by contrast with 'over-civilized' Europeans, eradicated artifice and brought an ability to dispense with reason and science to capture the joyous 'essence' of humankind. Constantine's playing of cricket was natural, simply an expression of himself: 'To say that he plays cricket … is to say that a fish goes swimming.' Though not all of the press reporting of West Indian cricket in this period indulged in such image making, the idea of Constantine almost as an *enfant sauvage* was nevertheless a common one that remained with him during almost the whole of his playing career.[8]

It was appropriate that Constantine was one of the first cricketers to excel in the art of fielding.[9] It is the least formal of the game's arts. As a young man he specialized in fielding at cover point, a position demanding swift movement to cut out boundary shots and deny batsmen quick singles. A clean pickup and accurate throw to the wicket keeper was essential. A good fielder in this position was indispensable to a successful team, as well as being a source of immense excitement to the watching spectators. Constantine was quick off the mark, with a fluid, easy gait. It was a pleasure just to see him move. In this role he fitted perfectly the Cardus idea of the uninhibited Negro. Constantine's suppleness and speed of movement underlined the notion of the natural rhythm of the black man. The cricket writer and broadcaster John Arlott described him as being 'so joyously fluid and … acrobatic, that he might have been made of springs and rubber'.[10] England captain and Yorkshire batsman Sir Leonard Hutton, in an obituary for Constantine, recalled: 'He was by far the best [fielder] I had seen … He ran as though his feet did not touch the ground.'[11] He was, indeed, jocularly known in Lancashire as 'electric heels', and 'electric' – with all its linguistic connotations of vitality and modernity – was the adjective most frequently employed to describe his play. 'There are no bones in his body' wrote Cardus, 'only great charges and flows of energy.'[12] His presence on the cricket field was sufficient in itself to draw the crowds, and during his time at Nelson he so boosted attendances in local matches that in 1935 all the clubs in the league joined together to stage a testimonial match for him.[13] While his big-hitting batsmanship and fast bowling were capable of producing spectacular moments of play, the popular memory of Constantine was often not so much his runs and wickets but the magical fielding skills that conjured up an amazing catch or an unconsidered run out. Thus an opponent from Colne in Lancashire recalled some thirty years afterwards one such galvanizing experience:

> Connie [Constantine] was fielding in the gully. I slammed the ball hard and low and expected four runs, but I turned round to find that Connie had caught the ball and put it in his pocket almost as everybody else on the field was looking for it at the boundary. It could not have been more than a few inches off the ground and Connie was only about four yards from the bat end. It was an unbelievable catch.[14]

As one speaker observed at the dinner in Nelson to mark Constantine's election as a Freeman of the Borough in 1963, he was a 'variety act'.[15]

There was an ambivalence about these perceptions of Constantine. On the one hand he was a source of wonder and admiration, someone unique in the cricket world; as many commentators have noted, Constantine was the equivalent on the cricket field of the nigger minstrel acts in the variety theatres. On the other, he defined white European-ness by being categorically neither white nor European. He was a member of a race imagined in contemporary minds as 'inferior'. The qualities the image emphasized were physical ones, those of the senses and youth, rather than rational or 'constructive' ones. They belonged to the same ideology of race that had generated the environmental determinist idea of tropical riches, from which it was inferred that black people were naturally lazy, lacked a work ethic, and were therefore 'underdeveloped'. It was an ideology that continued to inform some aspects of colonial policy, especially in settler colonies, in the first half of the twentieth century, and it was responsible for much of the discrimination experienced by black people in Britain.[16]

II

Cardus had Constantine as the quintessence of West Indian cricket. Did this mean that the entire game in the West Indies was fixed in an image of racial difference? To an extent, from a European perspective, it was. A striking illustration of this is seen by the mid-point of the twentieth century, when the term 'calypso' cricket became a common way of describing the West Indian style. In part it derived from the presence of actual calypso bands among the West Indies supporters.[17] But it also denoted an idea of difference, of an unorthodoxy that defied established notions of how the game should be played, and indeed watched. And it was underpinned by certain racial assumptions. A style was attributed to West Indians that would not have been applied to Australians or South Africans.

The idea of 'calypso' cricket is worth pausing over. West Indian spectators at the test matches between England and the West Indies in 1950 were accompanied on the grounds by calypso bands and performers who penned lyrics reporting the play. The most celebrated of these were Lord Kitchener (on guitar) and Lord Beginner (vocals), both from Trinidad, with 'Cricket, Lovely Cricket' their calypso of praise to 'those two little pals of mine' Ramadhin and Valentine.[18] Crowd participation at cricket was not a new thing. Spectators at northern grounds had long been renowned for their curmudgeonly comments on the standard of play, but these were individual, spontaneous and sometimes amusing, if unmelodic. When the Middlesex batsman Denis Compton, who was famous both for his stylish batting and for advertising a hair-styling preparation, was bitten by a dog that had run onto the field during a test match at Leeds, a wag in the crowd shouted 'rub some Brylcreem on it'. Association football grounds, later the site of chanting, sometimes witty but more often ribald and crass, were not before the 1960s known for mass singing. 'Abide With Me' at the Football Association (FA) Cup Final was exceptional, the very opposite of spontaneous.[19] While brass bands might play during the intervals at seaside cricket festivals, English cricket grounds simply did not have singing. And so, the calypso – a cultural creation of Trinidad – was a startling innovation. It represented a new way of being at the cricket; not just watching the play, though that was part of it, so much as making the whole occasion an experience to be enjoyed and celebrated. It was of course also a way of establishing the identity of certain parts of the crowd, those containing immigrants from the Caribbean who, during the 1950 tests, had arrived only a year or so earlier and were beginning to implant some of their own culture into English sporting life. These were England-based spectators, supporting the visiting team. It went much further than sport, though. Together with jazz, calypso was an early export from the Caribbean of a black music tradition that ran on to reggae, ska, blues and many other variants that were to shape British popular music in important ways.[20]

In the theatre of cricket the difference of the West Indies was also perceived in the way the team played. In the 1950 test series the home team was significantly outplayed. The West Indies had defeated England in individual test matches before, but had never won a series until 1950. Then, with England fielding teams that, for the most part, included seasoned professionals, some of high international standing (Hutton, Compton, Washbrook, Bedser, Evans), the West Indies had come with relatively inexperienced, and in many cases relatively unknown, players. Nonetheless in the batting Worrell, Weekes and Walcott, with strong support from Stollmeyer and Rae, dominated the English bowlers.

In the West Indies bowling two young spinners – Alf Valentine and Sonny Ramadhin – completely bamboozled the English batsmen. Before the tour Ramadhin had played scarcely any 'first class' cricket. The orthodox technique of these players could not be faulted; none of them dispensed with the basic rules of the coaching book, but they approached the game with confidence and a flair for attacking cricket. Constantine himself, in a lengthy preview of the tour for the *Daily Worker,* played up the differences in the approach to the game in the two countries: the West Indians exuberant, going into games with a joyful holiday spirit; the English professionals 'unsmiling' with 'grim-eyed officials sternly directing ... attention to averages, defence and the final day gate receipts'.[21] It seemed that England had been defeated by a more exuberant and inventive cricket team, and it came as a shock to English administrators and supporters alike. It might well have prompted the first appearance in 1952 of the *MCC Cricket Coaching Book*, aimed principally at youngsters in school and club cricket. 'It would seem that of recent years,' its editor noted, '[the] instinct for attack has tended to give place to a premature concern with defence ... with the resulting development of defensive technique in batting, bowling and field-placing the game is in danger of becoming *less vital and less enjoyable* for players and spectators alike.'[22] Vitality and enjoyment were what West Indies cricket appeared to have in abundance. The fear of English cricket becoming less 'vital' underscores the notion of a more dynamic racial essence at the core of the game played by what was by this time a predominantly black West Indies team. 'Calypso' cricket, therefore, summed up a style that set flair and excitement above obedience to approved technique.

These developments chime with some of C. L. R. James's thoughts about the game of cricket. James always felt strongly that cricket was an art form. Indeed, as far as Trinidad was concerned he sometimes claimed that cricket was its *only* art form.[23] In *Beyond a Boundary* he discusses at some length Bernard Berenson's ideas on the artistic qualities of painting, finding that two essentials – the tactile and movement – were both to be found in cricket, an art whose form also contained infinite dramatic possibilities. Thus cricket, like the 'high' art of painting, offered the combination of aesthetic line ('cricketers call it style' as James put it) and immediate resonance with the viewer/spectator.[24] James shared the views of Neville Cardus that cricket was art, though departed from Cardus in believing that cricket should not be relegated in a hierarchy of the artistic from 'higher' forms such as music. It was James who noted with displeasure that while Cardus the cricket writer could introduce musical allusions into his descriptions of play, Cardus the music critic never sought analogies from cricket.

Ideas about West Indian cricket contrasted with established notions of style. In the so-called Golden Age of cricket, roughly from 1890 to 1914, style had marked out the outstanding talents, especially in batting. There was a rough class distinction here: amateur players tended to be batsmen, the bowlers were more often than not professionals. For Cardus the Lancashire batsman of the pre-1914 era, the amateur A. C. Maclaren, was the epitome of style: 'I can still see the swing of Maclaren's bat, the great follow-through, finishing high and held there with the body poised as he himself contemplated the grandeur of the stroke and savoured it.'[25] Appropriately, considering the influences classical education wrought in late-Victorian discourse, Maclaren was to Cardus 'the noblest Roman'. In terms of style, Maclaren was matched by the Australian Victor Trumper: 'the most gallant and handsome batsman of them all; he possessed a certain chivalrous manner, a generous and courtly poise.'[26] In these terms, style was a white Anglo-Saxon attribute. We should remember also that until well after the Second World War cricket was governed by a peculiar set of imperatives that had little to do with commerce. Morality, Englishness, Empire and the beauty of the game were guiding principles.[27] It was not held that 'spectator appeal', with its implications of gate receipts and commercialism, be a *prime* factor in deciding how the game should be staged. Cricket got along quite effectively without becoming a fully commercialized project, in contrast to what it became in the later years of the twentieth century. The introduction of sponsorship in the form of the Gillette Cup (1963), and the further development of a money consciousness by Kerry Packer's World Series Cricket (1976–79) was a world away from pre-1914 thinking, when ways of playing were judged by the stylistic pinnacle achieved by players like Maclaren and Trumper.

III

Taking this long view – from the Golden Age to post-Packer – we may see that cricket has been subjected to differing aesthetics; that is to say, varying ways of thinking about and valorizing the game that determine what can be done and what, on the other hand, is unacceptable in the performance of play. Cricket in the colonial West Indies did not escape these imperatives. In view of the rigid racial and social controls that bound West Indian cricket and society, it should not be surprising that black cricketers did not figure in the classical pantheon of style. Like artists of any kind the 'language' through which they worked and the dominant aesthetic that guided them was part of the specific cultural circumstances that surrounded them. In the case of cricketers it was imposed by colonialism. Cricket in the Caribbean was a popular sport that brought together all levels of society but in a highly stratified form. Writing in 1912 Pelham Warner, a leading figure in English cricket both as player and later administrator, and who himself was from a Trinidadian Creole professional family, saw in the cricket of the Anglophone islands extensive enthusiasm for the game and much evidence of natural ability among of its players.[28] In international terms, however, the islands had a low standing. The Imperial Cricket Council (ICC) had been set up in 1909 to oversee the game internationally; it was comprised of representatives of England, Australia and South Africa, the countries that played each other in test matches at that time, and where cricket had developed into a 'mass', if largely male, sport. The West Indies were not admitted to membership of the ICC until 1926, playing their first test series in England two years later. Before then the Caribbean colonies were apprentices, judged by a white governing body according to how effectively they were building up to the level expected of 'test-playing' nations. The poor performance of the West Indies against England in 1928 caused some to think that their elevation had been premature, that the awarding to them of test match status had been a 'mistake'.[29]

In attaining 'test' level, exchanges over many years between cricketers in the West Indies and those of England had been very important. There were frequent tours to the islands by English teams of varying ability from the late-nineteenth century onwards. Before 1914 there were two tours to England, in 1900 and 1906, by West Indies teams of mixed race. The mixture, however, was singularly un-fluid. Teams, whether those representing individual islands or the combined Anglophone colonies, were stratified by race and function; that is to say, the batsmen were almost exclusively white and the bowlers black. The captain was always white. Most of the West Indies cricketers who attained the highest level of play in the early-twentieth century were members of either the English Creole/settler group (planters and merchants) or the small black middle class. Almost all – whether white or black – had been educated at elite schools such as Queen's Royal College (QRC) in Port of Spain or Harrison College and The Lodge in Barbados.[30] At these schools cricket was coached and played according to conventional techniques that would have been taught in English public schools (often by former English professional cricketers). C. L. R. James, an alumnus of QRC, was himself a product of this system. There was no greater lover of cricket than James, and he played the 'English game', sometimes very well.[31]

Before the First World War, and then during the tour of England in 1923, the most admired West Indies player was the batsman George Challenor, a member of a wealthy white planter family from Barbados. Learie Constantine's father, Lebrun, was the leading black player in the West Indies before 1914. He was an exception in that he played mostly as a batsman. When Pelham Warner played against him in Trinidad he thought him 'the best native bat in the West Indies.'[32] The journal *Cricket* also praised his other skills: 'A fine stalwart of black manhood ... he has all-round qualities ... is very useful as a change bowler, can keep wicket, and is a good field.'[33] His powers were acknowledged, but he was rarely, if ever, noted for a 'style'. He had not attended an elite school, and as a cricketer was very largely self-taught. As in later years, the West Indies produced some fine fast bowlers before and just after the First World War, possibly the best in all the cricket-playing countries at that time. Cumberbatch and Woods, both of Trinidad, received praise for their bowling before the war,[34] and on the 1923 tour George John and George Francis were fearsome. John, though by this time around forty years of age, was particularly effective. On the whole, though, their threat to the batsman was moderated by their adhering to contemporary conventions about their type of bowling: on a length, around off stump, aiming for catches in the slips or by the wicketkeeper. 'For years,' cricket historian David Frith has commented about quick bowlers, 'there was something dishonourable about bowling to leg.'[35] The West Indies teams were at this time always captained by the white Harold (H. B. G.) Austin, and played according to the 'honourable' conventions laid down by MCC.

These conventions, then, were formed of ideas about race, class, gender, style and empire. Learie Constantine was among the first to throw down a challenge to them. Unlike James he had not been schooled in the game at QRC; he learnt something from his father, and much from watching and imitating established players.[36] By his early twenties he was playing for Shannon and soon attracting attention, not only for his name but for the dynamic style he brought to the cricket field. Importantly, he produced the most arresting display of this style in England. As a junior member of the West Indies touring party of 1923 he had – aside from his fielding – achieved little with either bat or ball. A man who might also have blazed the trail that Constantine later pioneered had been omitted entirely from that tour. He was a player whose batting revealed the first flouting of a white-imposed orthodoxy and the creation of something peculiarly 'Caribbean'. He was the flawed genius Wilton St Hill, one of C. L. R. James's early cricket heroes, an exponent of remarkable individual talents that sometimes defied rational analysis. His art was encapsulated in his mastery of that most difficult of cricket shots, the cut.[37] St Hill's arrival in England came later, in 1928, by which time he was probably past his best. On that tour his batting failed to impress, he had a dismal summer. St Hill's brilliance was therefore appreciated at its fullest in the islands and in Trinidad in particular, where, alongside Constantine at Shannon, he had helped to shape the powerful team of the early 1920s.[38]

By 1928 it was the younger Constantine who caught the eye of English spectators. The team as a whole, captained by the Dulwich College-educated white man Karl Nunes from Jamaica, was accounted by Wisden to have been less impressive than its predecessor of 1923. Constantine, however, in spite of his failures in the three tests, was praised for his bowling, batting and fielding: 'great pace ... hit fiercely ... fast and brilliant in the field.'[39] The display of the Constantine brand hinged on one match – frequently cited in accounts of Constantine's career – in which he was not even fully fit. It was his performance against Middlesex at Lord's in June, when he rescued his team from a seemingly impossible situation by making 86 and then taking 7 for 57, before winning the match with 103 in his second innings. It was his 'breakthrough moment'. It announced the arrival of a new kind of cricketer.

Constantine was, in many ways, a prototype for the form of cricket that was to appear internationally in the later twentieth century; the cricket of the one-day match, of limited overs, of attacking play, pleasing to spectators. But in his own day Constantine was something of an exception, difficult to categorize: a player who combined, almost in equal measure, all the cricketer's skills. Was he a batsman or a bowler? Or was he something even more unusual at this time, a player whose exceptional fielding skills made him almost indispensable to the team even without his batting or bowling? There had, to be sure, been all-rounders since the beginnings of the game. Some, like Gilbert Jessop, the Australian Warwick Armstrong, and Yorkshire's Wilfred Rhodes and F. S. Jackson, were expert batters and bowlers,[40] but no one had quite measured up to Constantine's calibre, and certainly not in the dynamic way he played the game. On his arrival in Australia in 1930, for what proved to be another disappointing test series, the crowds were charmed by his all-round skills. Though George Headley was acknowledged to be the better batsman Constantine possessed an intimidating presence on the field: '[he] is panther-like in all his actions. He never seems to do anything like anybody else ... Fielding had begun to look dull until Constantine came along ... He appears to be a law unto himself in the field, and makes batsmen uncomfortable.'[41] There are very few people (if any) still alive who saw him play in his prime, and there is little movie-film footage; what there is tends to be in fragments, mainly of Constantine batting. Photographs from the period are often posed stills. Film excerpts show a short-ish man, sleeves usually buttoned at the wrist, a quick mover, ready to have a swipe at the ball, sometimes in an ungainly fashion, and a bowler, often with a cap on, right-arm, gliding to the wicket and releasing the ball with a quick arm.[42] It is insufficient. Constantine lives on the page and in the memory. There is more – something that cannot be recorded mechanically. J. E. D. (Derek) Sealey, a Barbadian cricketer and schoolmaster, who for many years held the distinction of having been the youngest man to play test cricket, captured something else about Constantine – his *presence* on the field:

> He was not the best batsman, nor the fastest bowler I have seen and played against, but to be on a playing field with him was one of life's greatest and most exciting moments. To compare Learie's figures with other players is absurd, as mere figures cannot show his worth nor what he has done for our cricket in these islands and abroad.[43]

The English journalist R. C. Robertson-Glasgow, who had played for Somerset in the interwar years, considered Constantine's presence in a cricket match to be what most defined him. He was 'the magnet of the moment, whether batting, bowling or fielding … . Surely no man ever gave or received more joy by the mere playing of cricket'.[44]

It was this quality that seemed to contain something inherently West Indian that also seized C. L. R. James's imagination. When James described Constantine as a national hero in the Caribbean it was his cricket style that he was mostly taken with. What had been an English game as James had learnt it at QRC, an instrument of colonial control, was being strongly inflected by Constantine into something more authentically a product of the black Caribbean.

IV

Ironically, it was this that took him away from the West Indies. The story has been told many times of how Constantine was persuaded to go to Nelson as their professional for the 1929 season, the first West Indian player to appear in the Lancashire League;[45] of how his cricket that season drew the crowds, brought relief to a club needing to pay off debts, and led to Constantine staying on in Nelson for nine seasons of great successes for the club, becoming during that time a local hero. For Constantine himself the journey to Nelson was more than simply a step up the ladder, or a means of earning more money. It proved to be a liberating experience – it assured Constantine some financial security, and equally importantly gave him a status he would never have experienced in the West Indies.

Being a club professional meant that Constantine cut many of his links with West Indies cricket. Though he visited the islands from time to time during the winters, and played for the West Indies team in test matches, he left behind the club cricket in which he had grown up. Constantine described his former captain and mentor H. B. G. Austin as being 'cold' towards him over the decision to go to Nelson.[46] Austin, who had done so much to place the West Indies on the cricket map over the first quarter of the century, had played a key part in Constantine's emergence as an international player in the early 1920s. It was largely at Austin's insistence that Constantine was included in the 1923 touring party. It seems very likely, therefore, that he felt let down by Constantine's decision. Austin's coldness was probably to do, not so much with professionalism (though as a Barbadian he might have retained an old antipathy towards the idea of black professionals) as with his star player ceasing to be available as a coach and inspiration to youngsters in the islands. By going to England Constantine was shutting himself off to the game's further development in the Caribbean. The same could be said of the decision, a short while later, of George Headley to follow Constantine to Lancashire. On the other hand, however, both remained influential in international cricket. In the 1930s they were the names by which West Indies cricket was now known. Their eminence further registered the fact that the game was losing its white leadership. There had been a few good black batsmen before Headley (Lebrun Constantine, Joe Small for example), but he was the first to be the team's outstanding batsman.

This was a mark of a historic shift in world cricket, which Constantine further illuminated by his association with the dispute that rocked the game to its foundations in the early 1930s. This was the so-called bodyline controversy.[47] In a test series in Australia in 1932–33 the England captain Douglas Jardine, an amateur, had employed a particular form of bowling attack, designed chiefly to counteract the high scoring of Australia's leading batsman, Don Bradman. Jardine's plan was to use his fast bowlers, principally Larwood supported by Voce, to bowl short-pitched balls aimed on the leg stump at the batsmen's body, with a ring of close fielders ready to take catches as the batsmen sought to fend off the ball. The tactic succeeded. The ploy enabled England to win the series four matches to one. But, while successful on the field, bodyline failed off it. It caused diplomatic relations between Australia and England to become severely strained, with the Australians objecting that such cricket was dangerous and, what is more, contrary to the spirit of the game. The penalty for offending cricket's time-honoured conventions was that bodyline bowling was effectively abandoned in 1934. In a penetrating analysis of the controversy, Patrick McDevitt has shown how the dispute over Jardine's tactics turned on a number of interrelated issues that went far beyond cricket. Questions of social class, ethnicity, imperialism and gender fused together to form a powerful critique of the English team's sporting behaviour, quite at odds with the amateur ethos. Interestingly, what often came at the forefront of discussion was the question of gender: to be precise, notions of what was, and was not, 'masculine'. For their part the English authorities and players supported the argument put forward by Jardine in defence of his methods: that bodyline was a test of a cricketer's mental and physical courage, and that a good batsman should be sufficiently skilled and brave to withstand the attack. The inference drawn from this was that players who complained were cowardly, unable to fulfil the ideals of masculinity. Larwood was actually quoted as describing such complaints as 'an effeminate outcry'.[48] As against this position, the majority of opinion in Australia took the view that cricket should be played according to honourable traditions embodying the spirit of the game. 'Manliness' was to be found, not in intimidatory and dangerous bowling, but in good sportsmanship. The Australian viewpoint carried the implication, no doubt a valid one, that the English were simply indulging in casuistry, saying in effect that the end justifies the means – the end being an English victory at all costs, by fair or fell methods; the inference being that the English position was 'not cricket'.

In this immediate context the bodyline controversy appeared to have little connection with Constantine or the West Indies. It seemed to be a white man's argument. West Indian players had, it is true, applied tactics similar to 'bodyline' in the past – Constantine claimed in *Cricket and I* that George John had bowled it in island games in 1911,[49] while Constantine himself did in 1926 and again in 1928 against England. On the first occasion his bowling drew criticism from the English captain, F. G. Calthorpe, and in 1928 the English batsmen Hammond and Jardine found Constantine's bodyline decidedly unsettling.[50] In the far more prominent circumstances of the English season of 1933, immediately following England's successes against Australia in the bodyline series, Constantine, released by Nelson to play for his national team in one test match only, used a form of bodyline against the English batsmen. This case of the biter bit did not go unfelt, or unnoticed. The English players subjected to Constantine's deliveries complained of unfair tactics. Hammond, who never got on particularly well with Constantine in those days, was one victim, cut on the chin by a short-pitched ball from Constantine at Old Trafford.[51]

For Constantine the issue of bodyline had important ramifications: both for himself as a cricketer and a man, and for the West Indies team in international competition. One aspect of bodyline that is often overlooked is that it is a bowler's response to playing conditions that strongly favoured the batsman. One of Constantine's recurring criticisms throughout his playing career and afterwards, was about the imbalance in the game between bat and bowl brought about by the preparation of what cricketers used to call 'shirt-front wickets'; that is to say, pitches that were easy-paced and gave undue advantage to the batsman. It was a problem that had been recognized since the later 1920s, especially after the prolific run-getting season of 1928 in England when much doubt was cast on the preparation of wickets with various soil dressings.[52] Bodyline was, to an extent, designed to tip the balance the other way. As a fast bowler Constantine felt the need for some kind of change. In his first book *Cricket and I*, which appeared at the height of the bodyline controversy, he devoted an entire chapter to what he termed 'leg-theory and body-line bowling'. It is the most radical aspect of the book in a number of ways. First, he sought to establish that 'bodyline' was not a new thing – fast bowlers had always used it to keep the batsman guessing. It was, said Constantine, part of the game's subculture: '*These are the realities of cricket. These things cricketers know.*'[53] Second, he fiercely denounced Jardine's tactic of packing the leg-side field; it reduced cricket, he claimed, 'very nearly to a farce.'[54] The English approach to the game offended Constantine's sensibilities just as much as it did those of the Australians; it was contrary to 'the spirit of the game' – 'poor sport and no fun'.[55] Third, Constantine's chapter displays something more than a view on tactics; it exudes a self-confidence rooted in a racial identity that proclaims 'they are no better than we'. Constantine's bodyline bowling in 1933 was criticized in a variety of quarters: the English press, English county professionals (some of whom had been on the tour to Australia the previous winter), and even his own captain. He rebuffed it all. Constantine is saying, in effect: as a bowler I will bowl what I damn well please, no matter what the white bosses think. His defiant stance anticipated that of the West Indian team half a century later, when the similar tactics of its fast bowlers were disparaged in the British media.[56]

From this we might conclude that Constantine had sought to implant a new identity for West Indies cricket by the early 1930s: first by creating a style of cricket that departed from the conventions of the 'English game' as coached in the elite schools of the Caribbean, and secondly by espousing a tactic condemned by the cricket establishment, and attempting to justify its use by West Indies players. The effects of these personal and political initiatives varied. Bodyline was not persisted with in the West Indies team. The tactic not supported by Constantine's white captain, Jackie Grant, at the very time Constantine employed it. It was a bold, and largely personal, statement by Constantine that underlined his readiness to play the game in ways he chose. It was a form of kicking against the colonial status quo. But his style of play did persist and was universally admired, though it was a 'Constantine' style rather than one that characterized the West Indies players collectively. Few others followed him in this respect until after the Second World War. The 'English game', deeply rooted in Caribbean cricket through the colonial structures of sport, continued to influence. In the 1930s the best batsman by a long way in the islands was George Headley of Jamaica – often referred to in the press as 'the black Bradman' – whose style of batting, based essentially on playing off the back foot, was conventional but brilliantly executed. Constantine contrasted Headley with his own style. In a radio broadcast of 1939 Constantine was asked: 'Who is nearer the genuine West Indian type – you, with your tapping 'em hard and often, or George Headley with his comparative restraint and monumental patience?' In his answer Constantine played up to his stereotype: 'George Headley is a product of the modern age ... he represents a complete departure from the old West Indian tradition with which my own headlong style has more in common. Now that coaching is customary in the West Indies the old approach to the game is fast dying out.'[57]

Thus 'West Indian' cricket is swiftly characterized: a hybrid formed of old and new, spontaneity and artifice. It is an accurate assessment. The problem was, as we shall see in Chapter 5, that in his own writings Constantine, who observed many of the canonical methods of batting and bowling, became inclined to project his approach to cricket onto that of the entire West Indies and formulate a 'Caribbean' style: a dubious notion, though an interesting one.

4

Nelson

Without his knowing it Constantine could scarcely have chosen a more congenial environment for his new life in England. In Nelson Constantine took his first steps in casting off a colonial inheritance of racial subordination and becoming accepted as a 'black Englishman'. For the first ten years his habitat was the North of England, where he established friendships and connections that remained with him throughout his life. In the years after the outbreak of war in 1939, however, his networks widened. Constantine began a long association with a number of national bodies, the most significant and important of which, for him, was the British Broadcasting Corporation (BBC). His association with what was perhaps the most 'British' of institutions assured Constantine of a national status. But this was in a future that could not have been foreseen in 1929. At that point after his arrival from Trinidad, England meant Nelson. He arrived with no guarantees of success on the cricket field, and was faced with some racial hostility. Yet he and his family adapted to life there. He became as important to the town as the town was to him. Constantine's experiences in Nelson provided a personal lesson in racial 'assimilation', a notion that he was later, in the very different circumstances of mass immigration in Britain in the two decades following the Second World War, to formulate as a solution to race relations.

I

What kind of town was Nelson in 1929? An important question, because in a different urban environment Constantine might not have fared so well. Paradoxically Nelson, in most respects, could scarcely have been more different from the places in Trinidad where the Constantines had lived. It was a smallish industrial town of some 40,000 people, situated in north-east Lancashire, some four miles from the larger town of Burnley. Like all the settlements in this part of Lancashire it specialized in cotton manufacture. It was, unlike Trinidad's largely agricultural economy, a town given over almost completely to industrial production. It was, however, surrounded by open moorland country, rising to the Pennine uplands where Pendle Hill (1829 feet) dominated. On these moors farming accounted for a small proportion of the area's employment. The township of Nelson had been formed during the last phase of industrialization in cotton in the final quarter of the nineteenth century. It was, in effect, a 'new' town. Some 70 per cent of its labour force, which included a large female element, was engaged in the weaving trade. But, in spite of its late development, Nelson possessed none of the economic advantages often enjoyed by latecomers in other spheres of industry, notably those overseas, whence competition was later to present a problem. The town's growth was founded upon traditional forms of capitalization, business organization and technology. For the most part the cotton mills were small affairs, often subdivided into different firms, an arrangement based on what was known locally as the 'room and power' system. In effect, people with looms rented space and power from the owners of weaving sheds. It meant that manufacturers could set up quite easily with small amounts of capital. Weaving was done on the Lancashire loom, suitable for the finer cloths produced in Nelson, but it was technologically antiquated by comparison with the Northrop loom common in other countries. Of the larger undertakings in Nelson, James Nelson ('Jimmy Nelson's') was the biggest firm with over a thousand employees. By the 1920s its Valley Mills complex had discarded the old room and power arrangement and was operating exclusively with the firm's own looms. The owner, Amos Nelson (James's son), was already beginning a process of backward and forward integration in an endeavour to modernize his business and safeguard it against the world trade cycle. Amos Nelson had bought spinning mills in Bolton and Rochdale to secure his supply, and by the 1930s was looking to establish production in Tasmania to open up new markets on the other side of the world. By this time he had taken a major step to resist foreign competition by moving into the production of rayon. Jimmy Nelson's apart, however, the town's small-scale economy, with its old-fashioned technology and narrow capital base, was vulnerable when good trade turned to bad, as it could do quite rapidly. The local newspaper, the *Nelson Leader*, looking back in 1914 on fortunes in the cotton, noted a familiar downswing in trade: the 'exceptional prosperity and expansion' experienced a couple of years earlier had been followed by far less propitious conditions the following year.[1] Though local people were not to know it at the time, Lancashire cotton had reached its peak years in the four decades before the First World War. Thereafter the state of the local economy was more or less one of decline. To be sure, Nelson's cloth was of a finer quality – poplins for shirts and dresses, for example, which were well received in the Home Counties and North America – and therefore sold in dearer markets at home and overseas. This spared Nelson some of the harsher effects of the depression that came in the 1920s and, more especially, 1930s, shielding it for a time it from the foreign competition that undermined trade in the nearby centres of Blackburn and Burnley, where coarser cloths for colonial markets were woven. These relative advantages apart, Nelson experienced a characteristic that Constantine would have been familiar with from Trinidad: economic uncertainty. Cotton was like sugar – its economic fortunes were fickle. In the 1930s Nelson people became aware that the future might bring major problems, though it was to be another couple of decades before the bottom fell out of the cotton economy. When Constantine arrived, some people still retained an optimism nurtured in the pre-1914 conditions of boom, tempered though it was with a certain amount of foreboding about what lay ahead.[2]

Such circumstances placed big expectations on Constantine. His arrival was seen as an important event in sustaining the town's sense of direction. As in many industrial working-class communities sport formed a central part of Nelson's social life and civic identity. Sports clubs flourished in a town where mills, chapels, pubs and neighbourhoods provided the basis for a rich culture of voluntary association. Being relatively small in population Nelson lacked the resources to sustain a major League football club,[3] a key symbol of civic identity in larger urban communities. It was instead cricket that proclaimed the town through its sporting achievements. Fittingly, though, it was a form of cricket that bore some of the features of commercial football. The Lancashire League, an organization that had been formed in 1891 out of fourteen clubs in north-east Lancashire, had cultivated a competitive form of league cricket played during the afternoon and early evening of Saturdays. It was attuned to the needs of the local working populations in the towns and villages that made up the League, who left work at midday on Saturday. Local rivalry and keen spectator interest were the main features of the matches played. But in addition the cricketing prowess displayed by each club's professional player, usually a man of some national standing engaged as the local champion, contributed greatly to the excitement of the sport.

Nelson, as one of the larger towns in the League, had a history of success. Immediately after the First World War the club's professional was George Geary, a fine bowler from Leicestershire who was later selected for play for England on fourteen occasions. Geary was, as the Nelson chairman later commented, 'a most competent cricketer, but' and this is the key point, 'he did not attract the crowds.'[4] In response to this problem of spectator appeal Nelson Cricket Club, in 1921, had dramatically raised the stakes in the hiring of professionals by taking the unprecedented step of employing the Australian E. A. ('Ted') McDonald. McDonald had, in 1920–21, figured prominently in the back-to-back test series between Australia and England, in which the Australians won eight of the ten matches played (the other two were drawn). McDonald, together with his fast-bowling partner Jack Gregory, was the chief cause of Australia's success. So Nelson brought a world star to Lancashire. It was a bold move that anticipated signings of star players by leading football clubs. It was, of course, designed to secure Nelson's pre-eminence in the League, though it drew some criticism. The respected national sporting journal *Athletic News* judged it a risky venture,[5] and even the *Nelson Leader* did not hold back from commenting that 'the spirit of the game is made none the healthier by business transactions of this kind'.[6] It was, however, easy to see why Nelson wanted McDonald. He possessed the star quality that was to make footballers such as Dixie Dean and Alex James into crowd-pullers at football grounds in the late 1920s and early 1930s. McDonald was a dangerous yet graceful bowler whose art could be admired for both its aesthetic and its match-winning qualities. 'Whence does McDonald draw his terrible strength and velocity? His run to the wicket is so easy, so silent … A more beautiful action … was never seen on a cricket field, or a more inimical.'[7] Moreover, he was tall and lithe with dark good looks that gave him the allure of a film star. News of his signing produced a noteworthy increase in the number of female membership subscriptions at Nelson for the 1922 season.[8] The *Athletic News* had been right, however, to underline the financial risks involved in signing such players. McDonald, who played for three seasons before moving on to the Lancashire county club, and his white South African successor J. M. Blanckenburg (1925 to 1928) were expensive. McDonald reputedly cost Nelson £700 in wages for each of the three seasons he played.[9] They were popular players, but the gate receipts and increased membership they brought in did not prevent the club from falling into debt.[10] In Constantine Nelson saw exactly the kind of magnetic performer who would propel the club and the League farther along the distinctive path that had been embarked upon a few years earlier, and also wipe off at least some of the debt. The *Leader*, notwithstanding its earlier doubts about expensive professionals, hailed Constantine as a 'cricketer with a touch of genius', a 'super-player', and, most important of all, a 'spectator-bringer'.[11] Constantine was greeted with immense hope.

He himself knew little about Nelson. He was black, and had been brought up a Roman Catholic. From multi-ethnic Trinidad Nelson doubtless seemed a

strange environment. There were few Catholics, and no black people. Nelson
was a proletarian town with a radical political history and, in its religious life,
a strong nonconformist presence. Many social activities were carried out in the
context of the chapel. Although, as people of a new town, Nelson's inhabitants
were in many cases themselves immigrants or the children of immigrants
(mostly from nearby handloom-weaving villages in the Yorkshire Dales) internal
divisions based on place origin do not seem to have been significant cultural
barriers to urban cohesion. Nelson's social structure was compressed: most
people were workers, there was no marked class or status hierarchy. And, given
the nature of business ownership, there was no dominant local employer who
through patronage and public endowments might have assumed a seigniorial
role. Where other Lancashire towns had their civic identity bound up to a degree
with that of a prominent family in Nelson trade unionism, membership of which
had reached a near total coverage of the weaving workforce by the beginning
of the twentieth century, was the most obvious unifying force. The Weavers'
Institute was one of the town's leading centres of influence. Nonetheless, the
loyalties trade unions generated rested on an overall sense of capital–labour
conflict that could provoke hostility. An employers' Lancashire-wide lock out
of the weaving trade in 1911 exemplified the point. Moreover, during the First
World War, many Nelson people had adopted an anti-war stance. The socialist
Independent Labour Party (ILP), strong in Nelson, took the lead in condemning
the conflict, its meetings prompting pro-war demonstrations that sometimes
ended in violence. The war seemed to have brought to the surface tensions in
Nelson life that had previously been latent. The ILP was the main one of the
'many disruptive elements' in the town remarked on by the *Leader* at the end of
the war.[12] Amidst a growing sense of disharmony was the cricket club. Fittingly,
it was on its ground that the town's celebrations to mark the end of the war were
held. In a larger sense, the club offered a site where people of all persuasions
could meet together in relative harmony.

II

Initially Constantine's response to the town was lukewarm. He was plagued
with doubts over whether, as a black man, he might fit in. The first season was
difficult: although the cricket was a great success, he felt isolated socially. He
experienced problems of acceptance among some locals who were ignorant
of the West Indies and who had imbibed white conventional wisdom about

black people. Many anecdotes have survived about Constantine's colour. Most of them, though racist in essence, are mild attempts at humour.[13] Constantine accepted these without rancour, though he later admitted to having received rather harsher 'shots' (snubs) from people who objected to his colour. Many of these occurred on the cricket fields of Lancashire. Just before his death in 1971 Constantine told Noel Wild, the historian of Nelson Cricket Club, that matches against local rivals Colne were often particularly heated: 'It was not cricket; it was more like a bloody war.'[14] Racial abuse was part of it, usually in the form of verbal gamesmanship (what in later years came to be known as 'sledging') but with a clear racist overtone. Mostly it was limited to calling Constantine a 'black bugger' or something similar.[15] Others were more pointed. He did not hit it off well with Jim Blanckenberg, the South African whom Constantine had replaced at Nelson and who had moved to the East Lancashire club (Blackburn).[16] Constantine had heard 'second-hand stories' about Blanckenberg's racism, and felt 'furious' when the South African refused to shake hands at the beginning of a match. 'Hurt, insulted, but above all furious. And that day I bowled "bodyline" before the term had been invented.'[17] In 1938, when playing for Rochdale, Constantine reacted angrily to a racist remark made to him by an umpire, and sought to have it dealt with as a case of racial prejudice through the management structure of the Central Lancashire League. A different kind of intolerance extended to county cricket. When it was rumoured in the mid-1930s that Constantine might join the Lancashire club, as McDonald had done ten years earlier, the county professionals allegedly thought the idea 'ludicrous'. It was felt that Constantine and other West Indians in the local leagues would never play for the county 'because of their colour'.

> We Lancastrians were clannish in those less enlightened days. We wanted none of Constantine ... We would refuse to play. In all fairness I must say we had nothing against Learie Constantine personally. He was, in fact, very popular with us. There was no personal vendetta. But the thought of a black man taking the place of a white man in our side was anathema. It was as simple as that.[18]

Nelson, with its radical history, was generally a tolerant community, though not without pockets of right-wing politics. This was the time when Oswald Mosley was setting up the British Union of Fascists, a party that drew some support in the Manchester area. It was claimed by the pro-Labour *Nelson Gazette* that Constantine had been treated with scorn by a minority of 'snooty' people on his arrival in Nelson, just as the Labour MP Sydney Silverman had been the subject of anti-Semitic remarks when he first stood for Parliament for the Nelson and Colne parliamentary seat in 1935. The typescript autobiographical notes of a local worker, Nellie Driver, suggests a likely source of such opinion – a group of Mosley sympathizers, including influential members of the small but well-to-do business class. Driver and her mother appear to have helped organize a local branch of Mosley's British Union of Fascists, though the party never established itself with any real political force in Nelson.[19]

Taking all this into account it is not surprising to hear Constantine recalling in a radio interview some years later that at first 'we weren't treated too well [in Nelson] and that caused us unhappiness'.[20] He thought of breaking his contract and returning home. Had he acted upon this impulse he would have been remembered as one of a number of itinerant professionals who had spent a season or so with a club before moving on. What persuaded him to see it through was the attitude of his wife, Norma. She, as her husband always acknowledged, provided the backbone that Learie himself might otherwise have lacked.[21]

Little of this racial tension is evident in the records of the early 1930s. It resided in personal memories that Constantine expressed more openly in later years. When he did he sought to emphasize not the racial hostility itself but the manner of dealing with and overcoming it. His theme was perseverance in the face of problems. His remaining in Nelson was a vindication of his determination, with Norma at his side, to see things through. Opponents were won over; both he and they adapted to each other. The move to England had worked, not only on the cricket field but also in life generally. Racial harmony would ultimately prevail as a consequence of patience and tolerance on both sides. This was the moral that was stated emphatically in his later work in race relations, and which was inscribed in his book *Colour Bar*.

A good deal of this patience and tolerance came from the Constantines. The 'visitors' assumed many of the characteristics of the 'hosts'. They showed the willingness to adapt to local values. There developed what we might term the 'domestication' of Constantine. The 'animalistic' image of him seen in the descriptions by Cardus never left Constantine – it remained an essential part of his cricketing persona – but alongside the child of nature was created the idea of the dedicated, loyal and ambitious family man. It was a narrative that removed much of the discourse of race and replaced it with that of class and home. Constantine emerged from this as a solid middle-class paterfamilias who could readily be admired by respectable provincial society.

The local press had prepared some of the ground. To introduce him to its readers the *Nelson Leader*, a Liberal newspaper, ran full-page features with a prominent photograph at the time of his signing in July 1928, followed by an appreciation in April 1929 just before his arrival.[22] Together they construct an interesting and influential narrative. It begins with descriptions of the manner of Constantine's signing by the club, and provides extracts from several articles in the regional and national press as testimonials in praise of his abilities as a cricketer. The thoughts of two leading English players, Wally Hammond and Ernest Tyldesley, are quoted to underwrite the fact that Constantine was a dynamic and exciting player, and to confirm the astuteness of the Nelson club in securing such a catch. Beyond this, however, there are stories that serve to bring out those aspects of the man's personal qualities that had importance for local society. Constantine, it is noted, is a family man, married with a baby daughter (who, for the time being, would be staying with the family in Trinidad). He is shown to be respectful to his parents, who had brought up five talented children. The principal theme of an account of Constantine's early cricketing career is deference to elders; it tells of his willingness to learn, and to accept defeat with good grace. It presents him as modest but with confidence in his own abilities. Above all, Constantine has a self-discipline that ensures attention to success and self-improvement: 'I might say that conscientious training, exercise with chest developers, a love of fresh air and long walks help me considerably in my batting and bowling'.[23] Putting all this together: 'Constantine has that indefinable thing called personality; and this allied to great gifts should be of immense value to the club for some time to come'.[24] At the end of his first glorious season he and Norma left for Trinidad with a glowing testimonial from the *Leader*: 'It is no exaggeration to say that no cricket professional has left Nelson with happier memories, or left more behind. Amidst all the adulation and enthusiasm that has been showered upon him, he has had the good sense to preserve his balance, and success has not spoiled him'.[25] In view of what Constantine later said about this period of his career some of the paper's comments might be taken with a pinch of salt, but there is little doubt that from the town's point of view the man himself fitted the role of professional perfectly. If nothing else the gate money taken in 1929, a season blest with fine weather, enabled much of the club's debt to be cleared.[26]

What particularly reinforced this representation of Constantine was the idea of 'getting on'. From an early age his personal ambition was to make the transition from his occupation in Trinidad as legal clerk to becoming a qualified advocate. Encouraged by his wife and C. L. R. James, Constantine in Nelson enrolled on correspondence courses, and just before the onset of war in 1939 was employed by a firm of solicitors in Nelson with a view to becoming articled. The Second World War, in fact, was to bring quite different opportunities, but Constantine persevered with his law studies, eventually reaching his goal of being a barrister in 1954. Such dedication provided a point of contact, at least psychologically, with many people in Nelson. As a member of an incipient colonial lower middle class he could share some of the concerns about status and advancement of the small bourgeoisie of Nelson, for whom the cricket club was a natural focus of social life.[27] To a degree he also possessed a link with Nelson's working class. Though working men and women could, as Richard Hoggart has claimed,[28] be clannish, and certainly abhorred behaviour which seemed 'stuck up' from people who 'gave themselves airs and graces', they nonetheless respected a certain kind of ambition: it was a respect seen most clearly in the desire for sons and daughters to 'get on', and to have 'letters after their name'. Constantine could relate to this from his experience of the burning ambition of the colonial western educated elite to compensate for its racial insubordination by acquiring professional qualifications, and thereby a degree of independence.

The image of the man making his way in the world also helped to marginalize his racial otherness. The Constantine character became invested with 'good', one might almost say 'white', attributes. The qualities fashioned were important in two respects to local people. They were laudable in themselves, betokening sound character. But equally they signified his ability to discharge that character in a sociable manner, not as someone distant from his community. This was especially important in a radical town like Nelson. In chapel, factory and neighbourhood a rough-hewn egalitarianism prevailed. There was no tradition of paternalism or social deference. It was this that caused the Labour-dominated town council to refuse, in 1935, the granting of public money for celebrations to mark the King's silver jubilee.[29] In Nelson heroes had to be 'of' the people. In much that was said about Constantine there was ample reference to his heroic deeds on the field of play, but these exploits were generally framed in an image of the homely man. The language of home, family and neighbourhood was used to describe him. It stressed the very ordinariness of the Constantine household in Meredith Street, as the folks next door. C. L. R James, lodging with the Constantines in 1932–33, contributed to this image through an anecdote that seemed to him to sum up the local respect for his former hosts:

> Early one morning a friend turns up, has a chat and a cup of tea and rises to leave. "Norma, I am just going to do my shopping. If you haven't done yours I'll do it for you." Later Constantine said to me, "You noticed?" I hadn't noticed anything. "Look outside. It is a nasty day. She came so that Norma will not have to go out into the cold."[30]

In this incident, recalled many years later by James, there is inscribed in the rituals of daily life (cups of tea, shopping, nasty weather) a wish to honour someone who, though special, is also a neighbour whose door is open to visitors, and a person from an overseas world for whom the Lancashire climate could be intemperate. Is there also perhaps a hint of racial thinking there in the linking of race and weather: black people dislike the cold, just as they thrive in heat?[31] James's story is not an entirely fanciful confection dreamed up in later years. It sums up admirably the way Constantine was regarded in Nelson. He was invited to meetings and expected to participate in the life of the community. He willingly accepted the position of President of the young filmgoers' Mickey Mouse Club at the Regent cinema.[32] Nelson, it seemed, wanted to display him because it was proud of him. Moreover, Constantine *sounded* impressive. In such a simple matter as speech his 'beautiful English' was remarked upon, and compared to the 'broad Lancashire accent' of those around him.[33] He had brought esteem to the town, and in turn the town revealed its respect for a man whose race would, in many other places, have put him in an ambiguous position. Constantine responded appropriately, always ready to affirm Nelson as his home. He and Norma remained residents of the town, living in the house in Meredith Street, long after he had ceased to be a Nelson player. The house, if slightly up market, was not greatly different from the kind of dwelling in which most Nelson people lived. He returned there after cricket tours, visits to his family in Trinidad, and, during the Second World War, his work as a welfare officer in Liverpool. He only departed finally for London in the late 1940s, in the quest for his qualification in the law, once his daughter had completed her education at the local grammar school and at university in Scotland.[34] His departure from Nelson was consistent with the legend. He was leaving to 'get on'. But he could always return 'home'. In 1963, just prior to being given the Freedom of the Borough, he turned up in the town with letters after his name: he was now Sir Learie Constantine, MBE, High Commissioner for Trinidad and Tobago. '[He] came home again to Nelson on Tuesday' announced the *Leader*, in the course of a piece about renewing old friendships and visiting familiar places. It reminded readers that Constantine's route to fame had started, as they saw it, in their midst, and it was thus as much a story about the town as about its hero.[35]

Family was important, both in Constantine's acceptance by British society and for Constantine himself. It is mentioned in most of his writings, with particular emphasis on the influence of his father. But while Nelson became 'home' for Learie, Norma and Gloria, contacts with the Trinidadian members of the family became infrequent. Learie played cricket in the West Indies from time to time in the 1930s, though the number of visits back to the Caribbean in the English winter seem to have diminished during the course of the decade. Norma and Gloria did manage the journey in 1935–36 for the cricket matches against England, and Norma was no doubt able to see her own family – the Coxes – in which there were six daughters. Learie's parents, Lebrun and Anaise, also remained in Trinidad. Long after his own cricket career was over and he had left behind the cocoa estate, Lebrun took a post as a ward officer in the Aruca district. Upon their retirement Learie bought a house for his parents in Tunapauna. Both died in the early 1940s. Lebrun was honoured with a funeral at which several well-known people attended. Wilton St Hill was one of the pallbearers,[36] but Learie himself was unable to attend either his mother's or his father's funeral because of wartime travel difficulties. After that, contacts with his siblings seem to have been minimal. Younger brother Rodney – whose potential as a cricketer Learie rated very highly – had died young. Elias also grew up to be good at cricket and made an attempt, unsuccessful as it turned out, to establish himself as a cricketer in the northern English leagues in the later 1930s.[37] With his extended family now out of reach, Meredith Street became the focal point of Learie's family life. Elias stayed there when playing cricket, as did many fellow West Indians, cricketers and aspiring writers, who were visiting and in some cases seeking to establish a career in England. The house became, as Constantine's daughter describes it, 'like Grand Central Station'.[38] Learie's natural sociability made him a good host who liked to help whenever he could. His lodging of C. L. R. James ('Nello') for several months in 1932–33 was a typical example. Through his contacts in the cricket world, especially with Neville Cardus, Constantine was able to secure for Nello a job writing cricket reports for the *Manchester Guardian*. The house had only two bedrooms, though the one at the back was big and might easily have been divided into two. Learie had bookshelves installed and it became Nello's study while he was there. It was here that he worked on his Captain Cipriani book.[39] Later Gloria took it over as her own study, grateful for the shelving for her school and university work. With the frequent visitors and guests, Norma found that a great deal of her time was given over to household management and ministering to Learie. His cricket preparations demanded much of Norma's time. In a radio interview of 1950 she described very clearly her duties: cooking, helping him keep physically fit, washing his kit, ironing his silk cricket shirts, packing his bag before a match, accompanying him to receptions, and protecting him from visitors who arrived at awkward times.[40] She was a dutiful wife, whose time for her own interests was scarce. Norma was a very elegant woman of striking appearance, who always dressed well, and liked to decorate the house with flowers. Her hobbies included collecting china and silverware, and during the Second World War she joined the St John Ambulance Brigade, gaining certificates in first aid and home nursing, always ready for duty at the local first-aid post. She liked to travel, and embarked with Gloria on a visit to France and Switzerland in 1939 while Learie was playing for the West Indies in England. Gloria Valere speaks fondly of this trip, mother and daughter enjoying a splendid time until the imminent threat of war forced their speedy return to England. The West Indies team had already embarked (without Learie) on its return to the Caribbean via Montreal, and Gloria recounts how the three Constantines finally reunited at Euston Station after searching for each other at various London locations.[41] Norma was the perfect consort for the local hero and very definitely the guiding hand for Learie and Gloria in a close and loving family.[42]

What particularly endeared the people of Nelson to Constantine was the respect that the townspeople had shown to him. As a black man, respect was important. The affection shown when he announced his decision to leave the club in 1937 was remarkable. At the match against Lowerhouse in June, the Old Prize Band struck up 'Abide With Me'[43] and Constantine himself admitted to being 'amazed, and deeply touched, by the pressure that was brought to bear on me to stay. People whom I scarcely knew stopped me in the street and asked me to reconsider my decision'.[44] It was fitting that Constantine produced his greatest batting display for Nelson in one of his last games. It was a record-breaking 192 not out against East Lancs at Blackburn on August Bank Holiday Monday 1937. On a baking hot day, in a packed Alexandra Meadows, the match produced some outstanding performances, though none to surpass Constantine's. Dropped when he had scored only one, he first rescued Nelson from a poor start (65 for 5 at one stage) and then moved into a full-scale attack: 'He danced down the wicket to slaughter the slow bowlers, he slashed the ball to the ring off his back foot, he flicked the ball here and patted it there. A master, a tantalising autocrat among batsmen … Truly a day of days.'[45] An 'admirer' wrote an appreciation in the *Leader* shortly afterwards, which surely summed up the feelings of many people about local sporting heroes: 'apart from his cricket, Constantine has led a life which makes Nelson people proud to welcome him amongst us'. He continued:

> the people who object to him on account of his colour are very few indeed. For
> that Constantine is very grateful. It would be idle to pretend, of course, that such

an objection did not exist. It does, but Constantine has proved that a man need not necessarily be possessed of white parents to claim the title of gentleman.[46]

From T. E. Morgan, the chairman of the Nelson Cricket Club, came another tribute. Writing to Constantine from the *Nelson Leader* office, where Morgan was the editor, he praised Constantine for the manner in which he behaved as the club's professional: success had not spoiled him: 'You have never given me, as Chairman of the Club, a moment's concern – totally different to other experiences I have had … I hope Norma, Gloria and your self will be blessed with good health, and that the coming years will bring you much happiness and prosperity.'[47] Morgan's generous testimonial gives credibility to the loyalties and friendliness that writers have emphasized in explaining Constantine's long tenure at the Nelson club. In particular it reveals that, in addition to high standards of athleticism, a hero was required to demonstrate certain *moral* qualities. Learie Constantine did this by combining the virtues of a modest, respectable, family-centred life with outstanding skills performed in a spirit of good sportsmanship. One observer, seeing Constantine chaired off the field in 1937 after his final match, summed up perfectly the place he occupied in the minds of Nelson people:

> Connie was hoisted shoulder high and carried off the field … His personality is tremendous, wonderful … to say that he has been a "godsend" to Nelson is to put it mildly. He has, to all people, both living in and out of Nelson, *been Nelson itself.*[48]

III

Respect carried with it a financial value. Constantine's standing with his public was all the more remarkable given the very great divide that separated him financially from most Nelson people. It is not possible to be precise about the amount of his earnings with the club. The formal treasurer's balance sheets do not reveal the various material benefits provided by the Club over and above basic salary, or the frequent 'collections' he received from spectators following outstanding performances in matches. In addition, especially in the later 1930s, Constantine received payments for articles in newspapers.[49] For a relatively untried player he had struck a hard bargain when he signed for Nelson, insisting on a three-year contract, and it has been suggested that the opportunity of increasing his earnings through large 'collections' was a powerful incentive in his going to the Lancashire League.[50] Constantine's income levels were probably beyond those attained by leading professional footballers in the days of the maximum wage and are in stark contrast to the average weekly earnings of the mill workers who constituted Constantine's fan base. In the early 1930s, with many mills on short time, an individual weekly wage of 30 shillings (£1.50) would have been common. Constantine most likely earned ten times that amount by playing cricket for five months in the year. But, in contrast to some of the sporting stars of later years, his affluence was not flaunted in conspicuous spending.[51] Constantine recalled much later that when he first arrived in Nelson he had thought about buying a car. It was a difficult time in the cotton trade and a friend advised him to wait a while; driving around in a new car might not be sensible. 'So I waited and when I finally got my first car it was a second-hand Austin which attracted not a second glance.'[52] People would accept their sporting hero being a little out-of-the-ordinary, but not excessively so.

There is another side to the rewards Constantine earned. It was the money that he brought in to the League through attendances. Nelson with Constantine won the Lancashire League championship seven times and came second twice in the years from 1929 to 1937 (the club had never won it with McDonald). It was largely to compete on reasonably equal terms against this dynamic cricketer that other league clubs were drawn into a scramble to sign star players. With the contemporary English big names usually tied to the county and test circuit the gaze of league committees was turned firmly in an overseas direction. The League became a theatre of star performers. During the 1930s a clutch of Empire cricketers was drafted into the Lancashire League, in particular Manny Martindale, George Headley, Ellis Achong, Edwin St Hill and Constantine himself from the Caribbean.[53] The process was not without its critics, whose objections increasingly centred on the limiting of opportunities for young local players.[54] What, however, dampened criticism was the money that flowed from increased gate money. The overseas players brought in the crowds, none more so than Constantine himself. The admiration and affection that developed for him during the 1930s was amply revealed in 1936 when all the clubs in the League donated money for the staging of a match in recognition of Constantine's as a crowd-puller.[55] He took home around £500 from the proceeds of this event.

The internationalizing of the League created career opportunities for West Indian cricketers for whom professional openings in the Caribbean were severely limited. Playing cricket in the leagues brought financial benefits and equally importantly bestowed a degree of respect, accorded by employers and public alike. It would have been difficult for black people to find this in other walks of life, or even in other forms of sport in Britain, let alone the West Indies. In interwar Britain professional sport was a lowly form of labour, even for the more famous players. It was no more clearly illustrated than in the notorious retain-and-transfer system of the Football League, or in the way professionals were treated in county cricket.[56] In the leagues, on the other hand, the 'pro' was a far more liberated figure. He was valued both for his intrinsic skills and for the guidance and leadership he would exercise in the game. 'The players in his team' said Constantine, 'instinctively look to him when in difficulty'.[57] The 'pro' was respected as a man who somehow carried the reputation of the local community on his shoulders. In a small way, therefore, for a small group of men, the colour bar could thus be raised.

Constantine was undoubtedly money conscious. The emphasis that writers have placed on his loyal service to Nelson can obscure the fact that Constantine was a professional cricketer whose livelihood, and his status as a man, depended on his earnings. Much as he found Nelson to be a congenial place to work and live, he was always prepared to listen to offers from other league clubs that might pay him more. Money talked. Newspaper reports make clear that there were continuing enquiries from other clubs to which Constantine gave serious consideration.[58] As early as 1934 Rochdale Cricket Club of the Central Lancashire League was making overtures to entice him to leave Nelson, though the only effect at this stage seems to have been to persuade Nelson to increase Constantine's wages with a new three-year contract. On more than one occasion Blackpool Cricket Club expressed an interest in him; in 1937 the club clearly thought it had struck a deal, the Blackpool Secretary being plainly disgruntled when Constantine withdrew from negotiations.[59] Over the summer of 1937 he received an offer from the Canterbury Cricket Association of New Zealand to play and coach there. The sticking point again was money – £ NZ 450 was as much as they were able to offer, a figure only half what he could command in Lancashire.[60] By this time Constantine appears to have given Rochdale first refusal on his services, thus honouring a promise he had made 'some time ago', should he decide at any point to leave Nelson.

Constantine's arrival at Rochdale was accompanied with a very generous package deal. The terms, which Constantine asked should not be disclosed publicly, were to play in all League and cup matches for one season at a salary of £750, including two afternoons practice and coaching, with talent money at £1–10 shillings (1.50p) for five wickets or 50 runs.[61] He was also faced with a rather different cricket environment from the one he had become accustomed to in Nelson. The Central Lancashire League was composed mostly of small clubs from towns and villages in the south-east part of Lancashire around the bigger centres of Rochdale and Oldham, where spinning rather than weaving was the chief economic activity. The League operated on the same basis as the Lancashire League, with one professional employed by each club, although these pro's were on the whole less well known than those being recruited into the Lancashire League. Thus Constantine's capture was something of a coup for Rochdale, an ambitious club which saw in Constantine a means of achieving the status enjoyed by Nelson. By the time of his arrival, however, he was not the same player he had been ten years earlier. His fielding skills were now confined to close catching roles, and few were the occasions when he patrolled the covers with the lighting speed and deadly accurate throwing of his youth. Age had affected his fast bowling so that he now concentrated on medium-pace deliveries using swing, seam and subtle changes of pace; like many players before and since his days of fast bowling had left him with a persistent injury problem. He could still dominate with the bat, however, and when he 'came off' his hitting was as astonishing as ever. Taking all this into account his performances for Rochdale in 1938 were more than satisfactory. It was not his personal contributions that became a problem with his new club, so much as the attitudes of others towards him. Constantine never looked back on his season at Rochdale with anything like the affection he expressed for Nelson, or for his time playing in the Bradford League during and after the War.[62] He considered the standard of cricket in his new environment lower than in the Lancashire League, in terms both of the playing skills and the quality of pitches. He had an argument with the club over its attempt to deduct from his wages a fee for employing a replacement professional while Constantine was absent with a knee injury. He then spent some time in what proved to be a fruitless search to find employment that would enable his brother Elias to continue playing for the club as an amateur. But overriding all else was an unhappy experience of racial prejudice. Constantine claimed that an umpire, following a disagreement over a leg before wicket decision, had afterwards made comments in the tearoom 'indicating his prejudice and partiality'. Constantine wrote to the Rochdale club's secretary asking that the umpire should not stand in any matches in which Constantine featured in the future.[63] The matter was referred to the Central Lancashire League Committee but, as Constantine saw it, to no positive effect. He considered that he had had a 'raw deal'[64] and made no attempt to renew his contract with Rochdale for the following season. It no doubt came as something of a relief to Constantine when in 1939 he joined the West Indies party for its tour of England.

During the 1930s Constantine's commitment to Nelson had restricted his international cricket. In 1930–31 he went to Australasia with the West Indies team, a party of 'seven whites and eleven natives' who, it was emphasized by the West Indies management, 'should reside in the same hotels'. After some initial difficulties over accommodation the racial problem was overcome, though the Australian government insisted that the black players should not stay in Australia beyond six months.[65] In 1933 Nelson allowed Constantine leave to appear in only one of the tests in England. This seems not to have worried Constantine unduly; Nelson paid better wages. In 1939, however, he returned to the West Indies team for a full tour including test and county matches. He decided that, at his age, there would be no further opportunities to play test match cricket and, this being so, he would be willing to suspend League engagements for a season to have one last shot at the highest level of the game. However, respect and financial rewards were a serious consideration in this venture. Constantine was ever mindful of the loss of earnings the 1939 tour would involve. A protracted negotiation with the organizers over payments began two years before the tour started. Constantine's concerns were not only about earnings but also his status in the team: 'am I going to be the senior professional engaged, not merely from the point of view of age and experience, but also from the point of remuneration?'[66] He had a strong case, knowing that the tour needed his presence in the team to attract spectators and ensure some financial success for the venture.[67] He secured strong representation for his cause from T. A. Higson, the chairman of the Lancashire county club, who was brought in to mediate with the West Indies Cricket Board, represented by R. H. Mallett. Higson advised the Board to offer Constantine £600 and expenses for the tour, since, said Higson, Constantine could secure at least £750 for 'a much easier engagement' (i.e. in the Leagues).[68] The £600 figure was agreed, though Constantine later claimed that the West Indies Board had offered him £700, contrasted with £1200 he might have earned as a league cricketer.[69] The negotiations further illustrated Constantine's sense of status when he learnt that two other players in the touring party, George Headley and Manny Martindale, had demanded, and been given, the same money as Learie. Both were leading members of the team, Headley in particular having a just claim to be as important to the success of the tour as Constantine himself. Constantine's reaction was prickly. He saw the Headley/Martindale manoeuvre as a double insult: an undermining of his position by the Board, and a lack of respect from the two younger players for what he himself had done over the years for his fellow cricketers.[70] With Martindale in particular Constantine conducted a lengthy personal correspondence which, beneath its surface politeness, contained some vitriolic sentiments on both sides. Martindale irreverently dismissed Constantine's complaints as 'useless verbosity' and advised him to give his 'mental apparatus' a shake-up. For his part, Constantine was reduced to a final letter that bordered on self-pity: 'My reactions are only those of a man who has acted at all times not only in his own interests, but also in the interests of his Countrymen, receiving for his thanks a stab in the back.'[71] For once the affable Constantine revealed a sense of self-importance that no doubt soured his relations with two key players, and possibly with other members of the touring party.

IV

As things worked out Constantine's decision to accept the Board's terms, fees notwithstanding, proved a sound one, although the major consequences could hardly have foreseen. Membership of the touring party turned out to be a vital step in Constantine's future. In cricketing terms it took him out of local cricket and placed him once more onto an international stage. Although he was approaching the age of thirty-eight, his performances in the test matches were good, and in the final match of the series at the Oval, with war imminent, he was outstanding. He took five wickets in England's first innings, and then scored a rapid 79, recalling the explosive style of his youth. 'He ... hit a six off Perks, who was bowling from the Vauxhall End, to what geographically was the farthest part of the Oval, a stroke of immense power ... he had so disturbed the field that we were granted the unusual spectacle of a fast bowler, Perks, bowling without a slip fieldsman of any description.'[72] The reporter from the *Sunday Times* noted that Constantine was still his 'electric self' when, off his own bowling, he ran out an English batsman from a stroke into the covers.[73] There could have been no finer way to sign off, in what was to be his last big cricket match. With such reminders of his powers of former days it was fitting that the influential *Wisden Cricketers' Almanack* selected him as one of its 'five cricketers of the year', surely a mark of his achievements not only in this one season but over his entire career. Looking ahead, of greater importance than this accolade was what it led to. Constantine was brought into a relationship with the BBC that endured for thirty years and presented him with the opportunity to reshape his heroic standing in a field quite different from that of cricket.

5

Writer

Over a period of some forty years from the early 1930s nine books appeared under Constantine's name. For its time, a back catalogue of this extent was unusual. Sportsmen of that era might produce material (often 'ghosted') for the popular press, but before the 1950s they rarely produced full-scale books. Unless, that is, they were very famous. Jack Hobbs and Stanley Matthews were the most celebrated sports stars to enjoy such published esteem. But none could match Constantine's output.[1] With two exceptions (*Colour Bar* in 1954, and *Living in Britain*, which came out the year before he died)[2] the books dealt with aspects of cricket, a game that has over more than two centuries generated a vast literature and an equally large readership. What is surprising about the discourse created through this writer-reader relationship is the minimal attention paid to it in academic analysis. Not surprisingly, in view of this, Constantine's is a body of work now largely forgotten.

It is an unfortunate case of neglect, for writings on cricket connect to wider issues of social activity and relations. Constantine's work provides ample illustration of the ideological energy contained in cricket literature. Two particular themes stand out, both present in all his books. On the one hand, there is a contribution to a long-standing discussion, associated with many former well-known players and commentators, on how the game should be played. This is the 'instructional' theme. It places Constantine as an 'authority', someone with expertise passing on practical advice – useful knowledge – to those learning the game. In this respect the Constantine text has at one and the same time an immediate practicality, and a strong sense of the history and traditions of the game.[3] In fact, such features form the explicit purpose of the books; from a publisher's perspective they are their chief selling point. On the other hand, though, there is a latent theme, less readily apparent in a casual reading but interesting from an ideological standpoint. At this level the books reveal a concern with ideas of race and race relations, of the place of the black player in cricket, and of how that black presence might be understood. To achieve this they work to a large extent through an autobiographical form. They are always about Constantine, as much as they are about the game in general. In other words there is in the text a degree of what some literary critics would call 'self-fashioning'.

I

Constantine's writings have contributed to a particular personification of the man. Some commentators read this in a political sense and readily associate Constantine with the notion of a black Caribbean identity. Constantine becomes almost a champion of black liberation. Chris Searle, for example, has presented Constantine as an early advocate of black leadership in West Indies cricket,[4] an interpretation supported by the Caribbean's leading cricket academic Sir Hilary Beckles.[5] Both cast Constantine as having perceived the white captaincy of the West Indies cricket team to be a principal instrument of the social and racial control exercised over black people by white colonial elites. Christine Cummings has similarly pursued the same point and claimed that from the 1920s Constantine 'felt that the Captain of the West Indies should have been a black man', going further to suggest that he 'did not merely critique the system, he challenged it'.[6] The cricketer Everton Weekes, in his intriguing autobiographical account of the game in the Caribbean islands, compiled with Beckles many years after Weekes had retired from the game, regards Constantine as 'the intellectual leader of West Indies cricket' in the 1930s. Weekes remembers that as a youth he saw Constantine as a towering figure: 'I had heard that he was a no-nonsense, highly political man, and he wanted justice for all in the game.'[7] Such views chime with those of C. L. R. James who, looking back at Constantine from the perspective of some thirty years, places him as a 'national hero' in the Caribbean.[8]

How much validity should we place on these varied claims? All Constantine's books appeared after the Second World War, with one exception, *Cricket and I*.[9] *Cricket and I* is the only sustained piece of writing produced during his playing career, and, as its title suggest, it is very largely an autobiography. It was the first such book by a black player, containing the first detailed account of cricket in the West Indies. The book is essentially a chronicle of Constantine's background and progress through the cricket hierarchy of Trinidad and the West Indies. It registers also the place of West Indies cricket in the world, something no previous publication had properly done.[10] It thus celebrates the achievements of both black and white cricketers who until then had been little known outside their own islands. It offers therefore a unique insight into the problems encountered by a poor black man entering a sport controlled by white men.

These are all significant innovations, and earned the book generous reviews on both sides of the Atlantic. A number of leading cricket writers in Britain, among them Neville Cardus, who contributed the book's preface, and R. C. Robertson-Glasgow, praised *Cricket and I* for its clarity and refreshing honesty about the modern game. The chapter on 'bodyline', the hot topic in cricket at the time of the book's publication, was especially well received.[11] In terms of any overt *political* content, however, *Cricket and I* is unremarkable. Readers expecting an overt critical perspective on racial and political themes would be disappointed. The book does not justify some of the claims made for Constantine's influence in either political or racial matters. In view of Constantine's position in 1933, and particularly in view of the claims made for him in the writings of C. L. R. James and others, *Cricket and I* might seem to present a person who was either non-political, or who was concerned to conceal his political ideas. The book makes no reference at all to the important political unrest that had been unfolding in Trinidad since the War. For a man credited with a keen political awareness this might appear surprising. Furthermore, from a man who had escaped the racial confines of his upbringing, and found a liberating role as a sporting hero in England, a more hostile commentary on the clearly racial and class nature of West Indies cricket might have been assumed. It does not appear. It seems that Constantine is content to let his text reflect the persona by which he was known in these years – a courteous, personable, dedicated professional sportsman who avoided bringing controversy into his public life.

This is not to say that the book is without undertones of questioning and challenge. A chapter on 'West Indies Cricket and the Future of the Game' considers the obstacles to be overcome if cricket in the Caribbean is to realize its full potential. Constantine points to a number of inhibiting factors: the shortage of organized cricket at the local level, the geographical dispersal of the major centres of the game, the rivalries that exist between the islands, the selection of too many inexperienced players (a very veiled hint at the appointment of white players in leadership roles) and the need to develop the necessary psychological toughness – the 'professional' mentality – for a team competing in test matches. All are put forward as the principal problems holding back West Indies cricket. It might be inferred from this that Constantine is asking for a team of black cricketers, selected solely on cricketing merit, and led by a black captain, as the way forward. But nowhere is this made explicit, and Beckles seems to overestimate the import of Constantine's observations on the lack of a spirit of solidarity in West Indian teams when he says '[The] division was political and had to be resolved by political means.'[12] Constantine himself does not go that far, and while, in another chapter, his thoughts on bodyline[13] suggest a degree of truculence that kicks against the system, readers searching for the roots of the politically conscious Constantine of later years will find little in *Cricket and I* as evidence of early radicalization. Featherstone's suggestion that in Nelson Constantine was developing 'radical anti-colonial politics'[14] must also be doubted. There is in fact little to suggest a man of any strong political views.

The circumstances surrounding the book's preparation and publication are important, and explain a restraining influence. Gerald Howat has argued persuasively that, at this time, Constantine wanted to live an 'uncomplicated' life in Nelson.[15] In contrast with Beckles, Howat's biography plays down the political side of Constantine, and has good reason to do so. It is not, as we have seen, that Nelson was an environment uncongenial to radical political views: quite the opposite in fact. By the time Constantine had arrived in Nelson the Labour Party had become the dominant political force in local politics, and by the late 1920s the press was beginning to refer to the town (misleadingly) as 'Little Moscow'. It suited the propaganda of anti-Labour forces that were re-grouping into what was in effect a Conservative–Liberal coalition in municipal politics. There was undoubtedly a politics of working-class solidarity and progressive thinking in the town.[16] Whether, though, it would have accommodated a politics of race is another matter. Constantine no doubt felt it diplomatic to leave that area untested. He was a newcomer, a public figure, nominally a-political, and in any case had received some hostility on account of his colour on first arriving in the town. 'He had', says Howat 'no illusions about the implications of being a coloured man.'[17] Looking back from the 1960s Constantine himself said that the early days in Nelson had been difficult ones: 'My God, I wouldn't like to go back on the first two years.'[18] Equally, if not more, important was the position of his employer, Nelson Cricket Club. As a leading institution in the town the club served as a symbol of civic unity, standing apart from the political and industrial conflicts that were otherwise present among the populace. This was in any case usual for sports clubs, big or small, and the people whom they employed. Being drawn one way or another politically would jeopardize their relationship with the game's followers and the financial support they provided. But in another respect the club, as a group of individuals who made up its officials, committee and at least some of its membership, had very clear political loyalties. In Nelson's case they very likely leant towards the anti-Labour side of the political spectrum.

The local Labour newspaper, the *Nelson Gazette*, saw the cricket club committee as having a very definite political standpoint, and there was no love lost between the club and the paper.[19]

Constantine's political stance at this time is most clearly illustrated in his involvement with the League of Coloured Peoples (LCP), an organization founded in 1931 to voice the concerns of coloured people across the colonial world. It was moderate in its aims, which covered the promotion of the social, educational, economic and political interests of its members; the improving of relations between the races; cooperating with other organizations sympathetic to coloured peoples; and providing when possible financial aid to 'coloured people in distress.'[20] It sought to avoid any hint of extremism in either ideology or action. Led by Harold Moody, a medical doctor from Jamaica, the majority of its more prominent officials were African and West Indian students and intellectuals based in and around London. C. L. R. James had joined, though sceptical of the League's likely influence,[21] and Howat suggests that Constantine followed his lead.[22] Learie was indeed mentioned in the first edition of the League's journal as having made a donation: he himself commented that 'our people are badly misunderstood in this country and I am trying to keep my end up in the North.'[23] Quite what this amounted to is uncertain. There are frequent references during the next few years to Constantine and the West Indies cricket team yet scarcely any indication that he was involved in openly agitational activity. What he did contribute was his cricket skill and celebrity, as skipper of the LCP cricket team in its annual charity matches held each September throughout the 1930s. The fixture at Aberdeen in 1937 was a notable example, which raised a significant amount of money for the League.[24] Thus Constantine seems to have affirmed his support for the League's activities in as non-political way as possible. There would have been ample scope to write pieces for the League's journal, *The Keys*, but the opportunity appears not to have been taken. Such a one, for instance, might have been on the subject of the mounting labour unrest in Trinidad and throughout the West Indies in the late 1930s. A critical review of the British Government's reaction, in the form of the Royal Commission on Trinidad, might have been right up a politically conscious Constantine's street, but it was League member and economist W. A. Lewis who provided the critique.[25]

Cricket and I, then, appeared at a time and in a place that predetermined the book's main tone. This was so in spite of another aspect of its production. *Cricket and I* marked the consolidation of a friendship between two Trinidadians that was to continue on and off for almost forty years. In his Foreword to the book Constantine acknowledges 'my West Indian friend ... who has given me valuable assistance in the writing of this book'.[26] The friend was, of course, C. L. R. James, and his contribution probably amounted to rather more than just 'assistance'. 'I agreed to do the actual writing' James claimed much later in *Beyond a Boundary*.[27] To be sure, there is an unmistakably Jamesian tone in the prose, especially in the descriptions of cricketers and cricket matches. When he arrived in Nelson to stay with the Constantine's in the spring of 1932 James was already a freelance intellectual blossoming as a writer. Following his involvement in Trinidad with the 'renaissance' group of writers around the journal *The Beacon*,[28] James had travelled to England and served a brief time within the Bloomsbury circle.[29] He had not yet taken up the Marxist philosophy that informed his later work.[30] But since we have scarcely any contemporary evidence about the relationship between Constantine and James, it is difficult to know what influence James exercised over Constantine, and vice versa, at this time. The fullest account of the partnership is to be found in *Beyond a Boundary*, composed, it must be borne in mind, at least a quarter of a century after the event. James certainly gives credit to Constantine. As a cricketer he considered him to be outstanding, part of 'that distinguished company of men who ... influenced the history of their time'.[31] This is some praise. And it was not only Constantine's technical skills as a cricketer that James was admiring, but his mental focus, his application, his ability to learn and to improve his technique, exemplified first of all in his astounding ability as a fielder: 'one of the most brilliant covers ever seen in the West Indies'.[32]

James also claimed to have recognized in Constantine something altogether different, something that is certainly not apparent from a reading of *Cricket and I*: that is, Constantine as a political animal. In fact, a man of forthright political opinions who was responsible, indeed, for moulding James's own thinking.[33] Other writers have taken up this point. Anthony Bateman, for example, has noted that it was Constantine who was 'instrumental in [James's] radicalization'.[34] By the early 1930s the two had known each other for a couple of decades. Constantine would have been familiar with James's appearances on the cricket field for Maple. But the early friendship was confined to cricket and does not seem to have become an especially close one before the early 1930s. According to James, Constantine had been eager to produce a book as a way of expressing his feelings about what he had imbibed from cricket experiences on both sides of the Atlantic. It appears that James had started a draft before he left Trinidad, and taken it, together with other manuscripts, to England.[35] On arriving in Nelson he found in Constantine a strong race consciousness and a striving for racial respect, together with the germs of the idea of West Indian self-government. James claimed that, in conversations while working on the book, Constantine's repeated refrain on black–white relations was 'they are no better than we'.[36] Thus James claims to have exposed a political undercurrent that was to be developed into something far more explicit. As James put it, with a somewhat heroic flourish: 'We didn't know it but we were making history. This transcendence of our relations as cricketers was to initiate the West Indian renaissance not only in cricket, but in politics, in history and in writing … Up to that time [May 1932] I doubt if he and I had ever talked for 5 consecutive minutes on WI politics. Within 5 weeks we had unearthed the politician in each other. Within 5 months we were supplementing each other in a working partnership which had West Indian self-government as its goal.'[37] If this is so, it reveals how much the text of *Cricket and I* was muted to suit the conditions of its production. *Beyond a Boundary* is itself enigmatic in its account of these years. Quite how far the nature of his relationship with Constantine is a construct of later memories, compounded from hindsight with an understanding of how events had subsequently worked out, is difficult to estimate. We should beware – *Beyond a Boundary* gives us a picture of Constantine through a veiled lens.

Recent work by Christian Hogsbjerg suggests a different aspect to James's political conversion during his time in Nelson. It is certainly true that James turned explicitly to Marxism at this point in his life, though it is inconceivable that this was the result of talking to Constantine. Learie never expressed any Marxist sympathies, still less any knowledge of Marx's thought.[38] James's shift of political emphasis is to be understood, argues Hogsbjerg, in the political circumstances affecting the town of Nelson in the early 1930s, and in particular, to the place of socialist activists in influencing C. L. R's political thinking. James does not mention in *Beyond a Boundary* three local socialists, Harry and Elizabeth Spencer, and Frederick Cartmell, the man who introduced James to the writings of Trotsky. Much later, in the 1970s, James did acknowledge Cartmell, while incorrectly remembering his name. Something else James skates over is the effect of Nelson's radicalism, especially its industrial militancy and Labour socialism.[39] By the time he left Nelson in early 1933, James was moving towards the revolutionary Left, propelled in that direction by these influences rather than by Constantine.[40]

II

If we are seeking political thinking that is more authentically 'Constantine' it is to his writings of the post-1945 years that we should look. One book in particular – *Cricket in the Sun* – published just after the Second World War, encapsulated the core of ideas that were worked through into his later writings.[41] The timing was appropriate. Constantine was by this time free of any official entanglements with the game's authorities, and the ending of the war, followed by Labour's 1945 electoral landslide, brought about a wave of optimism for the future. In truth, *Cricket In the Sun*, rather than *Cricket and I*, became Constantine's Ur-text. As with all his writings, it contained the familiar mixture of history, anecdote and polemic. But also emerging from it was something far more compelling: a critique of both sides of the Atlantic cricket community, and the conventional wisdoms that were to be found in it. He rejected the organization and mentalities prevalent in English cricket, before mounting an explicit attack on the racial attitudes in the West Indies game. Both issues were radical interventions for the time.

The voices raised at the end of the war for a new approach to sport had been met with resistance in some quarters, not solely in cricket.[42] Constantine countered the traditionalists by pointing out the virtues of the League cricket system in the North of England. It possessed 'qualities that the county game should imitate': the willingness to defy the weather and play if at all possible; the presence of good but 'sporting' wickets that offer chances to both bowlers and batters; the equality within the teams, without the social division of amateur and professional that the county game perpetuated; the fact that the clubs act as focal points of the community and attract large crowds, encouraged by attacking cricket and the appeal of leading professionals; and, for the 'pro' himself, a fulfilling and sometimes lucrative form of employment. Of the Lancashire League, where Constantine for most of his cricketing time had been engaged, he said: 'I admired the spirit of the game they play, and would go so far as to say that I would like a lot of their provisions and manners to be translated to county and international games.'[43]

In this way, *Cricket in the Sun* carried great historiographical weight; it brought northern league cricket, previously hidden from the history of the game, into public prominence. The Birmingham League, for example, had been founded in 1888, the Lancashire League in 1891; both were based in areas that sustained the new Football League, set up in 1888. By the early years of the twentieth century, similar leagues had found their way into many areas of the north and midlands of England as well as South Wales. In their approach to the game they differed markedly from the equivalent level of cricket in the south of England, especially the Home Counties. Here, the competitive league nature of northern cricket was absent. Clubs preferred to pick and choose whom they competed with in a series of 'friendly' fixtures, usually arranged with social considerations in mind. The result was that the game became in part a means of preserving social networks and hierarchies, much as in rugby union. The northern leagues, by contrast, were attuned to the principles enshrined in the Football League and what, in the 1920s, became the Rugby Football League.[44] One consequence of these regional and social sporting variations was reflected in the writing of history. League cricket figured only very rarely in the literature of the game that appeared up to, and beyond, the Second World War. Cricket books were often fixated on tradition, heavily weighted towards ideas of the rural, accepted almost unquestioningly the leadership of the amateur, and resonated with social conservatism. In its designation of as 'first class', county cricket conveyed not only Oxbridge elitism but a notion of the game as embodying a hierarchy, much as the nation itself did. League cricket had no place in this world view.[45] Constantine sought to rescue the leagues from the disregard such thinking engendered.

Cricket's prevailing ideology was not confined to Lord's and the Home Counties. It extended to wherever the game was played, but was nowhere more firmly obeyed than among the white plantocracy and merchant class of the West Indies. Here, as we have seen, class and status sensibilities were intertwined with those of race. Constantine felt the contradictions of this keenly. By the time his international career ended in 1939 he was the Caribbean's most experienced international player.[46] Such eminence ought to have earned him the captaincy of a test team, but because of class and race prejudices Constantine was ruled out. In *Cricket and I* he had merely hinted at the problems caused by this state of affairs. In *Cricket in the Sun* he came right out and said it:

> I think the time has come to speak out plainly what I mean in this matter of West Indian captaincy. It is not only what I mean – every coloured player who has ever turned out in an international side has been conscious of it, and it rots the heart out of our cricket, and always will until it is changed. The West Indies teams, mainly composed as they always are of coloured players, should have a coloured captain.[47]

Constantine acknowledged that there had been occasions when a white captain was the best man for the job, H. B. G. Austin being the leading (perhaps the only) example. But he expressed criticism of all the other captains he played under – R. K. Nunes and one or other of the Grant brothers, Rolf and Jackie. In Constantine's judgment they were not sufficiently experienced, they lacked an understanding of the strengths and weaknesses of players, not only of those of the opposition but also of the men in their own team, and they tended to favour white players over better black ones. The captains had been chosen, Constantine averred, on the basis that 'a white leader was better than any black man'.[48] It is with this book that Constantine gained the reputation, credited to him by later writers, as the champion of the black cause in West Indies cricket. Yet it was to be another fifteen years before the principle of white leadership was rejected, and indeed refuted, by the successes of the West Indies touring teams of 1963 and 1966 under the captaincies of Frank Worrell and Garfield Sobers.

III

In the 1940s and early 1950s Constantine produced a series of books on cricket technique. In them, he continued the practice, started with James, of having someone to assist him. The writer and agent Frank Stuart became Constantine's collaborator after the war.[49] In addition to helping with composition, Stuart provided sound advice on various practical aspects of the publishing business, such as the timing of publication, the scale of advances and the relation between the pricing of a book and the royalties likely to accrue: 'royalties might be 10 per cent on sixpence – or 10 percent on 18 shillings.'[50] At times, it seems, Stuart was willing to take over the complete writing of a book. Thus, with *How to Play Cricket*, for publishers Eyre and Spottiswoode, he suggested, 'Not merely will I help – I will do the "Hints" book, if you like; if you are busy you need never even see it till publication!' The proviso was that Constantine needed to negotiate a good price and advance to cover Stuart's work.[51] Stuart took on the editing of Constantine's drafts (on one book he proposed to Constantine 'any objection to a prelim line "Edited by Frank Stuart?" '[52]) and his sense of urgency was an important part of the liaison, keeping Constantine to deadlines, about which the nominal author (Constantine was concurrently studying for law exams) could be dilatory. Overall the Constantine–Stuart partnership – the two worked together up to and including *Colour Bar* – was an important means of keeping Constantine's name before the public now that he was no longer active on the cricket field.

The years in which these books were produced witnessed especial anxiety about the state of cricket in England. Constantine's writings were an attempt to offer solutions to the problems, essentially in the form of a 'brighter cricket'. A prime concern was the financial viability of the game. It had been in question since before the Second World War: in the season of 1937, for example, it was reckoned that some £30,000 had been lost in county cricket. Attendances were dropping compared with earlier years of the century, partly because the game's administrators continued to pay minimal attention to spectators. Since the three-day format monopolized first-class cricket 'The English "national" game', as Richard Holt has observed, 'was largely played at times when the English nation was otherwise engaged'[53] (that is to say, matches were played when most men were at work – or unemployed, and therefore unable to afford the price of a ticket). County treasurers were, in some cases, forced to rely on the subventions of wealthy patrons to clear their debts. Yet there was a deeply rooted commitment on the part of those who controlled the game to preserve traditions, especially the prevailing ethos of amateurism, and resist any notion of 'commercialism' or 'modernization'.[54] A committee under the chairmanship of Sir Stanley (F. S.) Jackson, a former Yorkshire captain and a hero of the Golden Age, was set up in 1943 by the MCC, to consider changes that might be introduced in the post-war years. Its proposals were limited to county cricket and nothing very radical emerged. The idea of a knockout competition, for example, was completely rejected.[55] In the years immediately following the Second World War financial problems were momentarily eased as a result of an increase in attendances at matches, but this proved short-lived. Furthermore, at the very highest, and therefore most conspicuous, level of the game the performances of the English national team were largely uninspiring. Poor results in three consecutive test series against Australia were interspersed by the shock defeat at home in the 1950 matches against the West Indies. Although an improvement in results was seen in the years between 1952 and 1958 the methods by which they were achieved often involved dull, defensive cricket.[56] Len Hutton's tenure of office as the first professional captain of England in the twentieth century, although successful in terms of victories, was marked by slow over rates and cautious play. In spite of this test matches usually drew good attendances, at times other than holidays or when 'derby' matches were being played, spectator numbers for county cricket matches were generally low. People now had alternative, and possibly more attractive, leisure opportunities to pursue than watching boring games of cricket. The first-class game had reached a point of decline similar to that exposed in many other branches of British sport by the findings of the Wolfenden Report of 1960, commissioned by the Central Council of Physical Recreation (CCPR) in 1957 to investigate the state of the nation's sport in both a domestic and an international setting.[57] It is not at all a coincidence that soon after the Report's publication a modernizing initiative came to cricket. By 1963 the old social division between amateurs and professionals had been abolished, and the first one-day competition was introduced into county cricket. This – the Gillette Cup – was also the first step in commercial sponsorship of the game.

Most of the volumes Constantine produced with Stuart are attuned to this context. Two of them – *Cricketers' Cricket* (1949) and *How to Play Cricket* (1951) – are instructional manuals for 'young cricketers and small-club cricketers',[58] with chapters on all aspects of the game. Both are essentially the same text, with minor changes and different titles. A third book, *The Young Cricketer's Companion*, which was published in 1964, draws very heavily on *Cricketers' Cricket*, simply replacing case studies of players' technique with those of individuals with which younger readers would be more familiar: Gary Sobers and Ted Dexter, for example, instead of Bill Edrich and Len Hutton. There had been a market for this kind of publication ever since John Nyren's *Young Cricketer's Tutor*, published in the early 1830s, and Constantine's publishers sought to exploit it. At the same time as Eyre and Spottiswoode's *Cricketers' Cricket* and *How to Play Cricket* Stanley Paul came out with Constantine's *Cricketers Carnival*. Rather than a manual on technique it offered a fanciful confection of cricket history based around an imaginary match between all-time greats.[59] Richly larded with historical allusions and anecdote, and a print run of 10,000, of which something like three-quarters sold quickly, the book testified to the popularity of such publications.[60] There is a temptation, however, to dismiss them as insignificant for anything other than learning the game. Yet to do so would be a mistake. The coaching manuals contain a vigorous critique, developed through examples drawn from Constantine's own playing career, of conventional thinking about cricket. They attempt to inject fresh thinking into a moribund game with the aim of bringing back the spectators. They might even be regarded as a contribution to an anti-colonial aesthetic by 're-defining' in Helen Tiffin's words 'the moral assumptions behind the game'.[61]

IV

To understand some of the more latent aspects of Constantine's writings we should turn to the nuanced analysis offered by the Guyanese writer Frank Birbalsingh, one of the few authors to have subjected Constantine to a close textual reading. In a highly original essay Birbalsingh sees Constantine's meaning coming not so much in his overt statements about cricket as in the literary construction of his books. While impressed by both Constantine's style – direct, precise and informed by a deep personal knowledge of his subject – Birbalsingh is struck by the creation within the text of a particular Constantine persona. Much of Constantine's writing, says Birbalsingh, is concerned with the creation of a 'self', which in turn can be related to contemporary racial power relations.[62]

While Constantine was clearly responding to problems that bedevilled English cricket in the post-war years, in his work there is also a dialogue with the linguistic, racial framing of Caribbean cricketers evident in the writings of Cardus and others earlier in the century. The idea of a 'natural' approach and an absence of artifice in black cricketers, of a vitality present in their play that is absent in white players, is a theme that figures in Constantine's writing. But it figures sporadically, and when it surfaces is treated with a degree of ambivalence.

Aside from the obvious frontal assaults on the racist structure and mentality of West Indian cricket Constantine's writings do not conspicuously take up the issue of race. Indeed, the predominant emphasis is placed on 'correct' play. Constantine was considered by some to have been a reckless player, especially where batting was concerned, but as an instructor he does not advocate risky abandon. He teaches a studied approach. For the most part his advice on technique is conventional. He does not reject the tried and tested methods that had been established over the previous half century. The models of rectitude he admires are invariably famous white men – W. G. Grace, Don Bradman, Wally Hammond. There are no uniquely Caribbean mysteries revealed and, in spite of the success of the West Indies team at the beginning of the 1950s, the references to black players are few (usually only Constantine himself). He acknowledges that many a leading player has developed an element of unorthodoxy in his play – he instances his own particular favourite, the Australian batsman C. G. Macartney[63] – but sound technique is what he advocates for the young players. Watch, he tells his readers, the methods of better players, and apply them; learn from them, and prepare yourself thoroughly through constant practice – 'pay attention', the dictum of Constantine's own father, is the clear message in the text. But, he advises, do not be a slave to method. To be sure, playing cricket well requires a degree of imitation but it is in his advice on what might be termed the cricketer's 'mentality' that Constantine nudges his reader towards a critical viewpoint of contemporary play. In *How to Play Cricket* he advocates something more than imitation – an injection of one's own personal quality. Playing cricket well demands an almost existential search for that quality:

> There is no way of becoming a great bowler simply by copying someone else. As in music and art, so in cricket; each great bowling artist is so because he has something the others haven't got; it is that very quintessence of his own personality as expressed through the medium of his bowling hand that makes him famous … So I want you to think, not how can I imitate Butler or Spofforth, but how can I adapt their skill and make it serve my mind and fingers as well as my purpose.[64]

What this 'purpose' might be is to be expressed not so much in techniques as in attitude. Cricket is not just a set of methods for batting, bowling and fielding. It is an art practised for *enjoyment* – 'Playing Cricket for Fun' as the opening chapter of *How to Play Cricket* has it. If attained, enjoyment will be communicated not only to oneself but to others playing, and to those watching. 'The game today, perhaps more than ever in its history, needs enterprise and initiative; for doped pitches, average worship, financial considerations, and not least, I think, spiritual timidity brewed out of two wicked and disastrous wars, have made first-class cricket – *dull.*'[65] The batsman should, therefore, carry the attack to the bowler – 'hit those bowlers' as Constantine himself was urged by Macartney[66] – while the bowler's task should be to attack the batsman's wicket: 'there are fewer bowlers today than ever before who make a bold, hostile, and undisguised attack on the three now larger upright sticks.'[67] It is against this measure of attacking play that Constantine finds contemporary cricket wanting. In searching for the vitality that transforms the game of cricket from mere mechanical routines into an expression of human enjoyment Constantine's instructional guidance direct the reader's attention to the personification of the ideal – nowhere better expressed than in the author himself.

The precepts remained constant. Fifteen years separated the first and final editions of Constantine's instructional books. They are substantially the same. Some small changes are inserted in the later edition to acknowledge the emergence of new personalities in the game,[68] but the basic premise remains: there is too much caution in the English game, and from the very top (the MCC) the game is suppressed by a dead hand. The cricket establishment, says Constantine, has lost sight of its purpose and now exists merely to serve its own corporate and social interests. Like many other grand institutions the MCC has 'lost its usefulness.'[69] The effect of this is that cricket has remained dull, with pitches either so over-prepared that they suit batting rather than bowling, or so slow that they favour neither. County officials are so concerned with wringing what income they can from matches that they are drawn out to fill as long a time as possible: 'an extra day's receipts mean more … than leaving the public with a memory of fireworks and lightning.'[70] Constantine's remedies were designed to bring on the 'fireworks and lightning': a smaller ball, the banning of over-prepared of pitches, all scores up to a batsman's first 20 to be doubled to discourage a defensive mentality, a limit on the score a batsman can make (150 is suggested) before he has to retire, points to be awarded for a drawn game, and the introduction of knock-out cup competitions as in football (and, it might be added, in the northern cricket leagues). Above all he challenged the sanctity of the three-day match in the county circuit by advocating shorter formats.

By the mid-1960s Constantine had added to his now well-worn proposals for reform a new Caribbean inflection. The resurgence of the West Indies national team in the early 1960s, and its comprehensive defeat of England in the two test series of 1963 and 1966, had its effect. It doubly confirmed for Constantine the validity of his views, and gave them a new 'West Indian' stamp. In 1966 particularly, under the leadership of Sobers, the West Indies were simply so much better than their English opponents. To Constantine's eye the English players, timidly led, adopted a county championship mentality of waiting for the opposition to make mistakes instead of 'trying to induce mistakes as a result of their own positive actions'.[71] 'Safety-first cricket' impoverished a game that should be enjoyed by players and spectators alike, not simply endured. For Constantine, the 1966 series was a warning that the English game must change if it was not to perish, and it must change by adopting a Caribbean style of play. In so doing, what emerged from his writing was a re-fashioning of an environmental/biological determinism reminiscent of Cardus.

In the mid-1960s Constantine embarked on a lengthy chapter for a book co-authored with the journalist Denzil Batchelor.[72] The book takes a long view of the development of cricket. Constantine (with a recycling of much familiar material) follows a chapter by Batchelor examining the dynamics of cricket, giving due emphasis to the importance of preparing English cricket for the challenges posed, historically by Australia, and more recently by the West Indies. Batchelor attributes to both countries an undefined quality in their game 'that we [i.e. England] have lost with the passing of the years'.[73] In his own long chapter, 'Cricket in the Sun', Constantine finds that quality in the West Indies. Although the chapter is descriptive, and glories in many tales of legendary Caribbean players, within it the motif of the 'natural' player comes to the fore – 'we play the game for fun, we play the game according to our natural instincts'.[74] It is as if being 'in the sun' brings out unique qualities that are dormant in the cold English summer.

V

In his biography of Constantine Peter Mason has noted that his subject was not 'a man of letters'.[75] To be sure, Constantine was not a writer with the qualities of those other acclaimed West Indians – George Lamming, for example, or fellow Trinidadian V. S. Naipaul – who were making an impact in the literary world of the 1960s. Constantine was not a great stylist; his writings lacked elegance of prose and analytical refinement. Some might dispute that they even contained a body of ideas. Constantine wrote in a plain, straightforward language, more appropriate for the popular press than serious literature. Yet it was a style that suited its purpose: Constantine's pages, as Birbalsingh has shown, achieved directness, candour and truth.[76] They were pitched just right for the intended reader, often a young person, relatively unsophisticated, seeking advice on cricket with an accompaniment of anecdotes involving top players. Further, Birbalsingh draws out something else in the books, another direction in the writing, one that places the author's own personality at the centre of the text. The books, he says, are inclined to display a boastfulness, with 'lapses of immodesty and even gloating ... Constantine's claim of acute perception and elaborate strategic planning, either in his own play or in the performance of other West Indian players is, at best, a half-truth.'[77] What Birbalsingh has in mind are passages like the one in *How to Play Cricket*, where Constantine describes in detail a series of what he called 'traps', set to bowl out not only Don Bradman but five other leading Australian batsmen in a test match.[78] Here Constantine glories in his own ability to deceive and outwit his opponents. Of course, pride in such ploys is a not uncommon feature of sportspeople's memoirs; it is a means of underlining in the minds of younger readers the need for self-confidence, steely determination and clear thinking in order to succeed in games. In Constantine, however, it took on a further significance. It was, Birbalsingh claims, a means of showing that the black sportsman could think as rationally about the game as any white man. In an age when racial stereotyping and notions of white superiority were all too likely to represent the black sportsman as a creature of uninhibited spontaneity, here was Constantine rejecting the conventional notion of a volatile, irrational negro personality; and at the same time constructing his own character as an artful, calculating cricketer.

This theme in the writings should remind us of Constantine's constant assertion, recounted by C. L. R. James: 'they are no better than we'. While undoubtedly present in the writings this sentiment of racial equality is only a part of the whole and we should guard against overemphasizing it. In their totality the cricket books are not a paean to blackness; they pay a sober-minded homage to the cricket methods devised and practised in a white context, in public schools, county cricket and in the leagues of the north of England, as much as to a black provenance in the Caribbean. The books stand as much as anything as a textual representation, not of 'blackness' but of 'Constantine-ism'. In this respect they call to mind a concept used by the American cultural critic Stephen Greenblatt, who has defined a literary process of self-fashioning – 'the power to impose a shape upon oneself'.[79] What Constantine wrote in those few years after the Second World War, culminating in *Colour Bar*, was highly important in the process of self-fashioning. He had achieved recognition as a cricketer; now, his writings displayed new abilities that gave him a position of renown. He was known for something in addition to playing sport (even if that addition might be confined to writing about how to play sport). Constantine had become the first black cricketer to establish a new identity beyond cricket. His writings set out clearly his West Indian heritage, but they showed equally clearly that he was immersed deeply in English ways. He had crossed the Atlantic and now spanned two worlds. His self-fashioning confirmed the hybrid persona that had been developing for some years: 'black Englishman'.

Figure 1 With members of the Cricket Club committee, Nelson 1929: the young professional brought a Caribbean *elan* to the club (Constantine Collection, NALIS. Reproduced with kind permission of Mrs Gloria Valere.)

Figure 2 The 1929 season ended with a Championship title: Constantine could scarcely have had a better beginning to his career as a League pro. (Constantine Collection, NALIS. Reproduced with kind permission of Mrs Gloria Valere.)

GIFT OF 800 BAGS OF SWEETS BY L.N. CONSTANTINE, PRESIDENT, REGENT MICKEY MOUSE CLUB...

Figure 3 Off the field: Constantine, as president of the Mickey Mouse Club at the Regent cinema in Nelson 1937, bestows confectionary on club members. (Constantine Collection, NALIS. Reproduced with kind permission of Mrs Gloria Valere.)

Figure 4 The location is unknown (certainly not Lord's) but the action looks perfect. (Constantine Collection, NALIS. Reproduced with kind permission of Mrs Gloria Valere.)

Figure 5 Constantine (third left, front row) introduces a group of West Indian technicians to Minister of Labour Ernest Bevin (centre, front row), at the Ministry of Labour and National Service offices, St James Square, London, c. 1944. (By kind permission of the Imperial War Museum.)

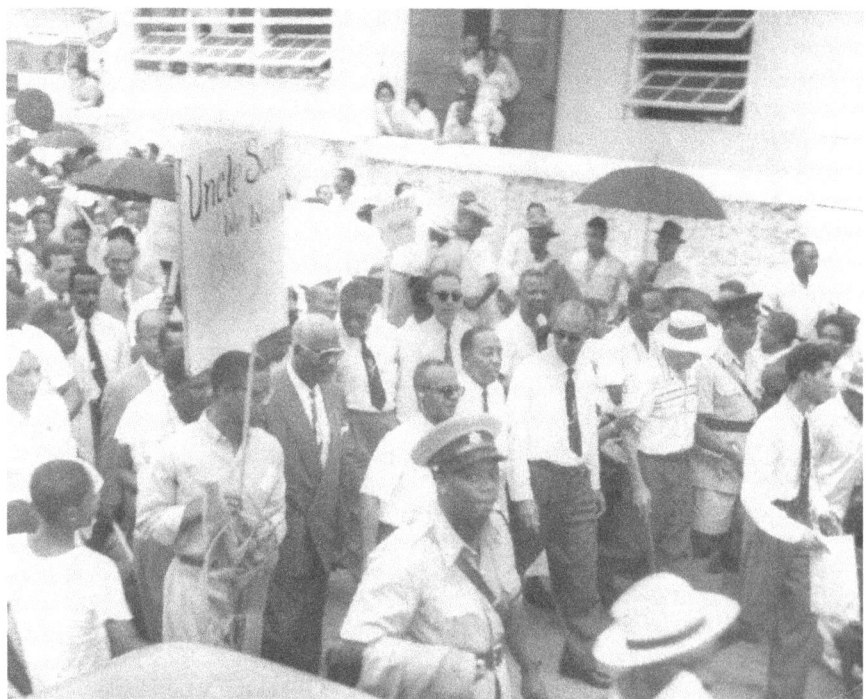

Figure 6 As a minister in Eric Williams's pre-Independence government Constantine (middle of front row) supports his prime minister (to his right) in the anti-American 'march in the rain' on Chaguaramas, 22 April 1960. (Constantine Collection, NALIS. Reproduced with kind permission of Mrs Gloria Valere.)

6

Race Relations

In the thirty years until his death in 1971 Constantine's experience of race prejudice changed. He became more aware of its impact upon black people positioned less favourably than him in society. Dealing with the problems of race on behalf of others broadened his mind to the nature of racial attitudes in Britain and took him into areas of life that had been closed to him in the confined world of cricket. It was a learning process that began when he was appointed as a welfare office for the Ministry of Labour in 1942, based in Liverpool.

I

Race and ethnic problems had a long history in Britain. Generally speaking, they had arisen from the movement of peoples along three axes – between Ireland and mainland Britain; between continental Europe and Britain; and within the British Empire. Liverpool had figured conspicuously in this history. Skin colour had not always been the cause of hostility. Irish Catholic immigrants had traditionally aroused the fiercest animosities. They had been arriving for generations, but were especially numerous from the middle of the nineteenth century onwards following the Great Famine of the 1830s and 1840s. Their presence provoked a reaction among the local population that was manifested not only in an ethno-racial form, but in a particular form of politics: a distinctive brand of popular Toryism, strongly infused with a Low Church, evangelical Protestantism and sustained by extensive working-class support. The Irish presence met its most hostile opposition in the form of an Orange faction headed by a group of 'bigoted, virulent and eloquent Irish parsons' who were Toryism's leading advocates.[1] This brand of sectarianism elided any kind of politics based on social class until well into the twentieth century.

Liverpool, a 'world city' with extensive Atlantic trade links, had in addition to the Irish a sizeable overseas population made up of men working in the merchant marine and various dockside trades. Among them Chinese and West African workers had a long association with the city and in many cases were permanent residents with families. Liverpool's black population, in fact, had been a continuous presence since at least the early eighteenth century.[2] This polyglot, cosmopolitan mixture of people might suggest the development in the city of an easy-going, tolerant racial attitude on the part of the local population, but the truth was less reassuring. The antagonism felt by locals towards immigrants was deeply rooted and evident in anxieties that were both economic and sexual. Violent disturbances had occurred at the end of the 1914–18 War when it was felt by some that black men were holding down jobs that should be open to returning soldiers. Such attitudes persisted throughout the interwar years. The outbreak of war in 1939 added new elements to an already divided community. John Belchem's exhaustive study of race relations in Liverpool has revealed the intractable and durable problems that existed in the city, which continued into the twenty-first century.[3]

In the light of this prehistory the duties of Constantine's posting to Liverpool in 1941 presented him with, at the very least, some difficult situations. 'Among such problems' he later said, 'I walked warily'.[4] His presence had come about as a result of a joint initiative by the Colonial Office and the Ministry of Labour to deal at one and the same time with two problems: on the one hand the labour unrest in the Caribbean colonies, which had been especially severe in the late 1930s, and on the other a skills shortage in British wartime industry. Constantine's task was the oversight, as welfare officer, of West Indians who had volunteered to work on Merseyside in the munitions and engineering factories. The Colonial Office hoped that by providing work experience and training to black workers, who would then return home and add their skills to the local economy, Britain's commitment to the strategy expressed in the Colonial Welfare and Development Act passed by Parliament in 1940 would be assisted. It should always be borne in mind that the British government's policy in response to the unrest in the Caribbean was to develop the colonial infrastructure to achieve better jobs and living conditions for local people. It was a policy whose influence endured in the public mind well after the end of the War. When, in the 1950s, migration from the Caribbean to Britain aroused alarm from whites, a popular reaction was to advocate further economic development in the islands. This, it was assumed, would prevent the need for West Indians to come to Britain to find work.[5] Thus the arrival of black people during the Second World War, as workers in factories and servicemen, was regarded as a short-term measure only. Fundamentally, the scheme was predicated on the belief that the voluntary black workers would return home ('repatriation' was the term used) at the war's end. From the Ministry of Labour's standpoint, the scheme was intended to support the necessary expansion of the British workforce in response to the demands of war. Factories in the Liverpool area, where the local economy was based largely on the shipping trade, simply needed more of the skilled work that appeared to be in ready supply in the West Indies. In all, therefore, an initiative of this nature offered a mutual benefit to both colonies and 'mother country'. Liverpool was favourably located in relation to wartime production centres, added to which there was a belief that local people were accustomed to living among a range of different races and would therefore receive workers from the Caribbean with, if not open arms, at least a degree of equanimity. As things turned out, however, race relations during the war had proved difficult, though contrary to expectations roughly a third of the workers chose to stay on and seek continuing employment in Britain. The experiment therefore exposed an assortment of the problems of race relations that were to develop in Britain in the second half of the twentieth century.

To begin with, an issue often overlooked in race relations was the potential for discord within the immigrant population itself. This was most likely to occur in Liverpool between the newly arrived West Indians and the older-established West African population.[6] In terms both of earnings and status their situations contrasted markedly. Many of the Africans, originally from Nigeria, the Gold Cast and Sierra Leone, were permanent residents in the port.[7] The shipping firm Elder Dempster, whose vessels plied the route between Liverpool and Lagos, employed many of them, often rather harshly.[8] By contrast, the newly arrived West Indians were better paid and often better housed. They were, in theory at least, skilled men and considered themselves deserving of greater respect. Relations between the two groups rarely ran smoothly. Following this difficulty, there was the question of integrating black workers with others. Various local and national organizations – notably the Merseyside Hospitality Council (MHC) and the Colonial Office's Advisory Committee on the Welfare of Colonial People in the United Kingdom (ACWUK) – attempted to ensure a congenial integration of the immigrant and resident communities, and to provide accommodation and social facilities that did not become too sharply segregated. They were supplemented by voluntary bodies providing welfare work on a limited scale, such as the African Church Mission run by Pastor Daniels Ekarte. Early in the War a former boys' club had been secured as a social centre for the West Indians, but Arnold Watson, the Ministry of Labour official who had pushed for this provision, came to doubt the value of what he saw as a 'segregated' approach. He preferred a more integrationist approach such as applied at the YMCA in Birkenhead, which housed a mixed group of transient seamen of various nationalities and races.[9] An ambitious scheme to make coloured workers feel more at home was launched in early 1943, inspired by John Carter of the League of Coloured Peoples (LCP), together with the Bishop of Liverpool, Albert David. It was aimed at creating a community centre of multiracial proportions near the middle of Liverpool itself. Crucially, the resident black population would form its core membership but with doors also open to all comers. Stanley House, as the centre came to be known, received moral and financial support from a number of bodies, including the LCP and the Colonial Office.[10] Cricket matches organized by Constantine brought in further funds from spectator donations. Unfortunately, though, the idea of putting multiracialism into concrete form was hard to realize. Problems of finance in particular hindered progress. By the time the war ended all that had been opened was a nursery for young children in Falkner Square. A new building was finally opened in Upper Parliament Street, but not until September 1946. Constantine, though he had been vice chairman of the initial organizing committee, did not attend the opening ceremony. He had doubts about the centre's physical location and its 'efficacy as a Cultural and Social Centre. The question of need is unchallenged. What is disputed is its isolation from a more cultured environment'.[11] Integrating the immigrants had succeeded only in segregating them from the local white community. In this way Liverpool presented a complex and often confusing picture of racial anxieties, with local and national agencies and their representatives each pursuing its own particular objectives, sometimes in unison, often in conflict.

Constantine's work was confined to helping the West Indian factory workers cope with their new environment. His activities reveal in detail the problem of 'race relations': both from the bottom up and, equally important from the top down, where officials for one reason or another seemed unable to give the colonial volunteers the support and protection they needed. Constantine had begun work with the Ministry of Labour in late 1941.[12] He was charged with overseeing the lives of the West Indian voluntary workers who had begun arriving on Merseyside earlier in the year. He and his small office staff had the responsibility of handling the various problems (in a broad sense the 'welfare') that the introduction of this new group of workers posed, both in the workplace and in broader areas of social and cultural life. He was, in short, a troubleshooter.

In 1941 there had been 188 arrivals from the West Indies, all save one from Jamaica. Over the course of the next two years the numbers increased to 345.

II

Although usually referred to as 'technicians' the West Indians carried out a variety of different jobs. Arnold Watson, the civil servant given overall responsibility for the scheme in the North West, listed the main types of work as motor mechanics, electric welders, machinists, electricians, pipe fitters and loco fitters (for which there was limited demand and some men were re-trained as millwrights and maintenance fitters).[13] Initially most of the work was located at three Royal Ordnance Factories on Merseyside, as well as at establishments run by the Shell oil company. By the time Watson had completed his report on the first year of the scheme, however, the West Indians had become dispersed across twenty-two local employers. The initial arrivals of 1941 comprised men who had been recruited in the Caribbean as 'skilled' craftsmen, but as the scheme expanded people with minimal qualifications were included; these men required training in England at Government Training Centres where they acquired knowledge that equipped them to be placed as semi-skilled operators in engineering workshops.[14] Much of Constantine's time was taken up dealing with the problems that arose among these varied types of workers in their various workplaces. An attempt visually to convey the nature of Constantine's work was made in a short, silent film produced by the Colonial Office towards the end of the war.[15] It shows Constantine arriving at a factory in his small car, being greeted by the management, going through the premises chatting with workers on the shop floor and having private talks with men who seem to be experiencing some problems. The presence of many black people in the short scenes seeks to underline the contribution of colonial workers to the war effort, with Constantine offering a reassuring support to them. From work, the film switches to leisure, ending with Constantine featuring in a cricket match played before a large racially mixed crowd. The intention of this sequence doubtless was to convey an image of the Empire's peoples united in their enjoyment of cricket and, by implication, in the pursuit of victory in war. Short though it was, the film reflects a concern present since early in the war at the Colonial Office that reports might filter back to the Caribbean that all was not well with volunteer workers who had come to England. Much of the effort put into securing accommodation and recreational provision for the technicians was motivated by the need to convey to those back home that black people in England were being treated fairly.

Relatively few difficulties were experienced in actually finding work for the West Indians. As Watson himself pointed out, the effectiveness of the scheme owed much to the wartime demand for labour.[16] Bigger problems arose once on the job. One of the most taxing concerned the expertise of the recruits. The men themselves held their skill in high regard and fought hard against any diminution of their status. Employers and their chargehands, however, often found that the Caribbean skills did not match up to the requirements of the job as demanded in England. Electrical welders, for example, were sometimes put onto oxyacetylene welding in aircraft assembly and were found to need further training before their work came up to Air Ministry standards. A problem of a different nature arose in the shipyards. The Boilermakers' Union, a long-established craft trade union, refused any workers who could not show that they had served a 'bona fide' apprenticeship, and this necessitated a search in the Caribbean for appropriate documentation, which was often not forthcoming. Closely related to such difficulties was the question of pay. As a general principle, the ministry held that the West Indians must receive the rate for the job and not be regarded by employers as a source of cheap labour. Nevertheless, what Anthony Richmond in his longitudinal study of West Indian workers in Liverpool calls 'misunderstandings' over pay were a source of dispute and anxiety during the entire life of the scheme. For example, the contracts signed by the original contingent of workers had included a misleading pay rate based on one exceptional firm in Liverpool that paid above the standard trade union rate. Once on the job there was naturally great discontent among the new arrivals, feeling they were being sold short. Their unease was not completely overcome by the payment by the Ministry of a £1 'expatriation' allowance, which proved to be less than the amount paid to white workers required to work in a town away from home.[17] Concern over absolute levels of pay were somewhat mollified by opportunities for overtime working once munitions factories had geared up to full wartime capacity. Weekly wages of £13–14 became possible for some skilled men. Wage differentials, however, remained a problem, especially among trainees who found that wage rates varied from place to place. This precipitated a scramble to move jobs to find a higher level of pay, a situation that worried officials, employers and white workers alike. There developed a feeling among the latter that the West Indians were treated too leniently, especially when they resorted to protest action such as refusing to pay their hostel fees, or ran up large bills, which the management was often unable to recoup. In more general terms, West Indian workers frequently felt that they were discriminated against in the workplace in relation to the jobs allocated to them, their promotion prospects and the attitude displayed towards them by white fellow workers, which was often influenced by popular stereotypes of the black colonial character.[18]

Such perceptions extended into the wider social relationships of the West Indians with the local population. Watson's summary of the early phases of the scheme, given as an address to a meeting organized by the LCP in London in March 1942, evinced an optimistic outlook. 'Making the West Indians at Home' had been a prime objective. While admitting that not all the new recruits behaved well he felt that the vast majority showed friendliness and a good spirit towards locals. Ingrained prejudices on the part of white people were, to be sure, a barrier to harmony but, as Watson put it, 'remove the fear of the white worker for his job, and you then get a chance to build.'[19] Watson recorded with particular satisfaction a cricket match in September 1941 between Eddie Paynter's XI and a team captained by Constantine, which attracted 11,000 spectators and raised £300 for the Lord Mayor's war charities.[20] He clearly regarded this event as a symbol of success for the scheme as a whole: 'We are witnessing,' he claimed 'the day-to-day elimination of racial discrimination.'[21] Later events, though, were to cast more than a little doubt on his optimism.

If anything, the more intractable race problems were to be found outside the workplace. These carried potentially serious political consequences. As John Carter of the LCP observed in a report on the social conditions prevailing in Liverpool in 1943: 'Like most West Indians [the technicians] refuse to appreciate anything that savours of colour discrimination and are never inarticulate or ambiguous in voicing their disapproval of any attempt to institute barriers.'[22] Housing was a sensitive area in this respect. Watson had earlier commented with some pride on the setting up of West Indies House, which lodged forty-five occupants. But generally speaking, such hostels acquired a poor reputation as the war went on. They became synonymous with the 'bad behaviour' of less respectable elements ('undesirables') among the West Indian workers.[23] And yet attempts by some to rent private housing prefigured the experience commonly found after the War, when black people were often bluntly turned away. A man interviewed by Richmond reported:

> Sometimes we had been given an address and assured there was a room vacant, but whenever we got there and they saw we were coloured it was found that the room had been taken that very morning! Sometimes the landlady was more honest and said, 'Well, I would not mind so much myself but I know my husband would not approve; and just think what the neighbours would say!'[24]

Although there was, of course, no formal segregation of the races in Britain, West Indians found themselves discriminated against in a variety of informal ways: for example, they were often ushered into the public rather than the saloon bar in pubs, or excluded from dance halls on the pretext that their presence might cause trouble. Some Roman Catholic West Indians found themselves refused the Mass in church and told to go to the mission instead. Race relations were often easier in sports clubs, where popular pastimes such as cricket and darts served as common ground for men of all colours. The local population's attitudes on race, however, gave the West Indians profound cause for dismay; their reception was quite different from what they might have expected as British subjects arriving in the 'mother country'. They were deeply resentful at being described by the near ubiquitous term 'nigger', and despaired of the public's general ignorance of the West Indies ('What part of Africa is Jamaica in?'). The police, it was felt, were biased against them, particularly in disturbances that had manifestly been provoked by white males.[25]

An especial source of anxiety was the sexual relationships between black men – invariably single, sometimes West Indians but often black American GIs – and white women. This was the area that exposed most clearly the difficulties of achieving racial harmony and was given emphatic treatment in Richmond's survey.[26] The problem of children born of these relationships – 'brown babies' as they came to be called – claimed a great deal of the attention of various committees in Liverpool at this time.[27] Much of the impetus in lobbying for action on brown babies and their mothers came from Pastor Daniels Ekarte, a Nigerian religious leader and long-time resident of Liverpool, who sought to provide facilities for a measure of care. Constantine was closely involved with Ekarte in a particular scheme to set up a home in Leeds for children of pre-war mixed-race marriages who had drifted into delinquency.[28] He was able to channel through the LCP some funds to the Leeds home from contributions made at cricket matches. But the money donated from such sources was never enough, and with financial support from government difficult to obtain the scheme eventually foundered.[29] The problem of the brown babies was one example of a social problem that came into full view during the War but which was never wholeheartedly confronted in official circles. Other such issues similarly arose only to be shelved in the expectation that once the war was over the problem would go away. The American presence threw up many examples.

III

The problems noted by Arnold Watson were greatly intensified and, at the same time, Watson's optimism significantly deflated by the arrival in the north-west of England during 1942 of large numbers of American troops, both black and white. The American invasion gave rise to a ticklish issue. The US troops had come to win the war, after some abject military failures on the part of the British. That being so, it was going to be difficult to say anything hostile towards them. But they brought with them their own racial antagonisms to add to those already present in the Liverpool area. White troops from the southern United States, whose antipathy to their black comrades in arms had been ingrained through traditions of race relations going back generations, found it difficult to accept the rather less intransigent attitudes found in Britain. Three interrelated difficulties emerged: hostility shown by white US troops towards their own black compatriots (the US Army was not fully de-segregated until the Korean War of 1950–53) when faced with them in pubs, cinemas and dance halls; the problem of the liaisons of all black men with white women and the response to this of local males; and the attitude specifically displayed towards the West Indian technicians under Constantine's charge by white American servicemen.[30]

Dance halls were a particular site of conflict. Race integration was especially difficult to stomach for white soldiers, particularly those from the southern states, when they were faced with the sight of black men dancing with white women. In such cases, Watson claimed, 'these American white soldiers go to dance halls with a positive aim of taking action – physical action if need be'.[31] In a quite detailed report of December 1943, Watson pointed up the difficulty of dealing with such relationships, and the problems they caused for the good will of the technicians, who expected action from the Ministry of Labour to protect them against discrimination. Having become used to Watson's 'welcoming' strategy, the West Indians began to encounter a colour bar. Certain respectable dance halls on Merseyside (the Grafton and the Rialto in particular) had been recommended by the welfare officers, in preference to 'dives' and 'low pubs', but following American pressure these more salubrious venues started to close their doors to the West Indians. One American officer, Captain Laing, had written that 'it is not our intention to dictate to privately-owned establishments, but in the interests of eliminating trouble … we will appreciate your co-operation in prohibiting Negroes from attending the dances'.[32] Segregation in leisure was the last thing Watson wanted, though he had to admit that, aside from a few 'palliatives aimed at appeasing' (Watson's words) the technicians (one of which was the practical step of placing some of them on foreman training schemes) he could offer no real solution to the problem.

Constantine's own experience underlined the presence of American prejudice. A few months after Watson's report, Constantine wrote to him about a situation he had personally encountered in London. He described sitting in a bar 'just off Oxford Street' with two friends (one the wife of the writer Arthur Calder-Marshall, whose book on Trinidad, *Glory Dead*, had recently been published):

> Two white Americans with their girl friends walked in and after hesitating near my chair (making it obvious what their feelings were) they proceeded to settle at a table. Then, one of them got up and had a conversation with the publican; in passing back he hesitated at my table the same way as before and moved on. Then the other man came through repeating the process and finally ended up by speaking to the publican. It was then the publican made it obvious by her statement, "If you do not like the people in this house, you know what to do. You can leave." The American returned to his friends and they all got up to leave; but in passing near my table one hesitated long enough to say within earshot of every one, "I would not have a bloody drink under the same bloody roof as any blood nigger."

Besides illustrating plainly a southern white-American mentality on race, Constantine's story was a demand for action. 'Everyone is hesitant to take action' against such 'blatant insults', he reported, fearing that if unchecked, situations like this would lead 'the Negro to take the law in his own hands.'[33] Quite what Constantine meant by this is uncertain. Possibly he feared some kind of direct action leading to street violence. Alternatively he might have had in mind organized radical action 'from below' (such as he was to encounter some twenty years later in Bristol), which might result in the initiative on race questions being taken out of the hands of moderate figures like himself. In any event, an urgent response was sought from the powers-that-be, since in his view this was more than a problem local to Merseyside or London.

Responses from senior civil servants varied, however. The troubles caused by the American presence were taken up, and rather bluntly stated, by Sir Frederick Leggett, a senior civil servant at the Ministry of Labour, in a letter to Sir George Gater, the Parliamentary Undersecretary for the Colonies, in March 1944. 'The colour-bar difficulties on Merseyside and at Manchester,' wrote Leggett, '*which have been stirred up by the Americans*, are seriously affecting the well-being and social life of the West Indian technicians and trainees, and Constantine recently came to London to express his very grave concern at the developments.' Leggett went on to describe the work Constantine had done in securing equal treatment for the technicians in 'a number of better class places of recreation'. All had subsequently been closed to them 'under pressure from the Americans'. Leggett was clearly worried that these developments were undermining the morale of the West Indians and might have the result of jeopardizing the entire scheme to which they had been recruited. He sought Gater's support at the Colonial Office in having the matter taken up 'at a high level' with the American authorities.[34] Gater, a former soldier who had come to the civil service from education administration, was concerned to 'give Constantine every support we reasonably can'.[35] His approach, however, was to treat the problem as a local matter and to look to a subcommittee of the Merseyside Council for Hospitality (of which Constantine was a member, alongside representatives of the Colonial Office's Welfare Department) to garner 'the facts' before making a high level approach to the US Army. This seemed, to Watson at least, a blind alley. He felt little would be achieved through representation by local officers to the MHC on a problem that, in agreement with Constantine, Watson saw as a national one. He urged the intervention of a Colonial Office man (suggesting the experienced John L. Keith) 'to put the case for the withdrawal of the colour bar in restaurants, dance-halls and public houses'.[36] Leggett backed Watson and Constantine to the hilt, writing to Gater that the two men were 'seriously concerned lest the forbearance hitherto shown may not continue … and may lay up trouble in the long run when they go back after the war'.[37] Touching as it did both on the diplomatically sensitive issue of British—American relationships and on the prospect of future strains in colonial relations, the letter prompted a speedy response.

The Colonial Office stance was, however, to recommend caution. Clearly, at the higher level, the maintenance of sound relations with the Americans was paramount. The extent to which the Americans were primarily responsible for the troubles was a subject around which questions circulated tentatively. Gater had looked in detail, in consultation with the Home Office and the chief constables of Liverpool and Warrington, at 'the facts'. The situation in six dance halls was reviewed and it was concluded that in most cases a colour bar had been operated by the management of the halls in the interests either of safeguarding their licences in the event of trouble, or of preserving the custom of American clients. In one case, the casino in Warrington, American civilian customers were said to have accepted a coloured presence once it was explained to them that neither the police nor the management was prepared to take action to exclude West Indians. Gater almost entirely absolved the Americans of any responsibility for a colour bar, and sought, somewhat unnecessarily since it had not been part of Watson's original report, to show that the American army authorities had played no part in demanding segregation in places of entertainment. His view was that official intervention by government departments with the American authorities was not the way forward on this issue. He suggested passing the ball back to the MHC and at the same time referring the problem to the newly-created British and US Liaison Board, of which the Conservative politician and Minister of Information Brendan Bracken was a leading member. Gater concluded by expressing sympathy for the management of the halls 'which have their own interests to protect and have in some cases undoubtedly had unfortunate experiences in their dance halls owing to the misbehaviour of the coloured people themselves, and it is perhaps understandable that they should take the line of least resistance by excluding a minority whose presence gives rise to difficulties.'[38] Since the Colonial Office response seemed to involve turning its back on the race problem by actually disputing some of the findings in Watson's report of the previous December, it might be imagined that both he and Constantine were, to say the least, dismayed by its tone. There seemed to be a sense in higher circles that the problems were temporary ones and that once everyone (Americans and West Indians) had returned home, things would settle back to normal.

In fact the normal proved to be as bad as, if not worse than, the temporary. In Liverpool the social climate of the immediate post-war period was a hostile one for all ethic groups. 'Liverpool,' says Belchem, 'remained at the forefront of concern about race relations ... into the 1950s.'[39] The attitude of the national and local authority was far less hospitable than it had been in the war, when Arnold Watson's call for 'making the West Indians Feel At Home' suggested an enlightened body of opinion towards race relations. With unemployment in Liverpool high after the end of the war the official position on immigration from overseas was to restrict it as far as possible. Repatriation was enforced for some of those already in the city. The official fear that the white population would react to scarce jobs being taken by immigrants, whether colonials or European Volunteer Workers, was not unfounded. The Chinese were the first to feel the effects of this, which soon caught up with other groups. During the August Bank Holiday of 1948, race tensions exploded into severe rioting in that area of the city most populated by black workers. The provocations came from white men, though in terms of arrests by the police it was black people who suffered disproportionately.[40]

A microcosm of the overall picture of race relations was provided in Constantine's domain, where the whole episode of the voluntary technicians scheme ended on a sour note. While Constantine was awarded an MBE for his wartime services, some of the technicians in his charge who had chosen to return home experienced something far less rewarding. In *Colour Bar*, Constantine describes problems he tried to resolve for 'about forty coloured workers' who were embarking on a ship bound for the Caribbean. They were being placed in accommodation inferior to that which the Ministry of Labour had paid for, and they were asked to carry out cleaning duties that were not part of a passenger's responsibility. In spite of assurances given to Constantine before the ship sailed, the accommodation provided proved to be less than expected. This 'meanness', as Constantine described it, was only one aspect of the racial attitudes that influenced the entire administration of the repatriation.[41] The voyage home could be problematical. As with Constantine's technicians, many other workers and ex-servicemen on the journey home encountered discrepancies between their expected accommodation and duties and what was actually provided. Anger was aroused over differentials in clothing allowances paid to those from different areas of the Caribbean. To cap it all, the prospect of unemployment when they arrived home produced a mood of disenchantment with the colonial order. One particular case – the *SS Bergensfjord*, sailing from Glasgow to Kingston via Port of Spain in March 1946 with over 1200 ex-servicemen and technicians on board – was the scene of a very ugly incident. Some of the passengers refused to take on cleaning duties, or to take part in the ship's inspections. Later in the voyage, tensions mounted and physical violence broke out. Some forced their way into stores and took rifles. Shots were fired, though no serious casualties were sustained. Finally, the ship's master declared a mutiny, and a naval escort was called for. Order was only finally restored on disembarkation, with the help of armed British troops at the quayside in Kingston. Norman Manley's People's National Party (PNP) protested at the incidents and the presence of what the PNP described as 'an army of occupation'.[42] For others, the arrival home, if less dramatic, nevertheless brought severe difficulties in re-settling into civilian life. Arrangements in place to receive them, which had looked exemplary when set out on paper, were far from satisfactory in practice. Above all the high levels of unemployment in the islands, particularly in Jamaica, made the finding of jobs for the returnees very difficult. This in part explains the return migration to Britain and the voyage of the *Windrush* in 1948.

III

Constantine's experiences in Liverpool were profoundly important in broadening his understanding of race, enabling him to witness the discrepancy between the respect he was often shown by white people and the treatment experienced by working-class black people. While he never openly expressed any negative views about his wartime-experience it might be conjectured that he regarded the experiment with the voluntary workers as a failure. Since his arrival in England in 1929, Constantine had lived a privileged and, it might be said, protected life: insulated within the world of cricket, living in a nice house in a little middle-class enclave of Nelson and the subject (aside from a few racial snipes) of the adulation of the local populace. In the colonial Caribbean he had known segregation and discrimination, though never in the rigidly institutionalized forms found in the southern United States. He was unused to the mentalities of white US troops stationed in England, though he had probably encountered something similar from American drillers in the Trinidad oilfields. What above all was new to him was the scale of the problem. Although the number of technicians under his charge was relatively small, it was nevertheless a bigger group, with a diversity of problems, than he had dealt with before. What had for him been largely a personal or family matter of race prejudice he could now envisage as a general social issue. Being immersed in the daily problems of West Indian migrant workers in Liverpool thus gave Constantine an awareness of how the problem of race relations might develop in Britain. It also prompted in him thoughts about how the problem of race might be tackled. Personal insults served to intensify such thoughts and translate them into action. The incident with the American serviceman in the pub off Oxford Street was one example. A similar one occurred at around the same time, also in London and also with an American connection. On this, Constantine decided to take a public stand.

In 1943, Constantine was refused accommodation at the Imperial Hotel on Russell Square in London. The incident was covered extensively in the newspaper press at the time and has since been well documented by historians.[43] A brief summary of the circumstances will suffice. Constantine had been chosen, along with other cricketers from the Commonwealth, to represent a Dominions team in a match against an England XI at Lord's in July 1943. He arranged to stay, with his family, at the Imperial Hotel in Bloomsbury, making a reservation for four nights with a deposit paid in advance. The hotel had been informed beforehand that the Constantine family was coloured. When they – Learie, Norma and Gloria – arrived, together with a colleague from the Ministry of Labour[44] and a friend from the cricket world, Charles Leatherbarrow, they signed in and took occupancy of their room. They were then told that they could stay only one night, after which they would have to leave. Constantine claimed that Mr Leatherbarrow was told that the Constantines' presence would offend a number of white American officers staying at the hotel: 'We won't have niggers at this hotel' was apparently the remark of the manageress, Mrs O'Sullivan.[45] This was not the first time that Constantine had encountered race prejudice in hotels and restaurants, as indeed had other famous black figures. In the late 1920s, Paul Robeson had experienced similar treatment at the Savoy Hotel in London. At the Imperial, however, Constantine was offered alternative accommodation at a nearby hotel, the Bedford, owned by the same company. The managing director of the company claimed that he had suggested that Constantine would be more 'comfortable' at another, smaller place. 'Mr Constantine readily agreed. There is no suggestion that he was turned out.' He added: 'there is no ban on coloured people at this hotel [the Imperial]. We prefer to cater for white people, but there is no question of coloured people being an inferior race.'[46] Constantine accepted the offer, having been advised to do so by his work colleague, who no doubt wished to avoid further embarrassment for the family.[47] On this issue, Arnold Watson later claimed that the comment about Constantine's presence offending white officers was invalid: 'The lying witness of Imperial London Hotels Ltd, foisted her own strong racial opinions on to some unnamed Americans, not one of whom could be produced or identified.'[48] The ironies and hypocrisies in the incident did not escape the more progressive elements of the press. In the *Daily Mirror*, the cartoonist Zec drew two coloured old soldiers, faced with a notice at the hotel stating, 'No Coloured People Admitted – By Order', exclaiming: 'We didn't see that notice in the trenches.'[49] The *Manchester Guardian* commented strongly: 'The men and women who want to impose their exclusive and intolerant prejudices on our society degrade us to the level of Nazis, whose doctrines they practise.'[50] But perhaps the clearest expression of outrage came in David Low's cartoon for the *Evening Standard*, which brought out the irony in the hotel's name and its implications for relations within the Empire.[51]

A short while later, Constantine decided to take a tort action against the hotel. In later years, there would have been statute law to be invoked against what Constantine felt was pretty clearly a case of racial discrimination, but no such law existed at the time so he sued for breach of contract and damages.[52] The case was heard before Justice Birkett in the King's Bench division in June 1944, 'without a jury in an improvised air-raid-shelter room in the Law Courts'.[53] Constantine's case was based on his having been turned away from the hotel contrary to the common law, which established that a 'common lodging house' had a responsibility to receive a guest unless there were reasonable grounds not to (e.g. that no rooms were available, or that the traveller was unable to pay). In

Figure 7 David Low's cartoon of September 1943 exposes the contradictions between Constantine's treatment at the Imperial Hotel, London, and his wartime work in seeking unity among imperial peoples. (Reproduced courtesy of the *Evening Standard*.)

Figure 8 An honoured gentleman: Godfrey Argent's photographic portrait of 1967 captures a Constantine proud of his life's achievements. (Reproduced courtesy of National Portrait Gallery, London.)

its defence the Imperial claimed that by offering alternative accommodation, which Constantine voluntarily accepted, there had been no breach of contract. In court, much emphasis was laid by Constantine's high-powered legal team (Sir Patrick Hastings and Rose Heilbron) on their client's status and respectability as both a world-renowned cricketer and a wartime civil servant of standing. By contrast, the representative of the hotel, Mrs O'Sullivan, was portrayed as unworthy, even described by the judge himself as a 'lamentable figure'. It was a difficult case, both for determining the legal nature of Constantine's plea and in dealing with evidence that was contradictory. Birkett found for Constantine, who was awarded an amount of five guineas in damages, a small sum but one that refuted the hotel's case that no damage had been proved. Costs were awarded to the plaintiff.

The case has been seen as a landmark in British race relations, with Constantine taking a stand against a clear case of racial injustice. At the time, Birkett's judgment was hailed by the LCP as a vindication of equal treatment for coloured people.[54] Not surprisingly, Constantine himself, writing some ten years later, underlined its significance: 'I was content to have drawn the particular nature of the affront before the wider judgment of the British public in the hope that its sense of fair play might help to protect people of my colour in England in the future.'[55] His biographer, Peter Mason, goes further, seeing the court case as 'a historic moment in the British battle for race equality ... one of the key milestones along the road to the creation of the Race Relations Act of 1965.[56]

Some of these claims demand closer scrutiny. That road to the 1965 Act was not a smooth one. There were to be many failed attempts in Parliament during the 1950s to arouse MP's interest in legislation to curb race discrimination before the act, itself a very limited measure, was passed.[57] While there is little doubt that the Imperial Hotel case highlighted the unfairness that could be meted out to black people, it is equally certain that Constantine's case did little to help most of them in the years afterwards. His victory in court and his hopes for fair play by no means halted racial discrimination, as the problems faced by black immigrants in the search for housing in the 1950s and early 1960s show all too clearly.[58] Although race was a prominent topic in courtroom discourse during Constantine's case, in legal terms race was a factor marked by its complete absence. Birkett's lengthy judgment illustrated this. He analysed several cases – some going back many years – in arriving at his decision. He gave close attention to one of 1918 (*Rothfield* v. *North British Railway Co.*), where a man had been refused lodging at an Edinburgh hotel. None of these cases involved racial discrimination, the main point at issue in them being the damage to the plaintiff that might have ensued from the specific actions under consideration: in the Edinburgh case, for example, Rothfield's having been turned away from the hotel. Nor was there any substantial evidence in the Constantine matter as to who might be at fault. Even the issue of failing to lodge the Constantines at the Imperial was clouded by the company's offer of alternative accommodation, which Constantine had accepted. This influenced the extent of damage that could be considered. In the final analysis, Birkett decided that Constantine's right to be lodged had been 'violated' and that a remedy was owed to him, though 'for nominal damages only'. His judgement, however, was a contentious one, not accepted by all lawyers. What might have determined the outcome was possibly a sensibility on the part of the judge to do justice to a man on account of his colour, when there was no legal sanction available against a refusal to accommodate people on such grounds. This is pure speculation though. Had Constantine's plea been heard before a different judge the verdict, on purely legal grounds with any race considerations set aside, might well have been different. The historian Anne Spry Rush has offered an interesting and quite different interpretation of the case that rests on something other than race: Constantine's social and professional standing. He was a respectable middle class man employed by the Ministry of Labour, a point emphasized strongly in the proceedings by his legal team. Spry Rush captures, perhaps, the essence of the matter: 'Without Constantine's class status and connection to high authorities, the incident would have drawn little attention.'[59] This may be so, for Constantine was certainly a very newsworthy figure. The inference is that, in contrast to Constantine, an unknown, and probably low status, black person would not have found a remedy in such an action. Such a person would in any case have been unlikely to be seeking lodging at the Imperial Hotel, still less taking it to court if that lodging was refused. Pubs, cheap hotels, rented accommodation and jobs were far more relevant for poor black people, and as Constantine himself was to learn when he later joined the Race Relations Board there was still ample discrimination being directed at them in these areas in the 1960s. Where does his leave the judgement in the Imperial Hotel case? Three points need to be kept in mind. First, it simply re-affirmed an existing state of affairs in common law: that a traveller could not be turned away from a common lodging house, except in defined specific circumstances, which had nothing to do with race, class, or gender. Second, a lodging house could choose to ignore this if its management was willing to risk of litigation, which might in many cases be a low risk. Third, the only sure remedy for the kind of problem that Constantine had encountered lay in statutory legislation that made it illegal for hotels to behave in the way that the Imperial had. So, the particular circumstances of the Constantine case illustrated nothing so much as the long-held view that the common law was an available course of redress, irrespective of race, provided a person had the financial resources to mount a tort action to affirm the law. As the old adage has it, the law was like the Ritz Hotel, open to all. In Constantine's case, so was the Imperial Hotel.

7

Colour Bar

Constantine's wartime work had augmented his understanding of race relations in a variety of everyday forms. The prejudice directed at the West Indian workers, for whose welfare he was responsible as a welfare officer, provided him with examples to add to his own personal experiences to create a wider perspective on the lived culture of race prejudice. It was from this that the idea for his book *Colour Bar* sprang. Published just before he left Britain in 1954 to take up a job in Trinidad, it was Constantine's most forceful public intervention on the subject of race.

I

The Imperial Hotel case had directed public attention to Constantine as a figure of more importance than simply a former cricketer. He was a man who would take a public stand for what he believed to be fair treatment in human affairs. By the time *Colour Bar* came out, his profile had been heightened through his writings on cricket and broadcasts for the BBC.[1] The new book took up a subject he had aired in many of his radio talks and developed it further as an unrestrained exposure of racial discrimination and prejudice. Since the war the term 'colour bar' had come more into common usage in Britain, although the subject of race was not so near the forefront of public discussion as it was to be a decade later. Outside academic circles, or pressure groups such as the League of Coloured Peoples, the subject of race was an issue for most white British people only in the sense that they objected to the relatively few coloured immigrants in the country (about 11,000 West Indians when *Colour Bar* came out).[2] In British cities where there had been a history of immigration, however, popular prejudices against black people were more deeply embedded in day-to-day life.[3] The increase in the numbers of immigrants during the course of the 1950s, and consequent incidences of racial conflict and public disorder, especially those occurring in Notting Hill (London) and Nottingham in 1958, in both cases focused on migrants from the West Indies,[4] brought race matters more fully into public consciousness. As far as public policy was concerned the response to this involved the controlling of immigrant numbers, rather than tackling the problem of prejudice and discrimination at social and cultural levels. Thus, the first major governmental intervention on race came in the form of the statutory restrictions on immigration in the 1962 Commonwealth Immigrants Act. Until the Race Relations Act of 1965, a Labour measure prompted by the success of a blatantly anti-black Conservative campaign in the Smethwick parliamentary election of 1964, there was no accompanying legislation on race relations.[5]

Considering, therefore, the relatively dormant atmosphere on race in the decade after the Second World War Constantine's book sought a breakthrough, forcing the race issue into the public sphere through its association with a famous name. Peter Mason, in the course of a perceptive discussion of *Colour Bar*,[6] attributes part of its impact to its unexpectedness, the fact that it was written by an unthreatening figure, a man commonly perceived as 'so charming, so unruffled, so suited to British society';[7] the implication being that matters of race had not been considered a fit subject for polite conversation, and it was a shock to read something so critical from the pen of such a man. Constantine claims that he was urged by various people – journalists, newspaper proprietors and 'humble English friends' – to write something down on 'the Negro's view of the black and white problem'. 'You know me!', he wrote; 'To one of my temperament, the invitation to knock a few over the pavilion is not to be resisted.'[8] What resulted is an easily readable volume that provides heaped examples of racial intolerance – some drawn from Constantine's own experiences in the West Indies and England, but most from a worldwide perspective. A few (but only a few) are taken from cricket.

The book takes it cue from the Universal Declaration of Human Rights, promulgated by the General Assembly of the United Nations in December 1948. The UN's aim, following the experiences of the recently ended war, had been to establish a canon of principles that all member states should strive to accept and promote to ensure that the fundamental belief enunciated in Article 1 of the Declaration became a reality: 'All human beings are born free and equal in dignity and rights. They are endowed with reason and conscience and should act towards one another in a spirit of brotherhood'. The Declaration, while seeking 'universal' relevance, was clearly influenced by ideas that had come out of western politics and philosophy in the nineteenth and twentieth centuries.

The Declaration gave prominence to constitutional, political and juridical rights, but added other objectives such as the right to social security, employment, basic standards of living and 'the right freely to participate in the cultural life of the community'. The problem of how, in a world with an unequal distribution of wealth, such rights were to be fully assured, was not explicitly brought out. Ambiguities were starkly evident. A country such as the United States, the history of which had been shaped by the notion of liberty, still allowed a system of racial prejudice and discrimination to continue; it was most obvious in its southern states but in no sense entirely absent in other parts of the country.

It was this kind of lacuna that prompted Constantine's book: to show how far most areas of the world were from achieving the principles of equality and freedom enshrined in the Declaration.[9] Great Britain and its colonies in Africa, the United States and South Africa form the main geographical focus. Readers expecting South Africa and the southern states of the United States to bear the weight of Constantine's criticisms would have been alarmed to find Britain and British colonialism in Africa in the spotlight. In Britain itself, Constantine pinpoints those areas where black people live a virtually segregated life, regarded with something like contempt by large sections of the population. 'I ... think it would be just to say that almost the entire population of Britain really expect the coloured man to live in an inferior area devoted to coloured people, and not to have free and open choice of a living-place.' He goes on to claim that most British people would wish to avoid contact with black people in whatever context – work, transport, restaurants, homes – that such intolerance is more common in the 'lower grades' of society and that it is more noticeable among women than men.[10] As for the colonies, he calls to account Britain for failing indigenous people's right to equality. 'The excuse is always: "The African is not ready for responsibility." Nothing is done to make him ready, everything is done to prevent the majority of Africans from making themselves ready.'[11] America, where a civil rights movement had come together at this time to combat racism in the south, was equally subjected to Constantine's ire. The injustices of the system of segregation were summed up in the case of Dr Ralph Bunche, who had recently refused to serve as Assistant Secretary of State in the federal government, offering no reason publicly for his decision. 'But I can tell you why he refused', says Constantine. 'It is because, being a coloured man, he is not permitted to eat at any public restaurant in Washington, the home of the government in which he had been asked to serve!'[12] Some parts of the world, usually those without colonial possessions, are spared harsh criticisms. Scandinavia is one, though even here Constantine notes, 'there is a general impression that coloured persons should "keep their place".[13] Only in the Soviet Union, it seemed to Constantine, did a true equality of the races appear to exist. Some readers would no doubt have contested Constantine's assertion that 'the fact remains, and it is indisputable, that in Russia there is no colour bar, no distinction of any visible kind, between black and white.'[14] It was this kind of unsubstantiated observation that invited the charge from some critics that Constantine was inspired by communist thinking. Those who knew him found this charge wholly misplaced, but his electrifying observations were to many seen as tantamount to disloyalty in a Britain that had given him a home.

Constantine's chief purpose in the book is to expose the source of the ideas and practices responsible for creating racial inequality. He finds it in the notion of white superiority, which, when 'justified' by quasi-scientific evidence, permits the ascribing of different qualities to people on the basis of their skin colour. He sees this as the fundamental problem to be tackled in attempting to move towards liberating coloured people from the status to which they are almost universally demoted – whether through the colonial system, the forms of legal segregation installed in the southern United States, the more informal segregationist practices carried out towards native Australians and Maoris, or the nominally non-segregated countries like Britain. He is particularly severe on religions and the churches as accomplices in this process. Christianity stands as a prime culprit. Where, according to the precepts of Christ's teachings, inequality and discrimination should be least in evidence, there is an obvious ingrained sense of difference: 'I have had some of the most painful experiences of colour segregation that I have ever suffered in churches in America, the West Indies and England.'[15] He himself had rejected the Roman Catholic religion in which he had been brought up because 'I have suffered so much and seen my coloured friends suffer so much, at the white priests' and white Roman Catholic worshippers' hands.'[16] If you are searching for a true example of the Christian idea of 'brotherhood of man' in practice, Constantine says, do not look for it in the Catholic and Protestant churches.

So it continues, page after page: a remorseless exposure of injustice in the name of white racial superiority. It is a deeply depressing book in the sense that it presents what seems like an insurmountable barrier in the way of change; formidably entrenched systems of belief and practice creating levels of obscurantism that defy rational thought and action. But in another sense, Constantine's polemic is rousing and stimulating. It poses a challenge to be taken up by those of a liberal conscience, employing educational methods and teaching tolerance to remove the scourge of race prejudice. Unlike some later race polemics, Constantine's book does not advocate violence as a solution, though he suggests that the longer this world situation remains unaltered the greater likelihood there is that black people will adopt violent means to bring about change. This was the concern he had developed during the Second World War when the powers-that-be seemed lukewarm in their attitude to race prejudice. It was to be a keystone of his thinking for the remainder of his life, seen in his wariness of black movements whose street politics might erupt into violence. What pervades his pages in *Colour Bar* more than any obvious call to action or political ideology is a sense of moral outrage. In this, Constantine's writing carries the legacy of the moderate League of Colored Peoples (LCP), only recently defunct, with which he had been associated since the early 1930s. It is, as the reviewer in the *Spectator* observed, a statement of passion and anger about the race question. 'His warning, which should reach a wide public, is authentic, timely and sincere.'[17] In this respect, the book succeeds in its aim of putting across the 'Negro's view of the black and white problem.'

In other respects, however, the tone and message of *Colour Bar* raise questions. Constantine had initially intended to use the title 'Black and White' for the book, and the categories of 'black' and 'white' are counterposed throughout in a simplistic manner. He also betrays an implicit Eurocentric perspective in his perception of the stages of development of humankind – the 'progress' he advocates for the well-being of black peoples implies a moving on and up to a European pinnacle.[18] Herein is to be found an idea of 'assimilation' – of coloured peoples aspiring to adopt the habits of thought and behaviour of the white European. Moreover, the structure of the text does not help. There are problems with Constantine's overly descriptive approach. It becomes too rich a pudding, overloaded with examples at the expense of a chronological or a thematic pattern, a separation of causes from effects and an overall argument. Only towards the end does it become clear that Constantine's solution to the obvious injustices perpetrated by white people is the rather naïve one of 'love'. Ideologically, the book is a plea to white people's reason, to behave better by fulfilling the demands of the Human Rights Convention, by legislating for equality of opportunity in work, under the law and in voting rights, together with the abolition of segregation and the recognition of the dignity of the human being. It is a call for non-violent action through persuasion: for the races to live together in a spirit of tolerance, with the initiative coming from white people themselves to set in motion a progressive programme of change. Looking back on *Colour Bar* from a twenty-first century vantage point, its approach to race might seem jejune: it is offered to the reader in an unproblematical way, lacking any nuance of class, race or gender identities and how they might interact in opposing race prejudice. The world is presented as divided simply into black and white. And yet, crude though Constantine's conceptual approach might seem, it surely communicated through its hammer blows the sense of the moral outrage needed in the first instance to inspire a movement for change.

As may be imagined, the reception of *Colour Bar* was mixed. There was much praise from reviewers for the book's main purpose, that of bringing the subject of race to the fore. At the same time there was ample criticism. It would not be surprising to know that for many British readers Constantine's dismissive view of colonialism in the British territories of Africa aroused particular animosity. In a colony-by-colony account Constantine identifies a multiplicity of wrongdoings, including unfair land distribution, the displacement of black people to reservations, low wages and harsh taxation. The worst excesses, he claims, are to be found in the 'Red Road' – that stretch of British power that 'runs from south to north of the continent, slightly to the right of middle'.[19] Kenya, with its obdurate white settlers, is seen as the epitome of misrule, one consequence of which was the recent Mau Mau uprising (continuing as the book went into circulation). Constantine portrays a continent on the verge of rebellion against the injustices perpetrated to its black population – 'a deadly dangerous picture'.[20] 'A word is creeping about that immense continent of 11,000,000 square miles and 160,000,000 people, nearly all of them coloured. The word is 'Communism'.[21] And, says Constantine, 'it is no use shouting at the Negro that Democracy is better than Communism. It may be better for you. It is not better for him. He only knows what Democracy does to him when it makes him carry Passes, shuts him in slums, pens him in land-sick Reservations, half starves him and his wife and children.'[22] Constantine thus made use of the contemporary 'red scare' to broach a problem, which, some twenty years later, had become a major concern in international politics – the place of Africa in the Cold War.

Some British critics were stung by these comments. The idea of communism being present in British colonies raised the hackles of many an old-school imperialist whose life's work had been aimed at preventing such an un-British outcome.[23] In the *Daily Telegraph*, the Africa hand and Conservative politician Dennis Herbert (Lord Hemingford), who had spent some twenty years teaching there and had recently been Rector of Achimota College in the Gold Coast (Ghana), was quick to respond. He was supportive of Constantine for exposing the gaps between the ideals of race equality and the actual state of affairs in the world – 'few of us', said Herbert, 'are safe from complacency' on that issue – yet felt that Constantine had not been fair, especially in regard to education. He had claimed, noted Herbert, that the education of 'bright' Africans was inadequate, reserved for those who were 'docile' and obedient to white control. 'How angry the undergraduates of Africa's four university colleges – at Khartoum, at Ibadan, at Achimota and at Makerere – will be when they read that statement!' Herbert attributed this lapse to Constantine's ignorance about Africa, a continent he had never visited. His review therefore damned Constantine with faint praise; it was a patronizing dismissal of a man who should go away and do more homework.[24]

Such an attitude was not, however, representative of the general tone of reviews. On the whole there was sympathy for Constantine's general aims and purpose, indicating that by the mid-1950s his views were, perhaps, becoming acceptable to some. To have opposed them outright would have been unlikely by this time, which made a hostile letter in the *Catholic Herald* surprising for claiming that black people were not 'by a long way' ready for 'full civilization'.[25] Criticisms there were, however, and came in various forms. Matters of factual accuracy frequently came in for comment, especially over what was considered to be Constantine's lack of knowledge on African matters.[26] The *Liverpool Daily Post* felt, correctly it might be thought, that the book failed to diagnose the 'root causes' of colour prejudice. 'L. B.' in the *Manchester Evening News* considered Constantine's argument too one-sided, which 'spoiled his own cause'.[27] The Rev. G. Needham in the *Sheffield Telegraph* was more dismissive than most: he confessed to disappointment with a book that contained 'nothing much new'.[28] The *Birmingham Post*, which adjudged the situation in Africa to be less bad than Constantine had portrayed it, nonetheless considered *Colour Bar* 'a fair and sensible book on a shameful and senseless situation'.[29] In the same city 'M. C.' in the *Birmingham Gazette* was unstinting in his praise. Noting that Constantine had declined an offer to stand as a Liberal candidate in the 1950 general election, M. C. felt he should have accepted the invitation: 'the House of Commons, bedevilled by colonial problems, badly needs advice – and an occasional angry outburst – from someone like himself.'[30]

Constantine could at least have taken comfort in the fact that his book had been widely noticed. It said as much about his public standing as about the timeliness of the topic. But his leaving of England a few months later deprived Constantine of the chance to follow up the impact of the book. In Trinidad political life seems to have presented him with little opportunity for writing. For almost eight years his name was absent from the British press, and by the time he returned from Trinidad in 1962 the book was looking dated. His own explanation for its publication – that it was the expression of one black person's subjective feelings about race, written at the suggestion of friends and colleagues – had rendered it something of a personal statement, the relevance of which might now seem inadequate in very changed circumstances. Its methodological naivety and unawareness of political tactics weakened its effect. To be sure, *Colour Bar* had once been part of a new consciousness of 'race relations'. By the 1960s, however, the field had been occupied for some years by specialist academic analysts. Pioneered by Kenneth Little, Ruth Glass and Sheila Patterson the field of race relations became one in which answers not confined simply to limiting immigration were sought to the problem of race. The discourse that this work generated was conceptual and 'scientific' in ways that Constantine's book was not. In many cases the idea of 'assimilation' was proposed, derived from earlier American work on race problems that configured the notion of a 'melting pot' in which the different races would be integrated. But, by the later 1960s, this paradigm had itself become subject to new questionings: did races exhibit particular characteristics, how did 'race' as an analytical tool of social analysis compare with concepts such as class and gender and did the idea of a race consciousness even correspond to actual lived practices?[31] In the light of what these later notions brought to the understanding of race relations, Constantine's book came to be seen, by those who remembered it, as an early, somewhat lightweight intervention in the subject. It had set out no scientific methodology, still less any persuasive theory, though it might have served a useful polemical purpose. *Colour Bar's* influence was not a lasting one, and as the years passed it became rare to find it referenced in the work of specialists in the field.

A vital point, and simultaneously a major weakness, in Constantine's thinking about race throughout these years, concerned how the race question might be dealt with politically in a country like Britain. It was all very well striking a moral pose on a question of social justice, but a very different matter to fashion a means of tackling the problem. Constantine's experience of political activity in Britain was in any case limited. He had on occasions been approached by both the Liberal and Labour parties to consider standing as a candidate for Parliament, but always declined the invitation. His avoidance of direct involvement with British political parties had confined him to lending his weight sporadically to individual causes. The case of Seretse Khama in the early 1950s was an interesting example. Constantine became a member of the Council for the Defence of Seretse Khama, a body composed of figures from a wide span of opinion. They were united in opposing the British government's refusal to permit Khama to take up his official position as King of the Bamangwato people in the British protectorate of Bechuanaland. Constantine and others were suspicious that pressure had been brought to bear on the Labour government of the day by the

South African authorities to banish Khama because of his marriage to a white woman. It was felt that Khama and his wife were victims of a blatant injustice. The case fitted precisely the kind of racial intolerance that Constantine was to rail against in *Colour Bar*, where he gave a lengthy account of the matter. 'We approached Parliament, lobbied MPs, held public meetings, even tried to appeal to the UNO Committee of Human Rights.'[32] It was all very respectable tactically, and Constantine was surrounded by some prominent figures from politics, sport and the churches. A role that always suited him is well described by a note from Fenner Brockway, the anti-colonial Labour MP who was active in the campaign, inviting Constantine to attend a gathering at the House of Commons in honour of the birth of the Khamas' child: 'You *must* come to relieve the dullness of us politicians! Seretse and Ruth want you especially.'[33] One may imagine the genial Learie enlivening the occasion with a few jokes and some cricket chat. In the end, though, it was high politics in defence of an African aristocrat and had little relevance to the problems of the man and woman in the street. And for all the close parliamentary and social networking that went on the attempt to help Seretse Khama was ultimately unsuccessful. Constantine's own (politely worded) verdict was: 'we might just as well have whistled to the wind.'[34] The Seretse Khama campaign connected with another race issue of South African origin: namely, apartheid. It goes without saying that Constantine was always an opponent of the Nationalist government in South Africa, which on coming to power in 1948 had systematized the country's racial laws to create a thoroughly racially segregated society. Yet international opposition was slow to develop. Constantine himself took time to form his views on the problem, and when he did the impetus came not from Britain but from Trinidad.

III

Shortly after the publication of *Colour Bar*, Constantine had returned to Trinidad where he joined the People's National Movement (PNM) led by Eric Williams. It was the first time Constantine had been actively involved in any political movement for a sustained period of time. In a critical period between 1956 and 1962, Williams steered Trinidad and Tobago through a stormy passage from Crown Colony through internal self-government to full independence. In spite of its name the PNM, which only emerged as a serious political movement in the mid-1950s, never enjoyed the universal appeal achieved by similar parties in other countries. It was in essence a black party and failed to win over the large Indian population in Trinidad. Much of its success at this time depended on Williams's personal magnetism as a public intellectual-cum-party leader, capable of bringing together a group of black politicians and at the same time keeping a firm hand on the party's organization. Williams insisted that the PNM was a *nationalist* organization, not a class, religious, or ethnic-based party. Indeed, he insisted that it was not a political party in the conventional sense of the word at all – it was a *movement*, and the idea of a 'national/popular' crusade was reinforced in the title and pages of the party's weekly newspaper, *The Nation*. Members were expected to be activists: each was urged, in Williams's words, to be 'agent, canvasser, propagandist of the Party ... in your daily rounds, in taxis and buses, at work, in clubs and friendly societies and fraternal organizations, on and off playing fields, at fetes and functions of all sorts.'[35] In the late 1950s, Williams's largely unchallenged political and moral authority in the party was neatly evinced in his regular weekly column in *The Nation* – 'The Doctor Says'. There was a sense that when Williams spoke his views were ex cathedra. He encouraged a mass involvement by members in the task of spreading the party's message and ensuring that everything possible was done to recruit voters.[36] His outstanding contribution to the country's political education came in the use of the busy park in central Port of Spain as a meeting ground for lectures and discussion on the big issues of the day – he named it the 'University of Woodford Square'.

This, then, was the situation in which Constantine spent the next eight years of his life, serving as a minister in the PNM administration leading up to full Independence in 1962. He remained a faithful member of the party, committed to its aim of bringing about the end of colonialism and installing an egalitarian society it its place. His hopes were not entirely fulfilled, however. Personal animosities within the party leadership, and an eventual falling out with Williams, resulted in Constantine's leaving Trinidad and settling back in England (Chapter 8). The time he spent in Trinidad might be regarded as time lost: less important for what he achieved in the Caribbean than for what he missed in Britain. Having made a name with *Colour Bar* as a spokesman on race he removed himself from British society for a period of important political changes: Suez, the formation of the Campaign for Nuclear Disarmament (CND), the race riots of 1958, Labour's electoral defeats of 1955 and 1959 and the gradual emergence of a new kind of black politics that surpassed the stance of the old LCP. There were opportunities aplenty to be involved in political and social movements that might have shaped a quite different Constantine from the one who came back as High Commissioner for Trinidad and Tobago in 1962.

One aspect of his work in Trinidad has been somewhat overlooked, however, and deserves consideration for what it reveals about race antagonism in the Caribbean islands. It concerns a subject on which he had a certain expertise: cricket. In the particular circumstances of Trinidad politics in the 1950s, sport played an influential role. The successes of the largely black West Indian cricket team in the earlier part of the decade had a political effect, encouraging a new self-confidence among black cricket followers, which in turn seemed to swell the tide of black power in the politics of the larger islands such as Trinidad and Jamaica. In response to these political and sporting developments, however, white opinion in the Caribbean stiffened. Opposed to the move towards self-government and the onset of Independence white residents adopted a posture in which sport became a vehicle of their symbolic defiance. Rather than supporting the West Indies against England in the test matches in the 1953–54 tour, and again in 1959–60, the plantocracy and allied groups looked for a sporting assertion of whiteness in victory for *England*. In this sense, cricket became a weapon in what Beckles has described as 'anti-black racism'. It was a sufficiently visible phenomenon for it to be viewed with some surprise even by visiting whites. Australian touring teams appeared to have been offended by it, while British cricket writers not otherwise known for their progressive views were prompted to comment. The *Daily Telegraph* correspondent E. W. Swanton, for example, noted with some distaste the 'shade distinction' he encountered among Caribbean whites during the 1959–60 MCC tour.[37]

Such developments brought an element of race hostility to the cricket ground. During the visits of the English touring party in both 1953–54 and 1959–60 there were incidents among black spectators that stopped play.[38] On the earlier tour at Kingston there was a disturbance in the crowd on the occasion of the run out of a West Indies player, and at Georgetown in the third test of that series an umpiring decision appeared to provoke unrest. As *Wisden* reported it, 'sections of the crowd hurled bottles and wooden packing-cases on to the field and some of the players were fortunate to escape injury.'[39] A similar demonstration took place in Port of Spain during the later tour. The British popular press – and, to be sure, sections of white opinion in the islands – was all too eager to ascribe such occurrences to 'crowd disorder', exacerbated by drink and gambling.[40] The Governor of Trinidad, E. E. Beetham, wrote to the Colonial Secretary Iain Macleod in March 1960, 'all Trinidadians were utterly ashamed by the display of hooliganism at the Queen's Park Oval.'[41] By complete contrast, and hardly surprisingly, a different light was cast on these events by C. L. R. James, by now the editor of the *Nation*. James argued that on both tours the crowd responses had very little to do with the state of the cricket match itself. Rather it was a case of small incidents in the game triggering a reaction on the part of black people to local white anti-nationalist feelings: 'That is the temper which caused these explosions and as long as that temper remains it will find a way to express itself.'[42] In other words, years of frustration over white dominance in both cricket and society in general was spilling over into the one public theatre where black and white West Indian relations were most clearly on view: the cricket field.

The incidents that occurred during the 1959–60 tour came at the time of the PNM's surge to power and should be seen alongside two other hotly debated issues: one was the Chaguaramas affair, which provoked deep popular hostility towards the United States for its continuing occupation of the Chaguaramas naval base in Trinidad;[43] the other affected sport and concerned the white captaincy of the West Indies cricket team. This was the issue that Constantine had declared his opposition to some thirteen years earlier in *Cricket in the Sun*. Now, it was his friend James to whom the baton was passed. In an open letter in the *Nation* to the elite, white Queen's Park Cricket Club in Port of Spain, written shortly after the demonstrations at the test match there, James pointedly stated that the governance of West Indies cricket should be placed in the hands of a democratically elected body. He added that responsibility for the crowd disturbances rested with the officials of the game, not the crowd: 'I have heard repeatedly that the bottles should have been thrown, not on to the ground but into the pavilion.' James accused the cricket authorities of having neglected black players over the years, to the extent that more of them were now seeking employment in England. 'You who could have done so much for them have not only done very little. You stand accused of having *deliberately contrived* to deprive some of them of honours which in any other country under the sun would have been theirs.'[44]

This last point was a reference to the denial of the captaincy of the West Indies team to Frank Worrell. The retention of the post by a white cricketer had once been regarded as natural. Harold Austin, Karl Nunes, the Grant brothers, John Goddard, Jeffrey Stollmeyer and Gerry Alexander, all men from well-established white families, constituted an almost unbroken lineage from the beginning of the century. On rare occasions, and usually for just one match, a black cricketer had been given the job – Constantine before the War, George Headley after. By the 1950s, the white succession was coming to be regarded as a grotesque anomaly. It was therefore an event universally applauded by the black population of the Caribbean when, following strong pressure from James in the *Nation*, Frank Worrell, a leading member of the West Indies team since the late 1940s, was appointed captain in 1960. There was no question about Worrell's distinction as a player – he had proved over the years to be an outstanding batsman by world standards, his tactical acumen on the field was highly respected, and for the most part his demeanour both on and off the field was thought to fit exactly what was required of a leading representative of the islands (it also helped that he had recently studied for a degree at Manchester University). But similar qualities had been evident in previous black candidates for the position yet had failed to persuade the cricket authorities to break with tradition. What made the difference for Worrell in the captaincy stakes was the changed context in which his claims were being pressed; that is to say, the full-scale movement for Independence being spearheaded in both Jamaica and Trinidad. The captaincy question was now politicized in a way that had not been possible previously, and James sought to exploit the situation to the maximum.

His campaign was forthright, not to say ruthless. Much of his argument rested on the perceived inadequacies of the man originally chosen ahead of Worrell. F. C. M. (Gerry) Alexander – Cambridge University graduate, good cricketer (and very talented footballer who had played at Wembley in the Amateur Cup Final for Pegasus), and the incumbent wicketkeeper of the international team – had succeeded John Goddard in 1958. It was not so much that James considered Alexander as a player not up to test match standard as that he lacked, in James's opinion, the astuteness necessary in a captain. He was, James claimed 'a novice' by comparison with Worrell.[45] James cited several occasions on which the West Indies team had gained the upper hand in matches only to then loosen its grip at crucial moments as a result of the captain making a wrong decision. 'What has happened in match after match,' claimed James, 'is indefensible. In fact it is an absolute disgrace. This sort of thing will ruin any side. Let me make this clear once and for all by some figures.'[46] James then proceeded to analyse instances in test matches during the current series with England that supported his case. He also compared them unfavourably with the ability of the current Australian captain, Richie Benaud, to make the right decisions.

It might reasonably have been expected that Constantine (as a senior politician in Trinidad) would be in the van of this campaign. He was not. The 'peacemaker', as Winston Mahabir described Constantine,[47] seemed content to leave the leading role to James. Constantine offered supporting comment: 'Alexander [was] one of the finest wicket-keepers in the world, although as a captain he left most of us puzzled and perplexed.'[48] The next test series for the West Indies was to be in Australia in 1960–61. The team's recent performances had been disappointing compared with the earlier 1950s, and it seemed that two of the famous '3 Ws' batsmen – Everton Weekes and Clyde Walcott (the other was Worrell) – would not be present in Australia. The West Indies could not afford to make a poor showing there as a result of bad captaincy. In James's words: 'A great injury will be done to the thousands upon thousands of people here who want us to make the best of what we have and equally to the Australian cricketers and crowds. The history of W. I. cricket is a history above all of ruinous captaincy. It cannot continue.'[49] It was unfortunate that so much of the James campaign for Worrell rested on a personal indictment of Alexander, something with which Constantine was in disagreement with his old friend. As it was, Gerry Alexander accepted his demotion to vice-captain with good grace and played perhaps the best cricket of his career under Worrell's leadership. The test matches in Australia, beginning with a dramatic tied match in Brisbane, produced thrilling play – 'the most talked about series of all time'[50] – with West Indies playing what Constantine was delighted to call their 'characteristic cricket',[51] attacking with both bat and ball. The team was treated to a ticker-tape farewell by a large Australian crowd on its departure at the end of the tour. Few were distracted by the fact that the West Indies had narrowly lost the series. Two years later, again under Worrell's captaincy, they comprehensively defeated England, in England.

It seemed a fitting celebration, both of the status of black cricketers and of the impending arrival of Independence: a neat convergence of sport and politics. It also helped to dispel some of doubts that might have enshrouded Worrell's appointment. For the choice was not as clear-cut to some as James had figured. In his younger days, Worrell had been regarded by some people, not only whites, as somewhat swollen headed – early successes seemed to have made him behave in a superior manner towards others in the team. Born in Barbados, possibly the least enlightened island as far as race relations in cricket were concerned, he had left for Jamaica shortly after the War, partly for family reasons and partly because he sought a more congenial atmosphere in which to play the game.[52] On top of this, his decision to study for a degree in England (he was playing at the time in the Central Lancashire League) was unprecedented for a black sportsman. It was a double-edged weapon – he was educated and urbane, but simultaneously educated and radical. Of all the West Indian cricketers of the 1950s, he was the one most likely to shake the status quo with new ideas. One of them, however, might well have cost him his claim to the captaincy.

It came up in 1958 and certainly caused consternation within liberal opinion, Constantine included, in both England and the West Indies. On the initiative of the non-white South African Cricket Board of Control, Worrell had agreed to lead a group of black West Indian cricketers – said to include Sobers, Weekes,

Ramadhin and Valentine – to play against black and Asian clubs in South Africa. It was an extraordinary proposal; there had never been any cricketing exchanges between the two countries, and the idea of having one now with apartheid strongly installed created grave doubts. Constantine was in contact with leading anti-racism activists on the matter. One of them, John Collins, Canon of St Paul's Cathedral in London, founder of Christian Action and a well-known campaigner for a number of radical causes, including CND and the anti-apartheid movement,[53] sought Constantine's help over the planned tour, which had been brought to his notice by the liberal South African writer Alan Paton. 'Alan's point', wrote Collins to Constantine, 'is that to accept the idea of playing against an all-black team, however attractive on the surface it might seem to be, is in fact to play straight into the hands of those who are out for Apartheid.'[54] Dennis Brutus, the secretary of the anti-apartheid South African Sports Association was equally opposed. It was, however, noted that not all black South Africans were against the tour, a point that gave credibility to a view expounded by C. L. R. James who, ever the contrarian, felt that Worrell should go, that a tour would not only assist his chances of securing the West Indies captaincy but would help the non-white South African game by coming into contact with world-famous cricketers. Above all the tour would throw a 'pitiless light ... on the irrationality and stupidity of apartheid.'[55] 'BY ALL MEANS GO' was C. L. R.'s motto in the *Nation*. Not all agreed, however. James and Constantine were on opposing sides.[56] Eventually, the tour was called off, though not as a result of any direct pressure by Constantine or others from outside South Africa. The African National Congress, as the chief anti-apartheid party in South Africa, had doubts about the value of the tour, and the Indian Youth Congress had actually threatened violent protest if the tour went ahead.[57] A potentially disruptive issue was thus avoided, the tour was scrapped, Caribbean tempers were calmed, and Worrell's reputation was saved from potential harm. Constantine among others deserved some small thanks for that, though the episode provided no satisfaction that a political instrument to support a laudable moral position on race had yet been found. This was to be a constant feature of Constantine's place in race politics when he returned to England in 1962.

Nevertheless, he could always be relied upon to oppose sporting links with South Africa. In 1968, he roundly condemned a rugby match arranged at St Andrews University, where he was rector, with a South African university.[58] Later in the same year he added his voice to what became known as the 'Basil D'Oliveira affair', perhaps the most notorious piece of cricket politics in the twentieth century.[59] At the time, the late summer of 1968, Constantine had an opinionated column 'Sir Learie Constantine Says' in the tabloid *Daily Sketch,* for which he was covering that season's test series between England and Australia. It was not exactly demanding journalism, and in a dull series Constantine deployed his 'brighter cricket' philosophy to inject some vitality into his match reports. On the D'Oliveira issue, he was suddenly bowled a slow full toss. He was able to express what liberals everywhere considered exactly the right view on the selection of the Cape Coloured cricketer Basil D'Oliveira for the MCC tour party to South Africa that winter. The *Sketch,* to its credit and that of its chief reporter Brian Scovell, had firmly denounced an idea current in some right-wing circles that D'Oliveira be omitted lest his selection offend the South African government. When the MCC's decision was finally announced in August 1968, revealing that D'Oliveira had indeed been omitted, the selection panel rather lamely excused the decision on 'cricket grounds'. Constantine derided it: 'to say that he [D'Oliveira – 'Dolly'] is not in the best sixteen cricketers in England is nonsense. I am convinced that if Dolly was white he would be packing his bags.'[60] Constantine took comfort from the public outcry against D'Oliveira's omission: 'It persuades me that there is a sense of justice left in many people outside the boundaries of Lord's'.[61] The weight of public opinion caused the MCC to reverse its original selection, and D'Oliveira was installed in the party, only for the entire tour to be cancelled by the South African government.[62] For many the cancellation was a not unwelcome outcome: it represented a tactical victory for the anti-apartheid movement.

8

Race Politics

Constantine returned to England in 1962 after spending eight years in Trinidad, his longest residence there since leaving in 1929. He had initially gone back, having qualified as a barrister, to take a full-time post with his old employer, Trinidad Leaseholds (TLL). After existing on irregular earnings from book sales and broadcasting fees since leaving his civil service post in 1946, the offer of a job promised some financial security. As he put it in a letter to the radical priest John Collins in 1954, 'I shall not have to bother for the first three years at least where anything is coming from.'[1] But far from settling into his role as legal advisor for TLL, Constantine quickly became caught up in politics. He was invited to join the newly formed nationalist party, the People's National Movement (PNM) for which he was chosen as Chairman, and in 1956 was elected as an MP to serve in the new parliament set up as part of Trinidad and Tobago's self-governing status within the colonial system. Between then and the arrival of Independence in 1962, Constantine occupied the ministerial post of Communications, Works and Public Utilities.

It was a surprising departure for a man who had never been a full-time politician, nor indeed been involved to any extent in a political movement. Constantine was persuaded to take the plunge by his old friend, Eric Williams, whom Learie had known since the early 1930s when Williams was studying at Oxford. After a career as an academic in the United States and a spell as a civil servant 'Bill' (as Williams was known to his friends) had quickly graduated to becoming the first minister of the PNM government in 1956. He was to remain as Trinidad's prime minister until his death in 1981. Another old friend, 'Nello' (C. L. R. James), joined them in 1958 to edit the PNM's newspaper *The Nation*. However, in spite of old friendships, the experience was not a happy one. Williams wanted to dominate his government and had a capacity for alienating those he worked with. James fell out with him in the early 1960s, largely over the failure of the West Indies Federation and Williams's handling of relations with the Americans.[2] Constantine, a competent minister who was generally loyal to Williams, became disenchanted with the atmosphere of high politics, in which he was not accorded the respect he had been accustomed to in England. There had been some acrimony stemming from Constantine's fame, a valuable political asset to the PNM, which explains his initial adoption by the party, but which also provoked criticism and jealousies. As his daughter has pointed out, 'Trinidad is a small place':[3] an island of petty rivalries, especially within the political elite. Winston Mahabir, a close friend and fellow minister, offered a telling, if not complimentary, comment on Learie's part in the early years of the PNM:

> It is no desecration of a great man's memory to state that his ministerial talents did not match his cricketing abilities ... His role in Cabinet was characterized by affability, unflappability and a general inability to score. He seldom bowled a bouncer and he failed to hold some easy catches. But he was not an all-round disaster. He was the peacemaker, the father-figure, the symbol of loyalty, the good-humoured butt of many jokes.[4]

Gerald Howat, while more admiring of Constantine's record as a minister, concluded with a verdict on his life in politics that hit the mark: 'Constantine was not tough enough to be a politician.'[5] He had already planned to leave Trinidad politics when Williams offered him a place of refuge – the eminent position of High Commissioner for Trinidad and Tobago in London. It was a job that bestowed on the incumbent respect and a good salary.[6]

I

The return to England marked a new beginning for Constantine in a variety of ways. For one thing it set in train a succession of personal honours – a knighthood in 1962, followed in 1965 by membership of two newly formed, high prestige national bodies, the Sports Council and the Race Relations Board; in 1968 there came appointment to the BBC Board of Governors[7] and to cap it all in 1969 elevation to the House of Lords. Far from placing him out of touch with his public by this apparent establishment embrace Constantine's popularity seemed as buoyant as ever judging by the volume of invitations he continued to receive to speak at all manner of clubs and societies.[8] He seems to have been regarded (and he himself certainly thought it) as the best known black person in Britain. Yet, accolades aside, these few years marked a degree of decline as far as Constantine's practical achievements were concerned. To an extent this was explained by failing health. Bronchial illnesses certainly interrupted his activities, increasingly so by the later 1960s. At the same time, he was brought into contact with quite new currents of race politics with which he was unfamiliar, and to which, in his self-appointed role as a spokesman for black people in Britain, he found it difficult to adapt. The combination of illness and new political challenges presented a difficult barrier for him to overcome.

The Britain to which he returned was also different from the one he had left in 1954. Prominent among new concerns shaping domestic and international affairs was the sharp increase in immigration from the Caribbean in the later 1950s, together with the incipient political movements formed among those who had arrived. Compared with the decade after the Second World War there was now a new issue to be confronted; as Stuart Hall has described it 'the slow-burn trauma of racial discrimination had begun to take hold.'[9] The White-instigated riots in Nottingham and Notting Hill in 1958 prompted the formation of a bold form of anti-racist activity at street level, which sought new ways of dealing with social relationships founded on issues of race. The assimilationist ideas of the League of Coloured Peoples, still cherished by Constantine as a solution to race problems, were no longer seen by activists on the street to be an appropriate political response to prejudice and discrimination. They contrasted sharply with the stance on race that Constantine had adopted on his return to England. In a radio broadcast of December 1963 – 'No Stranger Here' – he spoke about the appellation now often applied to him: 'black Englishman'. It was not something he found offensive, in fact he regarded it as a tribute, but he reminded his listeners that he was still a West Indian, though qualified that by adding, 'I always try to remember that we have hosts'. In his original script he had also included a statement that was excised from the talk as broadcast: 'It is not our country in which we can adopt our own pattern of life. We must accept the conventions and attitudes of the English, although modifying them in our own homes and amongst our own people when it won't cause any trouble.'[10] It was a sentiment that was to characterize his position in the country for the remainder of his life.

Constantine's first foray into race politics on his return is indicative of a clash between old and new mentalities. He was at this time still High Commissioner, but his intervention has generally been accounted a failure. It occurred in 1963 in an industrial dispute in Bristol – a town, like Liverpool, with a history of deep involvement in the slave trade and strong residual racial animosities. The dispute concerned the refusal of the Corporation to employ black bus crews. To Constantine it was a straightforward case of the iniquities he had exposed in *Colour Bar*, and he plunged directly into an issue around which High

Commissioners should (in a phrase he had once applied in Liverpool) 'circle warily'. He did in fact assume his favoured Liverpool approach – when as a welfare officer during the war he would tackle problems in a convivial manner, seeking consensus, and if a bit of cricket gossip might help he would use it.[11] Constantine himself could see no wrong in this tactic. It had worked with the trade unions that had stood fast against the employment of West Indian technicians. The Bristol case seemed merely to demand a repeat of the same. 'If that is not my business I should like to know what is.'[12] Moreover, it appeared to be vindicated. Constantine attributed the eventual outcome of the dispute in favour of the black drivers and conductors to his own personal intervention. In his radio talk 'No Stranger Here', transmitted later in that year, he summed up his role in the dispute as having seen the people at the top (politicians, trade unions leaders) and got them to do the right thing and 'enforce their own convictions.'[13] It was as simple as that. Nor was he inclined to relent in this view. In truth, however, it was all rather more complex. Part of the problem, as others saw it, had been that the black workers concerned were from Jamaica, and technically therefore not within Constantine's jurisdiction. He found this to be an unduly circumscribed view. It was, he claimed, not a case of nationality, but of race, on which few were better qualified than he to speak. 'Because of the unique and privileged position I have with British public opinion, I am able to do these things more quietly and successfully than many others.'[14] But far from calming the waters, his action led instead to a bitter falling out with Eric Williams, who felt that Constantine had exceeded his authority. A rift developed that was never healed. When Williams refused to see Constantine after the bus dispute it offended Learie greatly and he resigned his High Commissioner post in September 1963 after barely a year in the job. He later told the *Trinidad Guardian* that he had resigned because he had received no support from his government over the Bristol dispute.[15]

Amidst the extensive press coverage of the decision, suspicions were raised about another matter that, if true, would make Constantine's resignation rather more of a political issue than simply a personal spat with his prime minister. The suspicion, most explicitly expressed in the *Sunday Times,* was that the British government, in the person of the Commonwealth Relations Secretary Duncan Sandys, had protested not only about Constantine's behaviour in the Bristol case but to his veiled criticisms of the British government's Commonwealth Immigrants Act of 1962. The *Sunday Times* reporter referred to a strong difference of opinion between Constantine and Sandys over the effects of this Act. Like others in the campaign for race equality, Constantine always referred to the legislation as the 'colour bar act', which he felt discriminated especially against West Indians. He was particularly incensed by a speech Sandys had made in Malta in June 1963, when he had claimed that there were 'thousands' of jobs available in the south of England 'for which British workers are not available' and for which, therefore, Maltese workers, affected by job losses at the Malta dockyard, might think about applying.[16] Constantine repudiated Sandys's statement, saying that it made nonsense of the 1962 legislation and revealed the Act's bias against migrants from the Caribbean. In July Sandys paid an official visit to Trinidad, during which nothing appears to have been said to him, openly at least, by members of the Trinidad and Tobago government in defence of Constantine's views. While Constantine publicly denied that he had any concerns over Sandys's behaviour, it seems very likely that his own government's silence made his position untenable, and that his resignation, which followed shortly afterwards, was a direct consequence.[17] The repercussions of this affair, together with the Bristol case, might also explain Eric Williams's complete refusal to entertain a proposal by the British government in 1964 to award Constantine a peerage.[18]

There is also more to the Bristol matter than Constantine's apparent maladroit handling of it, which has tended to be the focus of most previous accounts. His biographers see it as a case of Constantine's heart ruling his head when a man in his position should have displayed a more diplomatic approach to the bus dispute. Looking at the event from that personal angle, however, fails to convey the full breadth and significance of the dispute in relation to the wider politics of race. In the first place, the Bristol problem had a history going back to the mid-1950s, when the Bristol Omnibus Company, with the tacit support of the Bristol branch of the Transport and General Workers' Union (TGWU), had instituted a bar on the employment of black and Asian bus crews (though not workshop and canteen staff). In her excellent monograph on this dispute, Madge Dresser has shown how difficult it was, at this time, to achieve solutions to problems about which people like Constantine had expressed 'moral indignation'.[19] Local politicians of both main parties were reluctant to offend white opinion, and trade union leaders seemed equally afraid of upsetting their own rank and file, in spite of the TGWU's official policy of race equality. As in the Colonial Office during the war there was a certain amount of pussyfooting around questions of race to avoid offending white sensibilities. Attitudes among the white bus crews seem almost uniformly to have been anti-black. Dresser's account brilliantly dissects the roots of racialism in Bristol, a city that had not only a slave-trade past but a long tradition of hostility towards 'outsiders', whether they were of an ethnic or racial background, or even simply not locals: 'the Arabs', it was said, 'begin at Swindon.'[20] Even after the colour bar was eventually lifted, with the avowal to have 'complete integration without regard to race, colour or creed' white drivers and conductors frequently refused to speak to or eat with black workers. They effectively sent them to Coventry.

The resolution in the Bristol dispute came less from Constantine's moral pleading for understanding, and much more from a new kind of grass roots protest orchestrated by a charismatic local leader. The activist Paul Stephenson, a local teacher from a mixed-race family, took that position when he organized a boycott of the Bristol buses. The Bristol protest might be seen as a new British model of direct action for civil rights on race. It bore the influences of American campaigns of the 1950s, notably the Montgomery bus protest forever associated with the name of Rosa Parks. Stephenson himself had American contacts and might have visited the United States at the invitation of civil rights leaders just before initiating the Bristol campaign. He held Martin Luther King in high esteem as an inspirational figure.[21] Constantine was unfamiliar with such ideological influences and the agitational methods associated with them. They had rarely featured in his politics. The Seretse Khama campaign had little in the way of this kind of street protest. Bristol, by contrast, heralded the mobilization of a well-organized local black movement, supported by influential radical white opinion – in the persons, among others, of Bristol MP Tony Wedgwood-Benn and, briefly, the Leader of HM Opposition, Harold Wilson.[22] Constantine's involvement was mainly at this level, bringing his celebrity status to bear in helping to elevate the problems to a national level, using his contact with Frank Cousins, Secretary of the TGWU and attracting the attention of national newspapers. But the chief impetus came from the locality. Eventually, by the autumn of 1963, the combination of local and national pressure succeeded in overturning the status quo in the Bristol Omnibus Company's labour relations. Mike and Trevor Phillips have precisely summed up the importance of the Bristol dispute: 'it ... demonstrated that concerted action could change established customs, and it represented a significant advance in the scope of the demands that the immigrants might be prepared to make.'[23] In comparison with Constantine's legal victory in the Imperial Hotel case the Bristol dispute had a far more telling effect on race politics.

The Bristol example of black working people taking matters into their own hands was to blossom into a more extensive feature of the race politics of the later 1960s. Constantine could not turn his back on it without disconnecting himself from his public support. But, at the same time, events in Bristol illustrated how far race politics was moving away from the Constantine line. The rapid development of black activism served to place Constantine ideologically outside what was fast becoming a rich, if often diverse, body of organized opinion.[24] Furthermore, Constantine's connection with formal national bodies, notably the Race Relations Board (RRB) which, if not a governmental agency nevertheless operated in an official public sphere, doubly distanced him from street politics. From the mid-1960s onwards 'black power' entered more fully into the discourse of race. The Civil Rights movement in the United States was a major source of inspiration, even though the methods employed there were not always appropriate in the circumstances that prevailed in Great Britain.[25] The visits paid to Britain during 1964–65 by leading American activists Malcolm X and Martin Luther King Jnr had a profound influence on the various groups set up around this time, often by students, to counteract race prejudice and the oppression of black people. Indigenous activities and mentalities also played their part in changing people's approaches to the question of race. The hostility shown by whites to immigrant groups in the Nottingham and Notting Hill riots of 1958 produced a strong legacy. It was evident in the racist campaign conducted by the successful Conservative candidate in the Smethwick parliamentary election of 1964,[26] and carried through into Enoch Powell's poisonous intervention in race politics in 1968. While at the time both events were denounced by mainstream opinion – Powell, for example, was ejected from the Conservative Shadow Cabinet by Edward Heath – their influence continued to affect sections of white society well into the following decades. In their turn, therefore, they played a part in shaping the reactions of black opinion.

II

By the middle of the 1960s, there had been a proliferation of pressure and protest groups displaying a variety of tactics and ideologies on the question of race. Some of these were quite new – the Campaign Against Racial Discrimination (CARD), for example, was created at the end of 1964 following discussions between Martin Luther King and British activists, among whom the Labour Party member David Pitt was prominent. For a couple of years CARD became the leading civil rights organization in Britain, campaigning successfully for a range of initiatives on race discrimination in political and industrial life. Its pressure was largely responsible for the government's adopting the policy that produced the Race Relations Act of 1968. CARD's influence, though, was short-lived. The campaign was disrupted by a group of aggressive activists who sought to dominate the organization. Many local organizers left and Pitt was forced into the difficult position of attempting to hold the ring between the competing interests. By the end of 1967 CARD had declined.[27] Other groups included the United Coloured Peoples' Association, established in 1967 as a largely London-based Black Power group, and the short-lived Racial Adjustment Action Society, led by the Trinidadian Michael X (Michael de Freitas). With a rather longer provenance was the Joint Action Committee Against Racial Intolerance (JACARI), which had been formed in Oxford in 1956 and which, by the end of that decade, had some two thousand members. Oxford, in fact, was a wellspring of action in race politics. It was to Oxford that the American black leader Malcolm X went in December 1964 to make a famous speech to students at the Oxford Union, and it was in Oxford that other groups sprang up in the wake of his visit: Oxford Committee on Racial Integration (OCRI), for example, which was not specifically a student body and which owed much to the work of the writer Michael Dummett; and Student Conference on Racial Equality (SCORE), which drew its inspiration from the previous success of JACARI. From 1967 the Black Panther movement gained strength, mainly in London, clearly inspired by American precedents. After the visits of Martin Luther King and Malcolm X, the American-based Trinidadian Stokeley Carmichael came briefly in 1967 to speak at the Dialectics of Liberation conference in London, a gathering that served as a powerful ideological impulse in energizing black power in Britain. C. L. R. James played an important part in it, urging the movement towards a community-based, inclusive strategy rather than a more Leninist model of leadership of the kind advocated by another leader, the Nigerian writer Obi B. Egbuna. All these movements had a plentiful supply of youthful adherents and adopted a more international and multi-ethnic approach to race relations than had been customary in the past. They were aware of both the American and European dimensions of racism and sought to achieve a unity of purpose between West Indian, Asian and African peoples in Britain.[28] In approaching the overarching questions of prejudice and discrimination, their work targeted a range of topics such as housing, employment and, in particular, policing methods. The Black Panthers, formed in 1970, were to achieve their greatest impact in the Mangrove protests of the early 1970s, against police harassment of black people in west London.[29] Less headline-grabbing than the Panthers, but in their way equally as effective, were the advances made in local politics by black groups, seeking to raise awareness of the need for people to become active in municipal affairs and, at the most basic level, simply to turn out and vote in local elections. Mike and Trevor Phillips have pointed to the important grass roots work of Londoners like Sam King of Southwark, Randolph Beresford from Fulham, Ben Bousquet of Notting Hill, and from Manchester Euton Christian, men who were in many cases active trade unionists and ex-servicemen, who led the way by becoming town councillors and, in Beresford's case, Mayor of Hammersmith in the 1970s.[30]

Constantine shared some of the outlook of these groups. Only a minority of West Indians and Asians were committed to the more radical black movements, and there was still a space in which the opinions of people like Constantine could be heard. He himself was essentially West Indian focused, although he was not unaware of problems in Africa, and actually visited Nigeria during a difficult time just before the Biafran War.[31] But he tended to think within the boundaries set by British cultural and legal mentalities. As demonstrated in the Bristol bus dispute, his favoured tactic on race issues was the one traditionally associated with the Fabian Society, lobbying through a network of high-level contacts to effect changes. Constantine had certainly cultivated the network necessary for this approach, so much so that his methods caused some of his opponents to see him as a 'Jim Crow' figure.[32] The idea was given credence by Constantine's frequent resort to his 'black Englishman' identity. He was reported in the *Express*, a Trinidad paper, as making the point in his maiden House of Lords speech that 'the West Indian was different from any other person with a colonial background ... He is in essence a black Englishman. When slavery took the African to the West Indies the owners destroyed everything that was African ... my grandparents were Nigerian but I am named Constantine.' He could, he said, easily live in England 'as he did not know any other language or customs than those here.'[33] That being so, it was equally easy for him to advise that the black people who came to live in England should be prepared to accept the laws and customs of this country. 'Once people are here, they should behave like good guests.'[34] Even in Trinidad this viewpoint was coming to be regarded as anachronistic. Noting the decline of the old pro-British feeling in the country the *Express* claimed, 'There is a psychological clash between a generation which once sang "Rule Britannia" (and meant it) and a generation which sees [rebel activist] Cuffy in Guyana and [Uriah]Butler in Trinidad as heroes and Sir Walter Raleigh as a common pirate.'[35]

III

The *Express*'s point was underlined by Constantine's membership of the Race Relations Board (RRB). As an agency, the Board met with distrust from many radicals in race politics. The Ceylonese (Sri Lankan) writer and activist Ambalavaner Sivanandan claimed bluntly in the late 1990s that the RRB and other similar organizations had not been set up 'to effect the integration of the mass of Black people in the country, but to create a tranche of Black middle-class administrators who would manage racism.'[36] Constantine had to deal with this mentality. He himself had been a member of one of the Colonial Office's advisory committees some twenty years earlier, and with the setting up of the RRB in 1965 he seemed a natural choice to become part of its small team of three. Alongside him was the Chairman, H. H. Asquith's grandson Mark Bonham Carter – 'pale, able, sharp-tongued … a man with an air of being the last of the reforming Whig oligarchs',[37] who had recently also briefly been Liberal MP for Torrington. Alongside Constantine and Bonham Carter was Alderman Bernard Langton, a Labour councillor and recent Lord Mayor of Manchester, who was closely involved in Jewish affairs in that city.[38] They had a staff of eight secretaries and administrators (increased to twelve in 1967). In judging Constantine's outlook on race questions it is not always easy to separate out his own views from the collective voice of the Board itself as it pursued its day-to-day business. The RRB was a relatively blunt instrument in that it was charged with enforcing the provisions of the 1965 Race Relations Act, but had to investigate complaints in a spirit of conciliation. It was not able to look into matters affecting housing and employment, and had no punitive powers, except in relation to incitement to racial hatred, an offence under the Act that could be prosecuted in the courts. In such cases the RRB referred the matter to the police and the Attorney General. Only when fuller legislation was introduced in 1968 were some of these shortcomings eliminated.[39] For all that, it should not be forgotten that the 1965 Act was the first instance of a government introducing statutory law to combat racial discrimination. It offered the kind of protection that had been absent twenty years earlier when Constantine brought his case against the Imperial Hotel. It established a massive precedent (albeit of ambivalent effect) for intervention in race relations by government in the future.

In the early years of the Board's life two issues dominated proceedings: receiving complaints about racial discrimination to determine whether they fell within the Board's purview; and, in company with that, the setting up of Conciliation Committees in eight separate regions of the country, which were to undertake the detailed collection of evidence on race relations within the terms of the 1965 Act. Many of the complaints received were to do with discrimination in finding jobs and housing, and – a problem of continuing relevance into the present day – the attitude of the police towards people of colour. In 1967–68 there had been 690 complaints received during the course of the year of which 574 were outside the Board's remit and which, doubtless to the dismay of those who had complained, could not be followed up. Of the remainder 'nearly three quarters' concerned public houses. Where complaints referred to such places of 'public resort' the Board's emphasis was on conciliation; that is to say, speaking to people, trying to educate them into fair treatment of immigrants and seeking to ensure that they would not continue to discriminate. It was a difficult procedure. Publicans and hoteliers could be obdurate. Board members grumbled that there were few sanctions at their disposal. Constantine in particular was astonished to find racial discrimination in publicly owned services: a British Railways guard, for example, had been refused employment at Euston station; and Manchester City Corporation would not allow its Sikh employees to wear turbans when on duty. Constantine felt that such cases, because the Board was unable to deal with them, placed it in a very awkward position, drawing criticism that was unfair.[40] Some issues dragged on. The case of the Gillott Hotel in Birmingham became one such headache for the Board.[41] Such experiences fuelled the Board's determination to lobby for more effective legislation. 'Simple, speedy and credible enforcement procedures are the prerequisite of successful conciliation' noted its Report for 1967–68.[42] At the same time much of members' time and energy was consumed in the creation of regional Committees. The work involved travelling around the country and seeking advice from local worthies in fields such as politics, religion, the professions and trade unions, as to people who might be suitable nominees for Committee membership. Once a likely candidate was identified, however, it did not follow automatically that the person would take the job, which was essentially a voluntary position. Committees were set up quite quickly in London and the North West but in other areas – Wales and Berks, Bucks and Oxfordshire for example – negotiations stretched over a considerable time before a final composition was arrived at.[43] This largely administrative business detracted from the Board's attention to matters of race.

Constantine himself seemed to respond quite readily to the Board's work at this stage of its existence. His role was not dissimilar to the one he had experienced with the Ministry of Labour during the war. With Board meetings usually comprised of four or five people (the members plus a secretary and legal advisor) the atmosphere permitted a relaxed and informal discussion of business. Both Constantine and Langton were willing to give Bonham Carter the lead in formulating decisions. In most cases they supported his line. Constantine would frequently chip in to add some of his 'local knowledge' on race matters to the discussion, or to recommend names for consideration as members of Conciliation Committees. There were several opportunities to visit schools to give talks on the work of the Board.[44] Although complaints of racial discrimination were supposed to be sent initially to the local Conciliation Boards Constantine, not unexpectedly, received many direct letters for help. One gentleman from Teeside, for example, was assiduous in seeking support in a case of alleged discrimination over his job applications for teaching posts. He felt that the Northern Conciliation Board was in collusion with the national Board to have his case rejected and asked Constantine to help him out. His view of Learie as 'the father figure of the coloured community' said much about the magic Constantine was still expected to produce.[45] As may be imagined Constantine became the resident expert in the Board on West Indian matters. When, for example, it was reported that comparatively few complaints of discrimination seemed to be coming through from the North West region the Board concluded that more publicity about its work needed to be circulated. As part of this initiative, Constantine and Alderman Langton were deputed to visit West Indian clubs in Manchester – 'to spend an hour or two, one evening' – to gauge the temper at the grass roots. Nothing much seems to have resulted from these visits, if indeed they ever took place. This rather casual approach summed up much of the Board's work in its early years, when even with its limited role it was ill-equipped with only three members to make much of an impact. Bonham Carter was a good Chair, and the Home Office (to which the Board was responsible in matters of finance) was relatively generous with expenses and other expenditure. But, looking at the operation dispassionately over its first couple of years, it was an amateurish approach to a problem of supreme magnitude. This is not surprising. To a degree the creation of the RRB had been something of a sop to the harsh immigration controls enacted by the Conservatives in the Commonwealth Immigrants Act of 1962, and maintained by Labour when the party returned to office in 1964. The same charge could also be true of the newly constituted Board of 1968. Its existence has often been seen as a device to counteract the dubious practices that had prevailed in the field of immigration control over previous years, and the further restrictions on immigration contained in the 1968 Commonwealth Immigrants Act. Geoffrey Bindman, the distinguished lawyer and civil rights campaigner who was the Board's legal advisor in Constantine's days, later commented that racial attitudes had been 'endemic' in the very processes of the Home Office itself at this time.[46] In this atmosphere it is doubtful whether the RRB, in either its pre- or post-1968 guises, could have made a great deal of difference to the state of race relations. Nor was the situation improved by the modifications made in the

1971 Immigration Act, with its 'infamous provision'[47] of a 'patriality' test, which sought to distinguish between immigrant British citizens on the grounds of their family connections with Britain. The test usually turned on an individual's race.

This is not to say, however, that the efforts of the RRB in its initial phase had been entirely worthless. Some successes were noted. For example, the Board's Report of 1967–68 showed that vital statistical information had been collected on matters such as the nature and extent of immigration (who lived where), the languages spoken by people, and the kinds of educational improvements that were needed to help the immigrant community. Much of this research was carried out by the Street Report on anti-discrimination legislation, published in November 1968. The report had been commissioned by the RRB, in company with the National Committee for Commonwealth Immigrants, and was conducted by a panel led by Harry Street, Professor of Law at Manchester University; it also included Geoffrey Howe QC and Geoffrey Bindman. Funding was provided from Marks and Spencer.[48] It was to a large extent the Board's insistence on the need to strengthen race legislation that led to the 1968 Act.

With the new Act came a rapid and significant change in the nature of the Board. The extension of work into housing, employment and finance meant that the Board became bigger, more bureaucratic and more professional in its business. Membership was tripled. Langton retired so only Bonham Carter (who continued as Chair) and Constantine remained of the original trio.[49] The local Conciliation Committees were expanded and reorganized to carry out most of the detailed work on individual discrimination cases, overseen by a series of subcommittees at Board level.[50] The preparation and discussion of reports and papers by Board members and permanent officials replaced the more intimate conversations of former days. Bonham Carter, concerned about the proliferation of papers and the growing list of agenda items, instituted 'pre-meetings' with the Board secretary and other officers in an attempt to reduce the amount of business to be got through in full meetings. Thus, with the Home Secretary's approval, greater responsibility was devolved to the sub-committees.[51] What most exemplified these changes was Bonham Carter's insistence that 'the present status of the Board is inadequate as compared with that of other statutory bodies'.[52] He introduced a new system of line management, with a newly appointed Chief Executive, to handle the various levels of work being conducted by an expanded body of permanent officials.[53] This new business climate at the Board saw the arrival of a different kind of member. L. T. Blakeman of the Ford Motor Company, for example, and more particularly Sir Roy Wilson, appointed by the Home Secretary in 1968 in anticipation of the impending new legislation.[54] More so than any of the three original members Wilson was a highly experienced public servant, a QC who had chaired various committees of enquiry in the past. In particular, he had overseen the very extensive investigation into immigration controls and deportation procedures subsequently known as the Wilson Report (1967). Its findings, among which was the proposal to have independent judgment of immigration cases, was of great relevance to the work of the RRB. Wilson was vocal in the Board, with a first-rate knowledge of national issues and procedures. Eventually, he succeeded Bonham Carter as chair, having earlier quickly become the chair of the important subcommittee on employment. This was a committee on which Constantine himself had expressed a keenness to serve, and for which he might possibly, in view of his length of tenure, have expected to be made chair.[55] As it was he did not help his cause by asking for leave of absence from the Board to travel to the West Indies for three months in 1967–68 to report on the MCC cricket tour.[56] Whether this was a decision prompted by his seeing which way the wind was blowing in the Board is difficult to say, though at this point in time it would have been unlikely that he could have foreseen his displacement from the Board's major decision-making forum. Later absences, however, this time through illness, further marginalized Constantine's position. He attended the Board on a regular basis in 1970 but his contribution at this stage (so far as one might judge from the Board's minutes) was slight.

IV

Constantine's association with the Board, especially in its newly found managerial guise, undoubtedly distanced him farther from the politics of the street, with which he had never been close. His official status at this time contrasted sharply with the life and politics of his old friend C. L. R. James, the relations between the two men serving to illustrate the divergences that existed in the wider field of race politics. Both were now in their sixties, and while Constantine had perhaps mellowed politically with age James certainly had not. A clear gulf had existed between them for some years. In *Beyond a Boundary* James remarked on a divide going back at least to the early 1950s: 'The Constantine I met again in 1953 was a very different man from the one I had first got to know in 1932.'[57] Constantine had been involved in a number of projects with which C. L. R. had little sympathy, one of them being the PNM, from which James had departed in a state of indignation. There was also the seemingly remorseless progression of 'honours' with which Constantine was bestowed in the 1960s. James made known his distaste for such accolades on several occasion. For his part James, after his American experiences in the 1940s, was still well to the left, and in the early 1960s was aligning himself in London with fellow Trinidadian black activists Marion Glean and Claudia Jones. The two, Jones in particular, were, among other things, fashioning a form of protest modelled on the US Civil Rights campaigns.[58] The Civil Rights Committee, as the group became known, aimed at lobbying MPs and setting up protests and pickets outside workplaces and other establishments known for racial discrimination. In response to such tactics Constantine had 'considerable misgivings about the emergence of this movement at this time'.[59] He felt that its methods were designed far too much along American lines that were inappropriate for Britain – they would simply provoke opposition and do more harm than good. He called instead for a more peaceful approach, working behind the scenes to influence policy makers while at the same time giving the recently elected Labour government – which he felt had the problem in hand with its proposed Race Relations Act – time to get on with the job.[60] To some, James included, this seemed a little too much like the advice of a man who had joined the establishment.

There was a clear difference of views here, though to portray it as a battle between two hostile camps would be wide of the mark. Constantine was not a person who provoked deep dislike. He had neither the personal power base nor the mental inclination to fight pitched battles. For their part James, Jones and others of their persuasion did not regard Constantine as a serious threat to their politics. Claudia Jones, whose death in December 1964 at the age of 49 deprived the black activist camp of one of its most talented voices, is a good example. In addition to organizing the Civil Rights Committee she had run the monthly journal *West Indian Gazette* since 1958, assisted by an editorial team that included Amy Ashwood Garvey, Sam King, Donald Hinds and Manu Manchanda.[61] Jones's work with her fellow editors helps to contextualize Constantine's place in race relations at this time. The *Gazette* was based in the Brixton area of London and had close ties with black residents and local businesses, helping to form around them strong social activities such as carnivals and women's groups.[62] The *Gazette* offered lively and varied content, not only political but also featuring the arts, music and sport. Its permanent writers included, alongside Jones herself, Daniel Hinds and sports columnist Theo Campbell, supported by 'guest' contributors such as the renowned Barbadian novelist George Lamming, Jan Carew, who later formed the journal *Magnet*, actor and playwright Errol

John (son of a famous Trinidad cricketer), and on occasions the historian Eric Hobsbawm. Close though it was to its immediate neighbourhood, the *Gazette* was remarkably international in its outlook. Developments in the Caribbean colonies were regularly reported and assessed, as were affairs in other parts of the world. Given her own left-wing leanings, Claudia Jones frequently included material on China and Cuba, as well as the nationalist movements in Africa. It was as much an international as a local Brixton newspaper. It embraced such a wide range of issues and causes – lobbying vigorously, for example, against Apartheid in South Africa, the Tories' 'colour bar' act of 1962, the race orientation of some of the candidates in the 1964 General Election, as well as a host of problems around the world – that it cannot be labelled as being linked to any particular tendency or cause in the fight against racism.[63] Jones's chief contribution to the whole debate about race relations was the idea of 'black self-organization' – that is to say, rather than relying on the work of state-sponsored bodies to provide integration, black people should strive to build up their own cultural institutions in the form of schools, theatres, newspapers, bookshops and information and legal centres to fight discrimination.

The *Gazette* was undoubtedly left wing, but Claudia Jones was willing to give space to the ideas that Constantine stood for. He could quite easily have been accommodated within its mantle. He was referred to from time to time, usually as 'Sir Learie'. Jones had interviewed him in an early issue, before he was 'Sir' Learie, during one of his trips to Britain on behalf of the Trinidad government.[64] Constantine took the opportunity to make some capital out of the PNM's achievements – 'truly a revolution in thinking and action is taking place at home' – and to defend Eric Williams against his detractors in the Trinidad press. Jones allowed him to reflect on one or two cricket matches he had played while in England, and to boast a little about his own performances on the cricket field for a man of his age. It was gentle journalism until, at the close, Constantine let slip a comment that, at this time of West Indian immigration to Britain, sounded like something from his welfare officer days. Asked for a message to his fellow West Indians in Britain, Sir Learie urged: 'Get your training, pick up your experience and profit by them and return to your native hearth to help in the battle to establish our nation.'[65] Perhaps he saw this as his own story, but for many West Indian immigrants in 1959 the myth of return was not an entirely appropriate notion. Four years later, the *Gazette* gave Constantine, now as High Commissioner for Trinidad and Tobago, space for a short piece on the advances, as he saw them, being made in Trinidad. He also sought to renew his links with the West Indian community in Britain in a rather more understanding way. He felt that all West Indians in Britain could 'help to increase the knowledge and understanding between our people and the people of our host country'. He went on: 'This might prove a difficult or irksome task, but it is essential if we are to identify ourselves as a well-disciplined people of high responsibility and unquestionable integrity.'[66] This was very definitely the Constantine story, and became his distinctive personal message on race relations in the 1960s. With its whiff of the humility expected of the 'good guest' it was not a message that the more radical black activists would have willingly endorsed.

A further indication that the conflicting positions occupied by Constantine and James did not preclude friendship or dialogue was provided when the two men got together in 1964 to work on a new book, to be called 'Living in Britain', for the publisher Michael Virtue. It was the first Constantine–James collaboration for over thirty years, since they had worked together on *Cricket and I*. The new project was prompted by the increasing population of immigrants from the Commonwealth and the various social problems that were felt to have resulted from it. 'Living in Britain' was aimed at the immigrant reader with the intention of giving practical advice and analysis of the many social, economic, political and cultural aspects of the society people from overseas would encounter on arriving in Britain. It presented Constantine with the opportunity of working out in practical detail the principle he had expressed amply in *Colour Bar*: that people should learn to live together in racial harmony. One of the chief tasks for the immigrant was that of adapting to customs and attitudes that already existed in the new country. In contrast to the multicultural philosophy that gained support in Britain in the later years of the century a crucial part of assimilation was, as Constantine saw it, for immigrants to respect the culture of the country in which they had come to live. They should learn, in Constantine's phrase, to be 'good guests'. The project took up a great deal of Constantine's time, becoming a strain that probably affected his health. James was not a helpful co-editor. He clearly developed reservations about the book. He was doubtless sceptical of the assimilationist tone of the proposed book, and of the editorial line that Constantine favoured, which dictated that much of the content would be descriptive information. At one point C. L. R. said he wanted it to be 'something more than a mere travelogue',[67] especially after Virtue (whom James had dismissed as 'a man of business' rather than 'a man of letters') baulked at some of the contributions James had commissioned. They seemed to the publisher to be overly 'political'. Perhaps James, after an initial surge of energy, had become disillusioned with the whole thing and simply wanted out.

His other commitments, of which there were plenty, began to take priority, and James eventually disappeared from the scene. Constantine then bore the brunt of the publisher's frustration at the book's laggardly progress. Originally slated for delivery in early 1965, it was still way off completion two years later, when Virtue threatened to replace Constantine as editor.[68] Eventually in 1970, with the help of Mabel Quin as assistant editor, the book appeared. '[It] deals', noted Constantine in his foreword, 'with every aspect of life in the United Kingdom … Welfare Services, schools, how to go about getting a job, where you can go for your holidays, and many other subjects.' At almost 700 pages it provided a remarkably thorough coverage of British life. It did indeed present an argument for assimilation; that is to say, there was strong advice to new immigrants on 'how to fit in', with information on such topics as queuing, manners, punctuality, hygiene, dress, and language. Immigrants, it was suggested, should strive to adopt British habits as far as possible and avoid offending the natives. Furthermore, as if to establish a yardstick by which to judge the mind of the locals, it sought to define 'British-ness'. Institutions such as the Co-op and trade unions were not neglected in the list of defining qualities and organizations, but at the same time, by drawing attention especially in the illustrations to the royal family, British history back to medieval times, and pretty rural landscapes, the book managed to give off a distinct echo of 'Merrie England'.[69] To be fair it fulfilled the intended purpose, though how many people consulted it (from a library copy, presumably, in view of the price) can only be guessed at. One assumes not that many. Perhaps for this reason, or simply because people do not know about it, *Living in Britain* is scarcely ever mentioned in writings on Constantine. It is overlooked by both of his principal biographers. It is his 'forgotten book'. Whether it was worth all the effort Constantine put into it, with the help of Quin, is questionable.

V

Yet, when Constantine's peerage came in 1969, James was not dismissive. The award elicited a warm and surely heartfelt response from him. C. L. R.'s tribute might well have summed up not only his own but the general public's feeling on his old friend:

> My dear Learie, I want to put it in writing that while I have no truck whatever with lordships etc, I am very happy to congratulate you in particular on making what is definitely a step up the ladder for most people … if anyone with our skin

would fill that post with positive achievements … I think not only that you are the person but that most people, particularly black people, would accept you as the one most fitted.

James concluded with a sentiment that transcended political differences and paid a touching tribute to their long friendship: 'If there is anything I can do that can be of assistance to you, you can depend upon me as it has been these 50 years.'[70]

9

The BBC

Constantine's long association with the British Broadcasting Corporation (BBC) came about adventitiously. During the West Indies cricket tour of 1939 he was approached to do some short radio talks on the matches and the players. He accepted (the pay was reasonably good[1]) and seems immediately to have taken to the medium. He was a fluent speaker with a pleasing voice and his producers quickly came to see him as a natural broadcaster.[2] Thus began a relationship that lasted for the remainder of his life. While not a frequent broadcaster he was heard on the wireless quite regularly, and later seen on television, over a period of more than thirty years. Working with the organization, which more than most represented 'Britishness', on serious topics concerned with matters of race, the Empire and cricket (cricket was in those days a serious topic for the BBC), ensured for Constantine recognition and respect as a national figure. If cricket had made Constantine's name it was his association with the BBC, along with his writing, that mainly kept it before the public once he had left the game. Where cricket had given him fame for his sporting achievements, Constantine's work with the BBC promoted him almost to a level of public intellectual.

I

The moulding of this new Constantine persona began following his appointment in 1941 to the full-time civil service post on Merseyside (Chapter 6). The significance of this work to the war effort, and in particular to relations with the colonies, suggested Constantine as the perfect contributor to wartime radio programmes going out to the Empire. Radio at this time was, of course, a monopoly of the BBC. It served a crucial propaganda role in the Second World War. The Corporation had to blend a variety of tasks: to instil civilian morale in the British population in the face of the various hardships being faced; to report the war and its many military reverses without incurring a loss of spirit among the troops; and to persuade colonial peoples that the war was worth fighting. This last task was a particularly sensitive one when racial animosity towards black people in Britain cast the war in an ambiguous light: if the conflict was about saving democracy, as the conflict with Nazi Germany was presented, why were black people not treated as equals? And, by extension, why were the colonies still only colonies? Alongside all this the BBC had simultaneously to keep on good terms with government while avoiding being regarded by its listeners as a vehicle for government propaganda. In carrying out these delicate balancing acts the Corporation also had to be aware of the legacy it carried. Since its inception in the 1920s, the BBC had developed a distinctive ethos that has been recorded and analysed by many historians.[3] Under the guidance of its first Director General (DG), John (later Sir John) Reith, the Corporation honoured principles that had been enunciated by two bodies set up in the 1920s to advise on the nature and purpose of broadcasting in Britain: the Sykes Committee (1923) and the Crawford Committee (1925–26). The airwaves, it was held, should be regarded in essence as 'a valuable form of public property.'[4] Working from this premise, with income provided by a licence fee set by Parliament, the BBC eschewed the model of radio being developed concurrently in the United States, which was based chiefly upon popular programmes drawing in revenue from commercial advertising. The imperative of 'easy listening' that this system demanded was not encouraged at Broadcasting House in the interwar years. The BBC's aim was loftier, 'to inform, educate and entertain'. Listeners were expected to be 'attentive' and receptive to a mixed output of programmes ranging from popular music and comedy to talks and symphony concerts. The idea of separating out listeners according to cultural taste, which was adopted after the Second World War with the creation of the Home Service, Light Programme and Third Programme, was not favoured in the days of Reith.

Such was the general context of British broadcasting when Constantine first became involved with it. During the Second World War, American influences became a matter of concern in a new sense that was especially relevant to the West Indies. The seas around the Caribbean islands became a major theatre of conflict. German submarines were active in the convoy routes carrying Trinidad oil to Britain and the North African campaign. Much of the land and aerial defence of the islands, Trinidad especially, was entrusted to American forces following the Lend-Lease deal with the British government in 1941. The American presence ushered in by these military arrangements had significant but at the same time contradictory consequences for the islands' politics and economy. Among these was the problem of 'Americanization'. It did much to undermine British colonial authority in a moral as much as in a physical way. American military and civilian personnel based in Trinidad served as a valuable, and not wholly unwelcome, stimulus to local economic, social and cultural development. The US bases provided employment for thousands of local workers, where in many instances they were treated better, and at better wages, than in the colonial labour market. One newspaper reporter from England observed that 'the workers have left the plantations to earn five times as much in the towns and camps ... the people of the West Indies never had so much to spend before'.[5] Even the normally staid Colonial Office annual report commented that with the arrival of the Americans in 1941 'a new Eldorado loomed on the horizon'.[6] And as in so many other colonial settings during the war, the presence of British or American conscript soldiers, in many cases ordinary people unlike the plantocracy or the well-to-do officials of the Empire, brought local inhabitants into contact with a different kind of white person, one who did manual work and who behaved in a less officious (if not always amicable) manner towards black people. This relationship put a different slant on the old idea of 'white superiority'. In addition to this, of course, the Americans represented a nation that in principle at least was committed to closing the door on Empire once the war ended. Awareness on the part of the British authorities of all these varied pressures ensured that colonial policy came to be framed in a more progressive tone than hitherto. It was important also that any American suspicions of a return to old-style colonialism after the war were allayed.[7] Thus, in a variety of ways, American influences were to be both welcomed and feared in London, and this duality was a concern that exercised BBC minds in wartime broadcasting to the Caribbean, as well as to the wider spread of colonial territories.

One response was that, in attempting to keep faith with colonial listeners, the BBC needed to revise its traditional policy of viewing the Empire from a metropolitan perspective. Before the war, radio had tended to be a conduit through which emigres to the colonies could be brought into contact with 'home'. The war necessitated some subtle changes to this Anglocentric philosophy of imperial broadcasting lest the support of colonial peoples for the war effort wane. There was also the challenge of short-wave broadcasts to the Caribbean from the United States to contend with. It was felt in London that such programmes might contain anti-imperialist sentiments likely to undermine the loyalty of colonial people towards the mother country. A new slant on programmes from London was needed, with a more pronounced emphasis on the idea of egalitarianism among all the Empire's peoples, united in the cause of a better British Empire in the future.[8]

A crucial innovation in this respect came with the voices of black presenters, speakers and producers: Ulric Cross, for example, from Trinidad, a serving officer in the RAF; the Jamaican feminist poet Una Marson, who became a producer of programmes to the colonies; and Learie Constantine himself, whose name and exploits were known to so many listeners at home and abroad because of cricket. Constantine's radio contributions, mostly transmitted initially to the Empire and North America, are indicative of these new emphases. Two programmes to the colonies, on which Constantine featured regularly, were 'Calling the West Indies' and 'Empire Brains Trust'.[9] He also featured in miscellany broadcasts such as 'Shipmates Ashore', 'West Indian Diary' and, for younger listeners, 'Radio Roundabout'. Following the success of these programmes, he was involved in a number of domestic broadcasts for the Home Service and the Forces Programme. His talks were usually short, based often on autobiographical reminiscences, but always with a clear message about the wartime unity of the Empire and its peoples. A case in point was his contribution of September 1943 to the 'Tonight's Talk' series. It reveals interesting effects of the war, both at the BBC and in Constantine's own character. His original script, considered for the Sunday *Postscript* programme for which J. B. Priestley had earlier had such an effect, was hard-hitting on racial problems and revealed an anger in Constantine that had previously been latent. In fact, the script as originally submitted began with his own family's background in slavery and went on to deal with the racial tensions he and his charges had experienced on Merseyside since starting work there in 1941. When received at Broadcasting House the Director of Talks (G. R. Barnes) deemed it 'too controversial': harmony, not disunity, was what the Corporation required at this time. Barnes suggested some light relief from the unremitting emphasis on the problems of coloured people: 'to show that a little of the joy of living peeps through sometimes ... for instance, some of the joy of first-class cricket.' Constantine was asked to look again at his text, which could be re-considered for broadcasting 'if Constantine's own Ministry and the Colonial Office will pass it.'[10] He willingly rewrote it and the modified script was accepted.[11] It went out as a fifteen-minute programme on the Home Service and, the changes notwithstanding, still carried a hard-hitting edge. Addressing his (white) audience as 'you', and thereby making each individual complicit in the problems covered, Constantine dealt with many topics – his slave ancestry, the lack of educational opportunities for the majority of negroes in the West Indies, who were not properly provided for because they were considered inferior, and his initial reception in Nelson, and in England more generally. On this, he said, 'We weren't treated too well ... We were met by a blank wall of ignorance that we thought we couldn't forgive.' When they first arrived in Nelson he and his wife were placed in digs, and it was made quite plain that nobody else would house them because of their colour. After a while, he said, the Nelson folk accepted them, so much so that the Constantines did not want to leave the town. Thus the talk moved on to a positive conclusion, avoiding any sense of discord, with Constantine claiming that racial prejudice was not as bad as it once was. Instead of the tensions he had emphasized in his first draft for the programme, he pointed to the treatment of the West Indian technicians on Merseyside being regarded as equals, getting 'the rate for the job'.[12] Soon after his talk the BBC received a warm response from the novelist E. M. Forster: 'I could scarcely believe my ears when I realised who he was and what his subject was. Pious disapproval of racial prejudice cuts no ice at all, what is wanted is something courageous and concrete like this'. Constantine's producer, Margaret Bucknall, rated it as 'one of the most significant contributions ever made by one to the cause of his people'.[13] This broadcast, though, was something of an exception. For the most part Constantine's wartime radio talks were limited to short pieces for 'Calling the West Indies', a programme with a wide-ranging mixture of items but with the primary purpose of allowing West Indian servicemen and women to keep in contact with their families back home. What was important was not so much Constantine himself, though he did receive several commendations for his broadcasting style and speaking voice ('pleasant and distinctive voice at the microphone',[14] 'your voices (sic) so quiet, so cultural in fact, attractive too'[15]) as the group of black presenters, all working for the war effort in one form or another and therefore casting the British cause in a good light to the colonies. Constantine, for example, did a series of two-minute programmes as Christmas messages on behalf of the technicians he worked with. He also made several contributions to another wartime programme, 'Empire Brains Trust', a version of the domestic 'Brains Trust' that had become a very popular programme with domestic audiences during the war. Panellists such as Julian Huxley and the conductor Malcolm Sargeant were brought into the imperial version, alongside distinguished figures such as Lord Hailey and the academic Reginald Coupland. Constantine had initially declined an invitation to speak on the programme, feeling that he would be out of his depth, until he was made aware that he would only need to deal with empire issues, at which point he accepted. He did in fact appear on an airing of the conventional 'Brains Trust', broadcast in May 1944.[16]

Many of the themes running through these programmes were condensed in a short film sponsored by the Ministry of Information in 1943 – 'West Indies Calling'. It took the radio programme 'Calling the West Indies' as its setting, showing various contributors, mostly black, coming together at Broadcasting House for a production. In essence, however, it was a film aimed not at West Indian listeners but at its British viewers. The idea was to feature for a British audience the work of Caribbean servicemen and factory workers in Britain, showing them carrying out essential and sometimes difficult and dangerous jobs (flying a Spitfire, for example) and doing so alongside white British people in a multiracial war effort. Learie Constantine spoke about the activities of his technicians in Lancashire, and Flying Officer Ulric Cross introduced film of a number of Caribbean men in various roles in the armed forces. Carlton Fairweather from British Honduras featured the little-known work of lumberjacks from his country working in forestry in Britain. Una Marson acted as the 'anchor' person. The film's musical background included the appropriately Trinidadian calypso 'Fight for Victory'. There was a good deal of emphasis on how these activities would hasten 'reconstruction' in the West Indies after the war, and yet more emphasis on how the war would bring about better relations between the races in the new world order following the defeat of fascism. In all likelihood, though, the film's greatest effect came over in a visual form. The camera's foregrounding of a large group of people holding a party at the BBC to celebrate a broadcast of 'Calling the West Indies' created a powerful image, suggesting that black and white, civilians and service people, and both men and women, could work and relax together in complete harmony.[17]

It was in this context that the Constantine persona was shaped by the BBC. His pleasant demeanour, always coming across as courteous whether on film or in sound, seemed to transform the message he was asked to transmit from propaganda into the avuncular advice of a good friend sitting by the fireside. An example of this came in the series 'The World Goes By', another of the BBC's miscellany programmes. It had run since 1941 dealing with a variety of people and issues in wartime situations, from the experiences of frontline troops, the role of French soldiers serving under de Gaulle, the work of the rescue services and many other occupations and activities. The presenter, F. H. 'Freddie' Grisewood later of 'Any Questions' fame, usually opened up a carefully prepared script with an observation designed to prompt his interviewee into a controversial response. The colonies were an obvious subject for this treatment and Constantine the obvious man for the job. Thus, on 8 August 1944 'The Barbados Conference' went out at 6.30 p.m. until 7 p.m. on the Home Service and the Forces Programme. The topic was an important one, if rather technical in nature for the average listener. The conference was an advisory agency created as part of the Anglo-American Caribbean Commission, a body set up in 1943 by the British and Americans to handle many of the issues arising from the joint wartime endeavours of their two governments in the Caribbean.[18] Eric Williams worked for the Commission from 1945 for some ten years. Its business highlighted some of the difficulties inherent in the relationship between the two countries over the future of the Caribbean, with Britain seeking to maintain its grip on the area and the Americans wanting change. But what made this otherwise recondite subject suddenly so important for the person in the street was the convening of the conference in Barbados in 1944. It was the biggest gathering of representatives of the various Caribbean islands that had ever been assembled, and it dealt with a raft of serious economic, social and political problems. The conference had clear implications for future British strategy and power. Grisewood began the programme by asking Constantine why a 'tropical paradise' should be demanding of such attention. Constantine replied wryly that the Caribbean was only a paradise for rich tourists; in reality it was a 'tropical depressed area', thus making reference to an economic status all-too-familiar to many British listeners with memories of their own recent history. He went on to outline the principal problems that needed urgent action – food shortages, unemployment, health, disease, living conditions; in fact all the problems that had been emphasized in the Moyne Commission report a few years earlier (the main points of which were not made public by the British government until after the War). Constantine's litany of failings in colonial rule was interjected by quotations from the official report of the conference. He ended by expressing the hope that the conference's resolutions would form a positive step in tackling and solving the various problems of the Caribbean, and not become simply a pious statement of aims that was then forgotten. 'I'm a West Indian and this happens to be my little corner of the "New World", and my part of the "century of the common man", which is what we're fighting for, or isn't it?'[19] His rhetorical question pointed up beautifully the paradox of words and action and, regrettably, anticipated the fate of the conference's findings. They were not received with any enthusiasm by the two governments concerned.[20]

II

Wartime broadcasting earned for Constantine approval at the BBC as a trusted performer, sound in microphone technique and with good sense in his opinions. It brought him frequent calls from the Corporation in the few years following the war, which became one of his busiest (and most lucrative) periods as a broadcaster.

Just after the war he drew on his experiences with the West Indian workers on Merseyside for radio talks, and later progressed to broadcasts for schools as well as unscripted discussions. He was interviewed on the relatively new medium of television by the popular broadcaster Wilfred Pickles on the subject of the colour bar, and received some good reviews.[21] Although the late 1940s and early 1950s was a time of intense study for his law qualification, Constantine responded to the promptings of BBC commentator Rex Alston to cover matches in the 1950 West Indies cricket tour of England. His broadcasts, particularly on the occasion of a famous West Indies' victory at Lord's, drew praise from the Head of Outside Broadcasts, S. J. de Lotbiniere ('Lobby'): 'I thought you did a most excellent job … what you had to say in your last broadcast after the 10 o'clock news made me feel that defeat [of England] was well worthwhile.'[22] Constantine's relaxed but perceptive style was acknowledged by other members of the Corporation, and by those outside.[23] His relationships with producers were cordial and in Margaret Bucknall and Jack Singleton especially he found two with whom he could work in particularly congenial ways. They presented him in talks and discussions as a beacon of quiet good sense and reasonableness, as when, for example, he chaired a discussion programme for the Third Programme in 1950 on the subject of the colour bar. The broadcast, which took as its focus the colonies and the prospects for change, expressed a liberal viewpoint. Constantine took the role of balancing the contrasting arguments expressed, on the one hand, by academics E. J. Dingwall and L. S. Penrose, and on the other by the Africanist Elspeth Huxley.[24] He confidently held his own in this company. In the early 1950s, he made numerous programmes on a variety of topics, often for younger listeners. He was even invited by producer Marguerite Scott in 1952 to do a talk for 'Woman's Hour' on how to dance the rumba. On this occasion he wrote a nice refusal back pleading the need to work for his impending Bar finals.[25]

The invitation from Scott, and one in 1954 to participate in what seemed a lightweight musical quiz programme, suggested that the BBC was now beginning to loosen his connection with race and Empire (which, in its way, his cricket broadcasting had preserved) and see him as a radio celebrity who might turn his hand to a number of topics. If this is the route his broadcasting work was going it was stopped short by his decision in 1954 to return to Trinidad. He signalled his departure with a broadcast on the Light Programme in March that year. It was called 'Return to Trinidad' and it went some way towards reinstating the themes he had explored during the war: looking back on his life and family, and recounting his experiences as a black man in England. In fact, the content of his script was little different from those he had prepared for 'Tonight's Talk' back in 1943, and a similar programme, 'Fields of Work and Play', broadcast by the North Region in 1946. Where it did differ, however, was in emphatically stating his gratitude for what his twenty-five-year residence in England had done for him; everything that he had achieved in life he claimed – 'materially, socially and intellectually' – he owed to England.[26]

Later, on his return to England from Trinidad in the 1960s, he resumed a busy broadcasting schedule. At that point he ventured into television, doing commentaries on Sunday cricket matches. Throughout these years his topics included race, the problems of youth and especially cricket. Cricket in fact took up most of his broadcasting time; race issues diminished, until in April 1968 he was called upon to do a short slot for 'Radio Newsreel' on Enoch Powell's notorious 'Rivers of Blood' speech in Birmingham. Not surprisingly the speech heaped fuel on the race relations debate: Constantine appeared with Corbett Woodall on 'News Time' with the topic 'Colour in Perspective', with Gordon Snell for Overseas Regional Services on the new immigration bill, and then a long question and answer session in May 1968 for the World Service. He seemed to be building up to a fresh focus on race when he was appointed a Governor of the BBC. This position demanded a degree of circumspection on controversial matters and understandably curtailed his broadcasting on race.[27]

IV

Constantine's appointment to the Board of Governors came in July 1968.[28] Among other things it had the important effect of completing the process of Anglicisation that Constantine had undergone since his arrival in Nelson some forty years earlier. By now, Constantine had already served on two other recently established national boards – the Sports Council[29] and the Race Relations Board. Both were important bodies, based in the capital city, working on essential aspects of modern society where previously there had been little public (as opposed to private voluntary) regulation. They operated close to central government and membership was reserved for distinguished leaders in the field. The BBC Board of Governors had a longer provenance, dating from 1927; it was similarly constituted, and possessed greater prestige. It was, potentially, the most important position that Constantine had occupied, and might have presented opportunities for Constantine to influence the Corporation's position on matters of race. Unfortunately, however, the appointment coincided with a period of worsening health for Constantine that prevented him from participating as fully in this role as might have been expected, considering the energy and enthusiasm he had displayed in all his previous ventures.

The role of the governors had always been a somewhat ambiguous one. They had been created as publicly appointed figures to serve as trustees of the public's interest in broadcasting, however that might be interpreted. Lord Normanbrook, Chairman of the Board until just before Constantine was appointed, expressed it thus: 'We have no purpose but to serve the public, and if we fail to serve them, or allow ourselves to serve some other interest, we forfeit our right to guide and influence this national service.'[30] In a more detailed sense, the board had executive power in that it appointed the director general, the administrative head of the Corporation, but governors did not sit in any specialist capacity; they were, as Charles Hill, Chairman when Constantine was appointed, put it, the 'amateurs' (in the best sense of the word), in company with the executive 'professionals' who actually ran the Corporation on a day-to-day basis.[31] In this way governors occupied an independent ground, even if they sometimes had to withstand the pressure of a determined DG seeking to bend the board to his will. The governors were also there to hold at arm's length the interests of government, and to ensure the neutrality of the Corporation in political matters, though on several occasions the chairman was appointed for political reasons. It was felt that Hill himself, for example, though a former Conservative cabinet minister, had been placed at the BBC by the Labour prime minister Harold Wilson to keep the Corporation in check.[32] These higher constitutional matters aside, the board's function in practice encompassed a wide brief, from the general to the particular; from carefully monitoring editorial policy to passing comment on ideas being canvassed by producers for individual programmes. Although the board had no executive role over programme making its views were important, and there were opportunities for governors, through their advice, to steer the direction of both policy and programme content.

The board met fortnightly at Broadcasting House with twelve members drawn from various realms of British life. In the late 1960s, they included nationally influential figures such as Sir Robert Bellinger, a prominent businessman and recent Lord Mayor of London, who was also a director of Arsenal Football Club; Tom Jackson, general secretary of the Union of Post Office Workers, who later sat on the Annan Commission into the Future of Broadcasting; the historian Glanmor Williams who was the national governor for Wales; and May Baird, a medical doctor and campaigner who took the position of national governor for Scotland. The vice chairman was John Fulton, vice chancellor of Sussex University, who chaired the committee that produced the influential Fulton

Report on the Civil Service in 1968. The chair, Lord Hill of Luton, was perhaps best known to most people from his role as the 'radio doctor' during the Second World War, before going into politics with the Tories. He was regarded as a tough character who would rein in the somewhat maverick DG, Hugh Carleton Greene. Shortly after Constantine's appointment, Greene was indeed eased out, and immediately, if unusually, joined the board as a governor.

In the 1960s, the BBC was still the only legitimate provider of radio, though in television there were, since 1955, competitors in the form of various independent franchises. These broadcasters – collectively known as Independent Television (ITV) – were funded by advertising revenue and in almost all cases adopted a 'populist' style of broadcasting. At the BBC the legacy of Reith had not entirely disappeared, though it continued in a far less strident form than in the 1930s. Nonetheless the idea of broadcasting as an educational tool still found favour among the nation's cultural elite. The Pilkington Committee, charged by Parliament to enquire into the state of broadcasting in Britain in the early 1960s, bore many traces of the traditional BBC outlook. Its report of 1962 came out, in a somewhat headmistressly fashion, with severe criticisms of ITV: commercial television's scheduling – with its emphasis on 'game shows' and a predilection for old American films – was considered to fall 'well short of what a good public service of broadcasting should be.'[33] ITV was, however, popular with its audiences and perhaps understandably the Conservative government to which Pilkington's report was delivered avoided implementing some of the more severe recommendations; too much tampering with ITV when a general election was due in 1964 seemed politically unwise. Nonetheless, there was ample Pilkington-ism present among senior figures at the BBC when Constantine arrived on the board.

For anyone with a lively interest in what was broadcast on radio and television a seat on the board of governors offered a challenging opportunity to engage in discussion of topics of real public concern. During Constantine's period on the Board, for example, a major topic, which anticipated changes in broadcasting over the next twenty years, was *Broadcasting in the Seventies*: a plan for the future of radio but with implications for television. Of more immediate import, yet equally controversial, was the question of the BBC's reporting of critical political events such as the troubles in Northern Ireland and the war in Vietnam. From 1969, for example, when the British government sent troops into the six counties of Ulster in an attempt to restrain the conflict between the opposing sides in the sectarian divide, the question of Ireland was well to the fore in board discussions. In September 1969, contrasting views about the coverage of 'extremist' opinion in Northern Ireland were voiced. There had been a proposal, anticipating a stance by the later Conservative Prime Minister Margaret Thatcher, to deny the IRA publicity for its activities through news reports ('the oxygen of publicity' as Thatcher later described it). It was felt among some sections of opinion at the BBC that the more radical wing of sectarian opinion should be omitted from the news lest it add a weight and seriousness to those whose politics seemed opposed to conciliation. Constantine himself expressed the view that coverage should be confined to what he called 'responsible leaders', that is to say, those being the most likely to promote the cause of harmony and peace. Prominent against him in this view were Greene and Glanmor Williams, who both argued that if 'extremists' were saying something significant they should be reported. Other controversial questions included the coverage of demonstrations against the war in Vietnam, and the BBC's own relationship with the political parties and government. This last issue was especially problematical; there was much discussion in the Board in 1968–69 of criticisms made by the prime minister, Harold Wilson, about the BBC's 'bias' in its coverage of the Labour Party. Other controversial topics included ethical matters such as the portrayal of sex or violence on television, and whether a film about Kim Philby, the spy who defected to the Soviet Union, should be broadcast.

At the same time, on a much more day-to-day basis, members' views were sought on whether they enjoyed or found worthwhile particular programmes; they were often asked to state their own preferences in terms of the balance of programme content. Two examples in particular stand out for the variety of opinion they reveal. The television film *The Big Flame*, about a fictional attempt to set up a workers' soviet on the Liverpool docks, written by Jim Allen and directed by Ken Loach, both left wingers, aroused considerable debate. The film had been opposed on political grounds by the campaigner Mary Whitehouse, and in the Board it received a scathing attack from the trade unionist, Tom Jackson. The second source of discord was Ken Russell's unusual film about the composer Richard Strauss, *The Dance of the Seven Veils*. Most members thought it was good, some said 'brilliant' but Constantine poured cold water over the proceedings by saying that it was 'rough and crude', that some passages should have been omitted, and that it ought not to have been broadcast at all. Lord Hill agreed with him.[34] There were many other occasions when programmes elicited a variety of opinions, and at these times the Board resembled a lively university seminar. It is difficult to imagine a more intellectually stimulating forum than the BBC Board of Governors at this period of the Corporation's history, with figures such as Greene, Williams, Bellinger and Jackson never slow to offer forthright and usually intelligent views on the items under discussion.

It is surprising, therefore, to see that Constantine's presence in the Board was quite low-key. At many meetings he made no intervention (or at least the minutes do not record him as having done so) and at other times what he had to say was of marginal value. To a considerable extent this appears to have been caused by Constantine's failing health. A few months after his appointment he was forced to apply for leave of absence from the Board in an attempt to recuperate in the warmer atmosphere of Trinidad from the bronchial problems from which he had been suffering in recent years.[35] He was not fully back in action until the early spring of 1969. There was a similar period of absence in the autumn of that year, which saw him miss several Board meetings until his return in mid-January 1970. It was sadly ironic, therefore, that shortly after his appointment Constantine had written to the DG assuring him that 'I shall always be doing my best'.[36] His absences meant that Constantine was unable to grapple in any depth with issues on which he had a weight of experience.

Race was the most significant of these, though it should be noted that the meetings of the Board provided relatively few opportunities to explore the subject. To begin with, before Constantine's first leave of absence, there was a discussion in the Board about the withdrawal of one of the programmes scheduled for a monthly television series that started to go out in late 1967 – 'Cause For Concern: Equal Before the Law'. The series dealt with several cases of alleged injustice. The particular programme in question, scheduled to appear later in 1968, dealt with the relationship of the police with the black community. 'Have we become too complacent with our image of the British Bobby?' as the BBC publicity put it. It highlighted cases of police brutality and abuse of power in relation to black people and was to have had senior members of the police in the studio responding to charges of racism. This was the concern that the black power movement was beginning to tackle, and which was soon to be inflated into a major national issue.[37] One aspect of the programme that particularly troubled the board was that the Metropolitan police had steadfastly refused to cooperate with the BBC in the making of the programme, and had indeed take steps to block it altogether. Legal advice had been received from the BBC's lawyers that the Corporation might be proceeded against in the courts if the programme were to be broadcast, though Constantine, a qualified barrister it should be recalled, questioned the validity of this advice and expressed concern on learning that the police had opposed the programme. He said that he knew of cases where the police had acted unfairly towards coloured people, who for their part might be 'disquieted by what appeared to be a BBC capitulation under pressure.'[38] The BBC had at first dropped the programme only to reinstate it a while later, partly no doubt as a result of Constantine's argument but more so because of the publicity generated by a protest picket outside Broadcasting House organized by the black militant Darcus Howe and others.[39] Howe, a Trinidadian with family connections to C. L. R. James, had become known in the Caribbean as a radical opponent of the Williams government, and having taken up residence in south London put his energies into local campaigns to achieve justice for black people. He was to become renowned for the leading role he took a few years later in the Mangrove affair, a court case which brought into full public view the problem of the behaviour of police towards black people. In 1968 it was the attempts by the Metropolitan Police, with its assistant commissioner Robert Mark to the fore, to block the 'Cause for Concern' programme that prompted Howe to organize his street protest on the pavement in Langham Place. Howe's biographers attribute both the reinstating of the programme and the effectiveness of the black speakers in the subsequent television debate to Howe's astute tactics and personal charisma, which, they claim, initiated his later career in broadcasting and journalism.[40] The juxtaposition of these two situations – Constantine attending board meetings inside Broadcasting House while militant black groups demonstrated outside the building – placed in stark contrast two different strategies in race matters at this time.

'Cause for Concern' had seemed a case to which Constantine's experience was well suited, and one from which he might not only establish a position in the board to argue for a greater attention in the broadcasting schedules to the problems experienced by coloured people, but also to make contact with some of the direct action groups from which he had so far kept his distance. As a public spokesman for the fair treatment of minorities it would have seemed eminently appropriate for him to undertake these roles. As it was the issue of race prejudice in the police was taken over by black power groups, and Constantine's subsequent absence meant that any possibility of his maintaining the momentum on this aspect of race relations was lost. A related matter came up in early 1970 when Constantine received a letter from Lillian Bader of Liverpool[41] asking for his support to have coloured people[42] more adequately represented on the radio programme 'Any Questions'. Mrs Bader described herself and her family as 'ordinary' people who felt that their views and feelings were not properly represented by those selected to speak on behalf of coloured people on the radio. It was a reasonable point, and one which people like Constantine should already have anticipated. If the BBC 'spoke' for the nation, was it doing so in a voice that authentically included black people? Constantine's reply was not especially encouraging for the Mrs Baders of the country. He defended the BBC's selection of speakers for 'Any Questions' as being decided 'on the basis of merit', and said he did not feel that panellists should be chosen simply because they were black (or, in other cases, because they were women); neither race nor gender were in themselves primary qualifications, so much as the ability to abide by the 'moral consensus on which society is founded' – an evasive and somewhat august statement.[43]

At about the same time a further problem, with similar implications, came up in the board. It was to do with the radio and television coverage of the planned tour to England by the South African cricket team in the summer of 1970. As we have seen, the question of sporting links with South Africa was another issue on which Constantine had taken a very public stand in the past, most recently over the non-selection of Basil d'Oliveira for the proposed England tour to South Africa in 1968–69. There was no question of Constantine's supporting any cricket contacts with South Africa so long as the system of apartheid prevailed there. In view of this, the position that emerged at the BBC in early 1970 over the coverage of the tour should have presented something of a moral dilemma for Constantine. As outlined by the DG, Charles Curran, the Corporation's policy was to be that the cricket matches would be covered on radio and television, though it was accepted that some staff might refuse to work on grounds of conscience. This seemed to comply with the stance of the trade unions involved. The Association of Cinematograph, Television and Allied Technicians (ACTT), for example, said it would give support to members who refused to work, while members of the National Union of Journalists and the Post Office Engineers would work as normal. Although the prime minister had suggested that the BBC could withdraw from coverage of the matches if it wanted to the DG insisted there was an obligation to broadcast 'events of public interest' and could not be swayed by matters of conscience that affected private individuals. To do so, claimed Curran, would be to embark 'on a most slippery slope.' The BBC was, to be sure, in a delicate position, but the idea that it could separate out so neatly 'public obligations' from 'private matters of conscience' was challengeable. It was felt among board members, with some justification, that much opposition to the tour would be aroused during the summer – there had already been demonstrations, violent in some instances, against a South African rugby tour earlier in the year. Lord Fulton, the Board's Vice-Chair, and Glanmor Williams were vociferous in their view that the Corporation should avoid any expressions of sympathy with the MCC, which supported the tour, and the South Africans in the coverage of the cricket matches. Some Board members were concerned, for example, that radio and television commentators might lean too far towards a pro-MCC stance.[44] Strangely, perhaps, Constantine was not much to the fore in these debates. His one positive intervention was to remark that the treatment of the tour in the BBC's programme 'Panorama', broadcast on 27 April 1970, had been admirable.[45] This particular edition of the programme had exposed some of the double standards that existed in South Africa. While indicating that there were pockets of opinion in favour of multiracial sport it juxtaposed the sense of fair play that prevailed among sportspeople with blatant racial inequalities in the apartheid system, thus cleverly indicting the conventional view among those who favoured sporting links with South Africa that 'sport' and 'politics' were separate entities. One interview in the programme – with the South African batsman Denis Lindsay – exposed the contradiction quite clearly. Asked whether teams of mixed race would be selected for South Africa in the future Lindsay was evasive. He offered no personal view. It was a question, he said, 'for the politicians': he himself was only a cricketer. His answer was roundly applauded by a group of white spectators standing in the background.[46] Constantine's own sentiments on this issue were therefore suitably expressed for him by the BBC's programme, though he himself avoided any direct comment.

Bearing in mind that Constantine's health was deteriorating rapidly at this time it is difficult to arrive at a balanced judgment of his contribution to the board. A harsh appraisal might raise the question of whether he was worth his seat. His attendance was affected by two lengthy gaps on health grounds, and his contributions to discussion when he was there were slight. It is important to remember why he was appointed in the first place. Certain basic qualifications – in the form of a 'distinguished' career – had always been required for membership of the board, after which its composition proceeded according to a rough balance of social interests. Tom Jackson, for example, was the trade union representative, and in a broader sense a voice of the 'working class'. There were explicit national representatives for Wales, Scotland and Northern Ireland (Lord Dunleath in the last case, who was a valuable contributor on 'the Troubles'). A balance between public and private sectors was also sought, personified in the contrasting backgrounds of Bellinger and Fulton. In this sense, therefore, there is little doubt that Constantine's appointment was part of a Labour government strategy for acknowledging the issue of race relations. In addition to the legislative enactments of 1965 and 1968, there was recognition of the need for some 'soft power', with representative figures from the black community in some of the nation's influential counsels. There had been a striking absence of such representation in the past and a start on the process was only just being made. Constantine fitted the requirement of the moment perfectly. It would have been inappropriate (and in any case impossible) for him to use the board of governors as a platform for polemics on race but, given that the ghost of Reith still stalked the corridors of Broadcasting House and with it the idea of radio and television as a national public service, it would have been entirely appropriate for a governor to use his or her influence on the board to ensure that the black community in Britain was properly represented in the programmes put out. This would mean, for example, giving black authors and actors the chance to figure in drama; recognizing Mrs Bader's point about the selection of members of discussion panels; thinking more sensitively about popular programmes such as 'The Black and White Minstrels Show' (surely an anachronism in the late 1960s); giving more space in documentaries to the social and economic problems of black households; and generally requiring programme-makers to have the notion of 'race' more firmly in mind when going about their business. Carleton Greene's stewardship in the 1960s had produced some refreshing innovations in many areas of the Corporation's output but in its underlying broadcasting philosophy the BBC remained conservative. By acknowledging even some of these injunctions the Corporation would be fulfilling its role as a public service to greater effect. A more perceptive and energetic Constantine might in this way have broadened the Corporation's racial boundaries.

His tenure of office therefore seems to have been something of a missed opportunity. There is a suspicion that, illness or not, he was a little out of his depth. It is interesting to compare Constantine's role as a governor with the person appointed to the Board at the very same time in 1968. She was Dame Mary Green, a teacher who had proved a success as the founding Head in 1954 of Kidbrooke School, a girls' comprehensive in London. She had been a member of the Central Advisory Committee for Education and sat on the Royal ('Donovan') Commission on Trade Unions and Employers' Association that reported in 1967. An experienced and forceful figure – she was described in her obituary in the *Times* as 'the last of the great "spinster headmistresses"' [47] – Molly Green appeared at first to be a rather lightweight presence at the BBC. As reported in board minutes, her chief activity was visiting local BBC offices and reporting back (usually with unstinting praise) on the work done by the staff. It seemed, as with Constantine, that she needed time to grow into the job. In contrast with him, however, she did so, becoming a more confident governor whose contributions to meetings became frequent and weighty. By contrast, it is perhaps a measure of Constantine's standing in the board that its chairman, Charles Hill, almost completely overlooked him in his broadcasting memoirs, published just three years after Constantine's death. There is only a passing reference to his having sat on a committee, and his name is even omitted from Hill's list of the Governors appointed in 1968. By contrast, Mary Green's contribution to the Board is highly commended.[48]

10

Black Englishman

Few people are honoured with a state funeral in one country and a memorial service in one of the main churches of another. Learie Constantine was. It is a measure of the regard in which he was held, both in his birthplace, Trinidad, and his mother country, England. In the historical record of both countries he stands unequivocally as a good man, universally respected. All those who have previously written about him have concurred in the view that his life and work were quintessentially admirable. The vast number of letters of sympathy, addressed to his widow at the time of his death, is testament to the regard in which he was held. They fill two whole boxes in the Constantine Collection.[1] It is all the more remarkable, especially in a country like England, which has never entirely emerged from the shadow of race and class prejudice, that such a status was accorded to a black man from a poor family.

It results in large part from Constantine's assumption of the role of 'black Englishman'. His is a story of acceptance and assimilation: of the immigrant behaving as 'good guest'. It was a story he projected as a model for all immigrants, though whether the vast majority of them accepted the model is another matter. For Constantine assimilation was a relatively easy process, but for many others the path he had beaten was a difficult one to follow.[2] In the early and middle years of his life he was admired as a cricketer, and once his playing days had finished his status was further buttressed by his public standing: an MBE, an author, a knighthood and finally a life peerage. All this followed work with the BBC both as broadcaster, and later, governor; with the Race Relations Board; and also with the Sports Council. These were national bodies on which respected figures, distinguished in public service, were invited to serve. In such company Constantine had undoubtedly 'got on'. Even now, in the twenty-first century, when black men and women have achieved eminence in many fields – politics, the arts, sport, business – people can still admire Constantine as a initiator of such advancement. This would have pleased him. He saw himself as a 'pioneer', a man whose wish was 'to leave something creditable behind'.[3] Seeing him in this way is to tell a story of success, of upward mobility in which boundaries that had debarred people of colour – and many not of colour – had been crossed. He achieved all this while cultivating a quality that was an essential component of Englishness half a century and more ago, especially for a person from a humble background: respectability.[4]

He did all this while retaining something of his Trinidad identity, a 'double consciousness' expressed in the title of his peerage – Baron Constantine, of Maraval in Trinidad and Tobago, and of Nelson in the County Palatine of Lancaster. It was not a strident racial identity in the manner of some campaigners of his later years, glorying in blackness and proclaiming 'black is beautiful'. He owed so much to England. In a radio broadcast of 1954, before embarking for Trinidad, he spoke of what he had achieved up to that point in life – materially, socially and intellectually – and ascribed it all to his having come to England.[5] A month before his death he acknowledged: 'My roots are all here. I have enjoyed a status I would never have had at home.'[6] In fact, the 'black' in the Englishman might seem little more than skin colour. The satirical magazine *Private Eye* referred to him as 'Learie Constantine, the former black man'.[7] In the days when pan-Africanism was in vogue, there was no sense of an African lineage transposed into British circumstances for Constantine. When C. L. R. James and his Trinidadian friend George Padmore (Malcolm Nurse) were both very conscious of an African inheritance, Constantine would surely have agreed with the writer and teacher Stuart Hall, from Jamaica and a whole generation younger: 'I wouldn't have understood myself as African in any meaningful, contemporary sense of the word.'[8] Constantine looked west. This was the axis of his double consciousness – a person (Joseph O'Neill's fictional character Chuck Ramkissoon, also a Trinidadian, is similar[9]) placed simultaneously within and yet to an extent outside established cultural norms. But for those coming from Trinidad, there was a sense in which they were already English before they ever set foot in the place. Like C. L. R. James and V. S. Naipaul Constantine recognized the absence of any native intellectual tradition in Trinidad. James clung to calypso as the one truly authentic cultural product of Trinidad. He was already a 'black Englishmen' by the time he had left Queen's Royal College with its Anglocentric syllabus of English history, literature, politics and cricket. People in the Anglophone Caribbean were in any case 'English' by virtue of being subjects of the Crown. Until legislation placed limitations on their status they were eligible freely to visit and live in England, the 'mother country'. So Englishness was not a strange concept for them. 'West Indian' was a stranger one for a people living in a fragmented group of islands. 'West Indian' existed primarily in the cricket team. Only when stirrings of nationalism in the Caribbean began to be felt from the 1950s onwards did new forms of consciousness start to conflict with 'England'. The immigrant's experience of actually living in England from that point in time queered the English pitch.

As he crossed his boundaries, Constantine relied greatly on his reputation from cricket. The game was the platform from which he achieved everything that came his way in later life. It was the source also of his Trinidadian identity. His relationship with cricket, however, was far from conventional. He was unlike the traditional heroes of the game, those outstanding practitioners whose on-field achievements were combined with loyalty to the cricket establishment. Jack Hobbs and Don Bradman were prime examples, both knighted for their services to cricket long before knighthoods for sportspeople became commonplace. Constantine, if not exactly a rebel, had challenged some of cricket's traditions. His style of play was unorthodox, and he went against the status quo so far as to advocate new forms of play in the search for 'brighter' cricket. He was the first black player to leave the Caribbean game at the height of his powers and take up a career in England as a professional. He called for the end of the established practice of giving the captaincy of the West Indies team to a white man. He stood out against the West Indies cricket management for better pay and status. In the last analysis, though, he remained within the fold, a serious critic of the status quo but ultimately too much a lover of the game to be a revolutionary.

The changes he called for were prescient. Largely designed to make the game more attractive for spectators they were well intentioned and have for the most part been achieved. Some of the consequences have been unintended, and how much Constantine would have approved of them is open to question. From the outset there was an implicit commercialism in much of what he advocated; it had the potential to contradict his basic philosophy – a belief in something called 'the spirit of the game' together with a wholehearted rejection of a 'win at all costs' mentality. Neither could be said to have been safeguarded in the new forms of limited overs cricket which, together with test cricket, now make up the game's chief source of revenue. From this, the earning potential for leading players has increased significantly. In fact, many have now caught up with and surpassed the real income enjoyed by Constantine in his Lancashire League days. He could scarcely have objected to that, though whether the career path of Chris Gayle, one of Constantine's charismatic successors in the West Indies team, would have met with approval by Learie is an intriguing question.[10] Gayle has effectively removed himself from the West Indies test team in order to pursue the greater financial rewards available in competitions such as the Indian Premier League.

In a more positive sense, what Constantine emphatically articulated through cricket was a discernable Caribbean identity. It was not the 'calypso' stereotype so often encountered in the popular press, but a more hybrid style; one that absorbed both the spontaneity that had characterized much of Constantine's own play, and the diligent attention to correct technique evident in the batting of players like George Headley and Everton Weekes. Caribbean cricket, in Constantine's eye, particularly achieved this hybridity once free of the racial controls that had held the game back in the West Indies. A few years before his death Constantine was able to glory in the success in England of a West Indies touring team playing, especially in the person of Garfield Sobers, a uniquely Caribbean brand of cricket that he saw as a vindication of his own thinking on the game over the previous three decades.

Constantine's success in floating upwards after he left cricket contrasted with the lives of other black sportsmen whose later years often plunged them into obscurity. There were, of course, black performers who attained a fame, fortune and recognition that carried with it a degree of tolerance from white society. Such people – footballer Walter Tull, for example, who died in the First World War, and singers Leslie Hutchinson and Elizabeth Welch – had moved into the middle class. As Colin Holmes has pointed out, the greatest racial discrimination was reserved not for people like these but for working-class blacks in towns such as Cardiff and Liverpool, the fear of racial intermarriage being a prime cause of hostility.[11] Constantine turned that which disadvantaged many black people – that is, their colour – into an opportunity. He was fortunate to live in a time of change. He benefited from the need after the Second World War to have a model black figure. With the move from 'Empire' to 'Commonwealth' and an acknowledgment of the requirement to confront the issue of self-determination in the colonies, it helped to be able to show that some black people now might have a new status and respect. What Constantine had done, others might also achieve. He was a poster boy for that long and difficult process of managing decolonization and the repercussions of it, chief among which was the problem of immigration into Britain. His work in Trinidad with the People's National Movement (PNM), though not a gratifying period of his life personally, strengthened this position. Trinidad and Tobago had been a 'good' decolonization compared with some other British possessions, and Constantine's loyal service there helped towards a peaceful transition of power. He always retained a loyalty to the idea of Empire and kept a low profile when his more radical boss, Eric

Williams, railed against the colonialists and their allies the Americans. In these ways Constantine acquired the status he did, not in spite of his race, but *because* of it. The photographic portrait of him by Godfrey Argent in the National Gallery, taken towards the end of Constantine's life, depicts a benign and evidently self-satisfied man, in an aldermanic pose worthy of a Victorian civic dignitary. Yet it carried more significance for him than simply personal glory. It was the part he felt he had to play to help fellow black people gain acceptance and prosper in Britain. He considered himself to be an exemplar of blackness. White people would judge other blacks by how Constantine behaved.

II

Constantine's approach to race and race relations was legitimized through white approval. It was the white establishment that had elevated Constantine to the eminence he enjoyed once he had returned from Trinidad in 1962, and his stature as the 'good' black man was perpetuated in the decade or so after his death. By the time Gerald Howat's biography appeared in 1975, the memory of Constantine had become a counterpoint to what were seen in some quarters as threatening forms of 'black power': groups of militants who took a more aggressive form of direct action to combat the injustices they perceived in contemporary race relations. A climate of apprehension about race conflict was generated. The late 1960s and 1970s saw black movements in the United States and South Africa deploy the street demonstration as a weapon in their campaign against the racial status quo. It was the era of the fearless black opponents of apartheid in the townships and of the urban disorder that came to American cities such as Philip Roth's Newark in the late 1960s.[12] Some of these methods were taken up in Britain: protests, for example, against continued police harassment of black people in the Notting Hill area of London produced confrontations between young black militants and the police. They led to the arrest and trial of the Mangrove Nine.[13] Constantine abhorred race conflict and always sought to avoid it. Although the links between British and American race activists were often close, the situation in Britain was relatively quiescent in comparison with that of the United States. There, at the height of the war in Vietnam in the later 1960s, a wholesale radicalization of younger black men and women was taking place. Clearly it had deep roots but its outburst at this time was precipitated in the war and the feeling that black men were being discriminated against in the American army. They were more likely to be drafted, and more likely to have to serve on the front line. Racism in the base camps was rife. Many came to feel that they were fighting a 'white man's war'. One sporting champion who had refused the draft, simply said: 'I ain't got no quarrel with them Vietcong.' 'I was determined', he later said, 'to be the one nigger that the white man didn't get.' Muhammad Ali (for it was he) joined Malcolm X's original party, the radical black Nation of Islam, but it was the Black Panthers who gained most from angry and disillusioned black brothers.[14] In this atmosphere Constantine was to many white people the perfect representation of the black man, an unthreatening figure who eschewed violence and sought race harmony through education and reasoned argument. The racial language with which Neville Cardus had described him some forty years earlier was now long gone.

Constantine's acceptance was helped too by his continued elusiveness in the world of politics. In spite of what C. L. R. James had attributed to him in the early 1930s, Constantine was always difficult to pin down politically. His writings reveal a concern for racial fairness but little that crystallized into a political platform, certainly not a party political one. Occasionally he suggested an allegiance: his conversations with the socialists in 1930s Nelson, which seem to have been little more than exchanges of ideas; his relationship with James, who pursued a radical path as much concerned with class as with racial politics (and Constantine never remotely indicated an interest in James's Marxism); the overtures made to him by members of the Liberal Party in the early 1950s, and again in the late 1960s by Jeremy Thorpe, whose party he never joined; and in his brief membership in the House of Lords, where he sat as a crossbencher. None of these was more than a passing fancy. The League of Coloured Peoples (LCP) was his most congenial political setting, where emphasis was on tackling the kinds of problems Constantine later highlighted in *Colour Bar*. But even with the LCP, whose Chairman he briefly became at the very end of the organization's life, he was never among the movement's most active members. Its founder Harold Moody would surely have welcomed more involvement from 'our Learie'. Essentially, though, he was not a joiner. His work with the People's National Movement in Trinidad was an exception and did not carry over in any sense into his life in England. Even in Trinidad he disliked the politics and had little impact in debate and policy formation. It is noteworthy how infrequently his name comes up in the major studies of Caribbean politics in this period.[15] Back in England in 1962, the stance he assumed was that of the man of the people, a spokesman in particular for the West Indian community in England. He was, though, never directly involved in popular movements at this time, and even seemed uncertain about what they might lead to. As in Nelson, he felt that neutrality in politics was demanded, as if a precise attachment to any movement might undermine what he regarded as the universalism of his appeal.

III

Looking back on Constantine's life shortly after his funeral, Sam Morris, his wartime assistant in Liverpool and later a leading figure in the Commission for Racial Equality, observed: 'To some of us Constantine's greatest role was in the field of race relations.'[16] What did he achieve? In seeking an answer to this question we must remember that, whatever Constantine's successes and failures, few if any have achieved much in this field. Race remains a monumental problem of contemporary British society.[17] Effective solutions are awaited in a whole span of key areas: at one end of the spectrum is continuing racial hostility, accompanied often by violence, as typified in the Stephen Lawrence case; at the other end there are unremedied disadvantages for black people in university admissions. A report by the Equality and Human Rights Commission in 2016 noted 'deep-rooted inequality' in Britain, and warned of widening social divisions and increased racial tension as a result. For young black people especially, it said, the situation had worsened over the previous five years.[18] Judging by the fears and hostility evinced over the issue of immigration in the 2016 referendum on membership of the European Union, the combination of xenophobia and racism is perhaps a greater problem now than ever before.

It is certainly true that race had been ever present in Constantine's own life, and in his own consciousness from the very day as a young child he was warned by his mother to be wary of the white man.[19] Race oppression was something he had to put up with and learn to handle. His outstanding achievement was in transmitting these concerns and placing the question of race as pressing issues at the forefront of British life; in particular, of presenting race relations not as a mere fact of life but as a problem in need of a solution. His welfare work on Merseyside gave him first-hand experience of the problem in Britain. The effect of *Colour Bar* in broadening awareness of it in the life and discourse of the British public was considerable. As a polemic on the subject it probably had as great an influence as anything previously published. He maintained, moreover, a position as a public figure, known as a campaigner on matters of race. He was always available for a comment on radio or television. This as much as anything helped keep race a live issue in Britain during the second half of the twentieth century and beyond. But Constantine's influence stopped at this point. He contributed little to the developing discourse on race. Theory had never been his strong point, as shown in *Colour Bar*. For him 'race' was a matter of white doing wrong to black, the solution to which was that people should learn to be more tolerant towards each other. He was committed to a basic assimilationist approach to the question of immigration, drawing much from the American notion of a 'melting pot', which had dominated the study of race during the 1950s. It assumed an integration of peoples from different cultures and backgrounds around a set of established, essentially white principles. The concept of multiculturalism and its positive and negative effects, which was beginning to interest some circles of policymaking in the 1960s, had little presence in his work.[20] His later years were a time of disappointment to him. Work for the RRB and the BBC was blighted by illness. Many colleagues noted that his contribution to meetings was less than it might have been had he enjoyed better health. He was sufficiently active to have made some kind of mark, however, and the dispassionate observer might be left to wonder whether it was ideas, as much as physical condition, that accounted for Constantine's relative quiescence at this time. It is pertinent to note that Constantine is mentioned only once – in connection with his legal case against the Imperial Hotel – in David Olusoga's compendious 'forgotten' history of black people in Britain.[21]

His impact also seems slight when viewed in comparison with some of his notable black contemporaries on the world stage. An Anglocentric viewpoint on race will sometimes mask the achievements of such men and women – the American performers Paul Robeson and Josephine Baker, for example, and the West Indian intellectuals C. L. R. James and Frantz Fanon; and another writer from the Caribbean, Una Marson. James, though most of his political experiments seemed to fail, is now better known than Constantine, his influence resting on a body of writings that have profoundly affected academic study in issues such as post-colonialism and literature. Fanon had a major role in the struggle for Algerian independence. An intellectual and qualified psychiatrist from Martinique, he was destined for the role of 'evolué' – black Frenchman – but rebelled against that and produced a series of books that exposed in one form or another the political, philosophical and psychological frailties of colonialism.[22] The less well-known Una Marson was a black Jamaican feminist poet who worked at the BBC during the War, producing *Calling the West Indies* and *Caribbean Voices*, the latter seeking to promote Caribbean literature in a way similar to James's involvement earlier with *The Beacon*.[23] Marson worked closely with Constantine at this time. She had important achievements to her name that, because she was a woman, have been unfairly neglected in the history of this period. Josephine Baker's career was not dissimilar from that of Constantine. Like him, she became famous as an entertainer, not of course on the cricket field but as a cabaret star in France in the interwar years. Her allure was fashioned around the same sense of magical negritude that Constantine brought to cricket.[24] But Baker had other sound achievements. She was decorated by the French state for her wartime work in the Resistance, served the civil rights movement in the United States, and devoted much of her later life to adopting poor children of different ethnicities. Most striking of all in this company is the towering figure of Paul Robeson, a man of immense talent in many fields whose struggle for black people's rights was truly international.[25] Many of these figures were, to different degrees, regarded with suspicion by the authorities for their radical views, and subjected to restraint and harassment: Robeson, a supporter of the Soviet Union, was watched and beset by the FBI for many years and had his US passport revoked; Baker and James were both deported from the United States in the early 1950s for political reasons; Fanon became a political opponent of the French state and, during the Algerian struggle, was forced to live outside its jurisdiction. Their lives were troubled, often uncomfortable, at times dangerous.

When the adult Constantine came to race relations it seemed that the future might be propitious for improvement. He himself was optimistic. Nelson comes into the reckoning here. It illustrates the impact of changing historical circumstances and changing racial perspectives. Nelson was, in a sense, the chief reception point for an Atlantic cricket migration into Lancashire, and from that, into English cricket generally. Constantine's success in Nelson created openings for West Indian players in the northern leagues, establishing, with the addition of men from Australia and India, a new form of internationalism in the English game. From the 1930s until the 1960s, most of the big names in the post-1945 Caribbean game were to be found, at one time or another, playing cricket in the Lancashire, Central Lancashire, Birmingham, and North Staffordshire/South Cheshire leagues. In the later 1960s, this flow of talent was diverted into county cricket. Clive Lloyd, who captained the powerful West Indies teams of the 1970s and early 1980s, typified the process; he moved from Guyana to play for Haslingden (George Headley's old club), before joining the Lancashire county club in 1969. Constantine was the person whose presence initially sparked this migration, which eventually served to remove the colour bar in first-class cricket that he himself had experienced from the Lancashire county professionals in the 1930s.

Nelson also had a deep personal influence upon Constantine. It was, after all, 'home'. It was the place where Constantine learnt how to adapt his views and behaviour and already-existing Englishness, to new surroundings. It was in Nelson that, for the first time, Constantine experienced an almost non-racial acceptance. In the 1930s he was a novelty, both in the style of his cricket and in his being black. Searching for the 'other' in Nelson at this time would have meant identifying not black people, but those who were ethnically and religiously different, such as the Irish (of which there were few). Because there were no black people in Nelson, acceptance of Constantine was relatively unproblematic; it is easy to admire a black man when he is, as well as being a sports star, the only one in town. His identity was made the more non-racial by Constantine's undoubted middle class-ness in Nelson. He occupied a social position more compatible with the colonial middle class, black and white. To put it more plainly in terms of the cricket club hierarchy in Trinidad, if Constantine had possessed the social placement he enjoyed in Nelson it would have entitled him to play for a club with a higher status than Shannon.

But if we believe that Constantine's presence brought out an innate tolerance in Nelsonians, a model for harmonious race relations, we should revisit the town and look at its present condition. It says something about what has been happening in England. The circumstances of Constantine's time in Nelson did not last. It was little more than an interlude in the town's history. Some ten years after Constantine had left the town and the local cotton economy ran into serious competition from overseas producers, a fresh wave of immigration brought an influx of workers from the Indian subcontinent. They were not so well received as Constantine had been.[26] A deep racial hostility was engendered, and has continued into the present century. It created a town divided along race lines, the population segregated geographically and culturally. With this came a new form of extremist right-wing politics. Not long after Constantine had been made a Freeman of the Borough in 1963, signs of the erosion of the old radical political culture were appearing. In the parliamentary by-election of 1968 following the death of the long-serving Labour MP Sydney Silverman, the Conservatives took the seat. A major reason for this political reversal was the state of the local cotton industry and the Labour government's failure to revive it. But there were rumblings too of Powellite anti-immigrant feelings with a nationalist candidate, Brian Tattersall, polling over 1200 votes on the promise to 'repatriate' immigrant workers who, he claimed, were 'disillusioned and unhappy' and wanted to go 'home'.[27] Tattersall's campaign was a foretaste of a gradual swing to the right in both parliamentary and local council elections in that part of Lancashire in the late-twentieth century. In the early years of the twenty-first century there were municipal election successes for the far-right British National Party and a little later for the United Kingdom Independence Party (UKIP). In the Labour seat of Pendle (formerly Nelson and Colne) the Conservatives tightened their grip on politics at all levels. In the EU referendum of June 2016, Pendle voted solidly for Leave, and narrowly returned a Conservative in the 2017 parliamentary election.

The respect that had been accorded to Constantine was signally lacking in relations with the new residents who had come to work in Nelson from the Indian subcontinent. One personal case dramatically illuminates the contrast with Constantine's reception forty years earlier. In 1973 Suresh had arrived in Nelson with his mother and father from India. His schoolmates called him 'Billy' because they said they could not pronounce his name. Their teacher, said Suresh, 'called us "Wogs"'. Suresh and his Asian friends felt a constant threat of violence towards them – for much of the time, in fact, they said they were 'totally terrified'. On one occasion, Suresh took his younger nephew to the cinema where they were physically assaulted by a group of skinheads. Suresh tried to defend himself and his nephew, but they were both punched and beaten. Suresh reported the incident to the police and to the head of his school – 'nobody did anything'. The police recorded the incident and said they would follow it up and get in touch – but 'they never called us'.[28] 'They never called us': it might be the leitmotif for many an immigrant to Britain from the arrival of the *Windrush* in 1948 onwards. Constantine would surely have been horrified to hear it. It happened only a few years after his death, and conflicted with everything Learie had worked and hoped for. In an interview with the young South African writer Lewis Nkosi in 1966, Constantine was asked about the future for race relations. Nkosi questioned whether racial prejudice in England was 'so deeply ingrained' that there could be little cause for optimism. Constantine demurred. 'Within my lifetime', he said, 'the relationship will so change' to bring about 'a world fit for my child and your child'.[29]. The prognosis was over-optimistic, but the sentiment remains the goal for any good society.

Notes

Preface

1 'A Knight at Old Trafford', *New Statesman*, 7 June 1963, 861.

1 Constantine

1 Most accounts give his date of birth as September 1901, though Constantine himself sometimes put it a year later.

2 Anne Spry Rush, 'Imperial Identity in Colonial Minds: Harold Moody and the League of Coloured Peoples', *Twentieth-Century British History*, vol. 13, 4 (2002): 377.

3 Constantine's life is covered in Gerald Howat, *Learie Constantine* (London: George Allen and Unwin, 1975), a study rightly described by Brian Stoddart as an 'excellent biography'. See Hilary McD. Beckles and Brian Stoddart, *Liberation Cricket: West Indies Cricket Culture* (Manchester: Manchester University Press, 1995), 253, fn 21, a book which itself provides many valuable insights into Constantine and his colonial context. See also Gerald M. D. Howat, 'Constantine, Learie Nicholas, Baron Constantine (1901–1971)' *Oxford Dictionary of National Biography* (Oxford: Oxford University Press, 2004); online edn, January 2011, http://dx.doi.org/10.1093/ref:odnb/30961. The case of Arthur Wharton, the first black sportsman to achieve some fame in English football and cricket, makes an interesting comparison. Wharton, who came from the Gold Coast (Ghana), played in goal for Preston North End and was a professional cricketer in the northern leagues at the turn of the century. He represents the antithesis of Constantine's success. He died in penury after working as a coal miner once his sporting days were over. He was buried in an unmarked grave. See Phil Vasili, *The First Black Footballer: Arthur Wharton 1865–1930: An Absence of Memory* (London: Frank Cass, 1998).

4 'Great Lives', BBC Radio 4, 7 April 2015.

5 See Chris Waters, '"Dark Strangers" in Our Midst: Discourses of Race and Nation in Britain, 1947–1963', *Journal of British Studies*, vol. 6, 2 (April 1997): 207–38.

6 David Olusoga, *Black and British: A Forgotten History* (London: Macmillan, 2016), 498.

7   See Paul B. Rich, *Race and Empire in British Politics* (Cambridge: Cambridge University Press, 1986), 171ff.

8   Anthony H. Richmond, *Colour Prejudice in Britain: A Study of West Indian Workers in Liverpool, 1941–1951* (London: Routledge and Kegan Paul, 1954).

9   Derived from the term 'colour line', coined by the American writer and activist W. E. B. Du Bois to describe racial divisions in the United States.

10 Learie Constantine, *Colour Bar* (London: Stanley Paul, 1954).

11 Kathleen Chater estimates that, apart from M. Dorothy George's references to black people in eighteenth-century London (*London Life in the Eighteenth Century*, London, 1925), there was no other book dealing specifically with black people in Britain until Little's book appeared. (Kathleen Chater, 'Black British History', *Making History: the changing face of the profession in Britain*, The Institute of Historical Research, 2008) (www.history.ac.uk/makinghistory/resources/articles/black_history.html. (accessed 23 June 2017). Among the leading texts on race in the 1950s and 1960s were: K. L. Little, *Negroes in Britain: A Study of Racial Relations in English Society* (London: Kegan Paul, Trench and Trubner, 1947); Anthony H. Richmond, *Colour Prejudice in Britain: A Study of West Indian Workers in Liverpool* (London: Routledge and Kegan Paul, 1954); Ruth Glass, *London's Newcomers: The West Indian Migrants* (London: Centre for Urban Studies/George Allen and Unwin, 1960); Sheila Patterson, *Dark Strangers: A Sociological Study of the Absorption of a Recent West Indian Migrant Group in Brixton, South London* (London: Tavistock Publications, 1963).

12 Waters, 'Dark Strangers', 217.

13 See, for example, Bernard Crick, 'Throw the R-word Away: We Should Attack Racism by Ceasing to Use the Word "Race"', *New Statesman*, 18 October 1996; Paul Gilroy, *Against Race: Imagining Political Culture beyond the Colour Line* (Cambridge, MA: Harvard University Press, 2000). As against Crick and Gilroy, see Harry Goulbourne, *Race Relations in Britain Since 1945* (Basingstoke: Macmillan, 1998), 147.

14 Karl Spracklen, *Whiteness and Leisure: Leisure Studies in a Global Era* (Basingstoke: Palgrave Macmillan, 2013), ch. 1.

15 Stuart Hall, *The Fateful Triangle: Race, Ethnicity, Nation*, ed. Kobena Mercer (Cambridge, MA: Harvard University Press, 2017), 32–33.

16 Hall, *Fateful Triangle*, 37.

17 Ta-Nehisi Coates, 'We Should Have Seen Trump Coming', *Guardian*, 30 September 2017: 37–39.

18 See Peter Kolchin, 'Whiteness Studies: The New History of Race in America', *Journal of American History* (June, 2002), vol. 89, 1: 154–73.

19 See David R. Roediger, *The Wages of Whiteness: Race and the Making of the American Working Class* (London: Verso, 2007 edn); Noel Ignatiev, *How the Irish*

Became White (London: Routledge, 2008). Jennifer Egan's recent novel *Manhattan Beach* (London: Corsair, 2017) gives an interesting reflection on this issue in describing the Brooklyn docks in the 1940s: 'Eddie was accustomed to seeing Negroes treated badly – on the West Side piers wops were regarded as Negroes and Negroes as something worse' (p. 304).

20 Katharine Tyler, *Whiteness, Class and the Legacies of Empire: On Home Ground* (Basingstoke: Palgrave Macmillan, 2012), 3.

21 Nicholas Lehmann, 'Who Was W. E. B. Dubois?' (review of Kwame Anthony Appiah, *Lines of Descent: W. E. B. Du Bois and the Emergence of Identity*, Cambridge, MA: Harvard University Press, 2014) in *New York Review of Books,* September 25, 2014.

22 Bryan A. Garrett and Isabelle Rispler, 'Introduction: Mirrored Sea – Reflective Glance', *Traversea*, vol. 3 (2013): 1.

23 Paul Gilroy, *The Black Atlantic: Modernity and Double Consciousness* (Cambridge, MA: Harvard University Press, 1992/London: Verso, 1993).

24 Gilroy, *Black Atlantic*, xi.

25 Gloria Valere, meeting with author, Port of Spain, Trinidad, 23 September 2016.

26 See Kwame Anthony Appiah, *Lines of Descent: W. E. B. Du Bois and the Emergence of Identity* (Boston: Harvard University Press, 2014).

27 Stuart Hall (with Bill Schwarz), *Familiar Stranger: A Life Between Two Islands* (London: Allen Lane, 2017), 140.

28 C. L. R. James, *Beyond a Boundary* (London: Hutchinson, 1963).

29 James Walvin, *Making the Black Atlantic: Britain and the African Diaspora* (London: Cassell, 2000).

30 Walvin, *Black Atlantic*, 169.

31 John Arlott, 'Lord Learie Constantine: The Spontaneous Cricketer', *Wisden Cricketers' Almanack* (London: Sporting Handbooks, 1972), 125–29. Also David Killingray, 'Learie Constantine,' in David Dabydeen, John Gilmore and Cecily Jones (eds), *The Oxford Companion to Black British History* (Oxford: Oxford University Press, 2007), 114–16. Ernest Cashmore, in his full-length book *Black Sportsmen* (London: Routledge and Kegan Paul, 1982), which explores the successes and failures of black men in the world of sport, surprisingly makes no reference to Constantine. His historical chapter concentrates chiefly on boxing and athletics; cricket receives scant comment (pp. 11–42).

32 Constantine himself provided some autobiographical material in *Cricket and I* (London: Philip Allan, 1933) and *Cricket in the Sun* (London: Stanley Paul, n.d., c. 1946).

33 Undine Giuseppe, *A Look at Learie Constantine* (London: Thomas Nelson, 1974).

34 Gerald Howat, *Learie Constantine* (London: George Allen and Unwin, 1975). An abbreviated version can be found in Gerald M. D. Howat, 'Constantine, Learie

Nicholas, Baron Constantine (1901–1971)', *Oxford Dictionary of National Biography* (Oxford University Press, 2004).

35 Peter Mason, *Learie Constantine* (Oxford: Signal Books, 2008).

36 Usually translated as: 'Men make their own history, but they do not make it just as they please; they do not make it under circumstances chosen by themselves, but under circumstances directly encountered, given and transmitted from the past. The tradition of all the dead generations weighs like a nightmare on the brain of the living.' (Karl Marx, 'The Eighteenth Brumaire of Louis Bonaparte', in Karl Marx and Frederick Engels (eds), *Selected Works* (London: Lawrence and Wishart, 1970), 96.

37 Lord Learie Constantine Collection (hereafter CC), Heritage Library, National Library of Trinidad and Tobago (NALIS), Port of Spain, Trinidad and Tobago, WI.

38 The South African C. B. Llewellyn had played in the Lancashire League, and also with Hampshire in county cricket, before and after the 1914–18 War; though often described as a 'black cricketer', Llewellyn seems to have been of mixed race.

39 See Donald McRae, *Black and White: The Untold Story of Joe Louis and Jesse Owens* (London: Simon and Schuster, 2014 edn).

40 Ian McCourt, 'Albert Johannson: First Black Footballer to Play in the FA Cup Final', www.theguardian.com., 28 May 2015 (Accessed 12 February 2016).

41 Valerie Wint, *The Longer Run: A Daughter's Memoir of Arthur Wint* (Kingston Jamaica: Ian Randle Publishing, 2011). On E. McD. Bailey see obituary by B. C. Pires, www.theguardian.com, 8 December 2013 (Accessed 13 March 2016).

42 *Lancashire Telegraph*, 18 May 2011.

43 See Tony Judt, *Ill Fares the Land: A Treatise On Our Present Discontents* (London: Allen Lane, 2010), esp. ch. 2.

2 Trinidad

1 Eric Williams, *History of the People of Trinidad and Tobago (HPTT)* (Buffalo, NY: EWord, 1962), 167.

2 On James, for example, see *The Nation*, 4 March 1960. On the social mix in Trinidad see Bridget Brereton, *Race Relations in Colonial Trinidad* (Cambridge: Cambridge University Press, 1979).

3 See Anne Spry Rush, *Bonds of Empire: West Indians and Britishness from Victoria to Decolonization* (Oxford: Oxford University Press, 2011).

4 The word only came into general use from the end of the nineteenth century; before that the area was known simply as the West Indies.

5 Creoles were people of varying degrees of status and income who claimed a long ancestry in the West Indies. In Trinidad this comprised black inhabitants descended from slaves as well as rich planters claiming either a French or English lineage.

6 Victor Bulmer-Thomas, *The Economic History of the Caribbean since the Napoleonic Wars* (Cambridge: Cambridge University Press: 2012), 153; for Trinidad sugar see Williams, *HPTT*, ch. 12.

7 Strictly speaking 'cacao', from which cocoa is the refined product; the refining was done overseas.

8 Brereton, *Race Relations* (2002 edn), 19–20.

9 Bulmer-Thomas, *Economic History*, 237, 240.

10 Bulmer-Thomas, *Economic History*, 112.

11 Learie Constantine, *Cricket and I* (London: Philip Allan, 1933), 8.

12 Brereton, *Race Relations*, 5.

13 Stephen Howe, 'Cyril Leonard Robert James (1901–1989)', *Oxford Dictionary of National Biography* (Oxford: Oxford University Press, 2004) online edition January 2011, http://www.oxforddnb.com/view/article/59637 (Accessed 9 June 2014).

14 C. L. R. James, *Beyond a Boundary* (London: Hutchinson, 1963).

15 C. L. R. James Papers, Rare Books and Manuscripts Library, Columbia Univ. New York, MS 1529, Series 1, Correspondence 1952–1990, Box 1, Folder 1, James to Grantley Adams (n.d. c. 1961).

16 Brereton describes the Jameses as 'somewhat snobbish' (Bridget Brereton, 'Introduction', in C. L. R. James, *The Life of Captain Cipriani: An Account of British Government in the West Indies* (London: Duke University Press, 2014), 5.

17 James, *Beyond a Boundary*, 17.

18 Ibid., 26.

19 Ibid., 14.

20 Ibid., 28.

21 See Constantine's comments in *Cricket and I*, 1–3.

22 Lebrun was not a small proprietor, of which there were several in cocoa growing in the late-nineteenth century. Much small-scale production had developed when the five-year contract system had been introduced in the 1860s. (Frances L. Bekele, 'The History of Cocoa Production in Trinidad and Tobago', in L. A. Wilson (ed.), *Re-Vitalisation of the Trinidad and Tobago Cocoa Industry* (Proceedings of the APAST Seminar-Exhibition, St Augustine, Trinidad, September 2003), 2–3.

23 *Saturday Chronicle and News* (Manchester), 15 September 1962.

24 Hinds later removed permanently to New York, and did well.

25 See ch. 3.

26 See Jeff Stollmeyer, *Everything Under the Sun: My Life in West Indies Cricket* (London: Stanley Paul, 1983).

27 James, *Beyond a Boundary*, 56.

28 Ibid., 61.

29 See Roy Marshall, *Test Outcast* (London: Pelham Books, 1970), 10–15.

30 Ibid., 11–23.

31 Brian Stoddart, 'Cricket and Colonialism in the English-Speaking Caribbean to 1914: Towards a Cultural Analysis', in Hilary McD. Beckles and Brian Stoddart (eds), *Liberation Cricket: West Indies Cricket Culture* (Manchester: Manchester University Press, 1995), 15–23.

32 Ibid., 25.

33 C. L. R. James, 'The Case for West Indian Self Government', in *The Life of Captain Cipriani*, 177, 181.

34 Bridget Brereton, *A History of Modern Trinidad 1783–1962* (London: Heinemann, 1981), 137–42.

35 Williams, *HPTT*, 181–88.

36 James, 'Case for West Indian Self-Government', 192.

37 Brereton, *History of Modern Trinidad*, 157–61.

38 Howard Johnson, 'The British Caribbean from Demobilization to Constitutional Decolonization', in Judith M. Brown and Wm. Roger Louis (eds), *The Oxford History of the British Empire, volume IV, The Twentieth Century* (Oxford: Oxford University Press, 1999), 604.

39 Brereton, *History of Modern Trinidad*, 170.

40 See O. Nigel Bolland, *On the March: Labour Rebellions in the Caribbean, 1934–39* (Kingston: Ian Randle, 2001); Johnson, 'British Caribbean from Demobilization', 603–15. One consequence of these initiatives was the wartime scheme of West Indian voluntary workers in Britain, on which Learie Constantine was employed in Liverpool (see ch. 6).

41 Gerald Howat, *Learie Constantine* (London: George Allen and Unwin, 1975), 33–34.

42 Constantine, *Cricket and I*, 17.

43 Ibid.

44 Howat, *Constantine*, 43.

45 Often referred to as 'Constantine Jnr' or 'Young Constantine' – e.g. *Port of Spain Gazette* (*POSG*), 4 March 1923.

46 Constantine, *Cricket and I*, 20.

47 *Wisden Cricketers' Almanack* (London, 1940) www.espncricinfo.com/wisdenalmanack/content/story/154641.html (Accessed 24 November 2014). He was nominated as one of the Five Cricketer of the Year for 1939. In 1923 one newspaper reporter, Fuller Pilch Jr, praised him for his enthusiasm in the field and his range of strokes (*POSG*, 8 July 1923).

48 *POSG*, 30 January 1927.

49 Constantine, *Cricket and I*, 93.

50 *POSG*, 12 July 1928.

51 Brereton, *History of Modern Trinidad*, 199–200.

52 P. E. T. O'Connor, *Some Trinidad Yesterdays* (Trinidad: Imprint Caribbean, 1975), 73.

53   Arthur Calder Marshall, *Glory Dead* (London: Michael Joseph, 1939), 244.

54   Howat attributes this to the intercession of the Trinidad batsman Joe Small, who was himself employed there as a store man (Howat, *Learie Constantine*, 45).

55   James comes close to this: his much-quoted statement that Constantine 'revolted against the revolting contrast between his first-class status as a cricketer and his third-class status as a man' suggests it (James, *Beyond a Boundary*, 110).

56   For example, Simon Featherstone, *Postcolonial Cultures* (Edinburgh: Edinburgh University Press, 2005), 80–84.

57   *POSG*, 12 July 1928.

58   The fund reached £750 by early September, but by this time Constantine had accepted the Nelson offer (*POSG*, 4 September 1928). It stood at £850 when closed at the beginning of October (*POSG* 1 October 1928).

59   *POSG*, 22 July 1928.

60   Ibid.

61   National Library of Trinidad and Tobago (NALIS), Constantine Collection, 2200, F. Grant to J. E. Scheult, 2 August 1929.

3 Cricket

1   See Anthony Bateman and Jeffrey Hill (eds), *The Cambridge Companion to Cricket* (Cambridge: Cambridge University Press, 2011), 1–10.

2   On cricket aesthetic see Anthony Bateman, *Cricket, Literature and Culture: Symbolising the Nation, Destabilising Empire* (Farnham: Ashgate, 2009).

3   Explored by Geoffrey Levett, ' "Englishmen Who Happen to Reside in the West Indies": Early West Indian Cricket Tours and Imperial Identity', paper delivered to British Society of Sport History seminar, Senate House, London, 27 January 2014. Levett has noted the tendency of white observers to ascribe to black cricketers a failure in temperament, most readily seen in fielding where a lack of concentration could lead to slipshod play. (Unpublished draft chapter 'Empire, sport and race in 1906 – West Indian cricketers in England', kindly supplied by the author.)

4   Neville Cardus, *Good Days* (London: Rupert Hart-Davis, 1948 edn), 33.

5   C. L. R. James, *Beyond a Boundary* (London: Stanley Paul, 1969 edn), 107.

6   Quoted in *Nelson Leader,* 6 July 1928.

7   Cardus, *Good Days,* 33.

8   See descriptions of innings by Constantine and Headley in *Blackburn Times*, 6 August 1937. For a fuller discussion of representations of West Indian cricketers by British writers see Anthony Bateman, *Cricket, Literature and Culture: Symbolising the Nation, Destabilising Empire* (Farnham: Ashgate Publishing Ltd, 2009), 158–61.

9   He did not invent high-class fielding; there were others before him – in particular, Gilbert Jessop, Jack Hobbs, and 'Nip' Pellew of Australia.

10 Benny Green (ed.), *The Wisden Book of Cricketers' Lives* (London: MacDonald Queen Anne Press, 1986), 178.

11 *Observer*, 3 July 1971.

12 Cardus, *Good Days*, 33–34.

13 *Nelson Leader*, 14 May 1937. It was also an attempt to forestall the possibility of Constantine's leaving the Lancashire League in favour of other northern leagues, where he had been made offers.

14 *Nelson Leader*, 26 April 1963. A letter to the BBC, sent in 1950 by an anonymous well-wisher from Southampton, praises Constantine on a recent broadcast. The writer adds: 'It was watching you in the field that amazed me. I have never seen anything quite like it.' (BBC Written Archives Centre [BBCWAC], Caversham Park, Reading; Constantine File, Talks 1, 30 June 1950.)

15 *Nelson Leader*, 19 April 1963.

16 See Colin Holmes, *John Bull's Island: Immigration and British Society, 1871–1971* (Basingstoke: Macmillan, 1988), 152–60; Stuart Hall, 'The Spectacle of the "Other"', in Stuart Hall (ed.), *Representation: Cultural Representations and Signifying Practices* (London: Sage Publications, 1997): ch. 4.

17 See Richard D. E. Burton, 'Cricket, Carnival and Street Culture' and Hilary McD. Beckles and Harclyde Walcott, 'Redemption Sounds: Music, Literature and Popular Ideology of West Indian Cricket Crowds', in Hilary McD. Beckles and Brian Stoddart (eds), *Liberation Cricket: West Indies Cricket Culture* (Manchester: Manchester University Press, 1995), chs. 5 and 22.

18 Beckles and Walcott, 'Redemption Sounds', 377.

19 See Jeffrey Hill, 'War, Remembrance and Sport: "Abide With Me" and the FA Cup Final in the 1920s', in Anthony Bateman and John Bale (eds), *Sporting Sounds: Relationships Between Sport and Music* (London: Routledge, 2009), ch. 9.

20 See Eddie Chambers, *Roots Culture: Cultural Politics in the Making of Black Britain* (London: I. B. Tauris, 2017).

21 Learie Constantine, 'Backwoodsmen on Tour', in A. A. Thomas (ed.), *Daily Worker Cricket Handbook 1950* (London: People's Printing Society), 9–14.

22 Marylebone Cricket Club, *MCC Cricket Coaching Book* (London: Naldrett Press, 1952), 7. Emphasis added.

23 Interview with James from the film *Every Cook Can Govern: The Life, Impact and Works of C. L. R. James*, Ceri Dingle and Rob Harris (London: Worldwide, 2016).

24 James, *Beyond a Boundary*, 191ff.

25 Neville Cardus, *Autobiography* (London: Readers' Union, 1949), 32.

26 Ibid., 182.

27 Jack Williams, *Cricket and England: A Cultural and Social History of the Inter-war Years* (London: Frank Cass, 1999).

28 P. F. Warner, *Imperial Cricket* (London: London and Counties Press Association, 1912), 450ff.

29   *Wisden Cricketers' Almanack*, 1929, www.espncricinfo.com/wisdenalmanack/
     content/story/151885.html (Accessed 24 November 2014).

30   See Keith A. P. Sandiford and Brian Stoddart, 'The Elite Schools and Cricket
     in Barbados: A Study in Colonial Continuity', in Beckles and Stoddart (eds),
     Liberation Cricket, 44–60.

31   James, *Beyond a Boundary*, ch. 2.

32   P. F. Warner, *Cricket in Many Climes* (London: William Heinemann, 1900), 5.

33   *Cricket*, 15 February 1913.

34   Both were considered to be very effective by Pelham Warner: 'quite unplayable'
     against Lord Hawke's team in 1897. Woods, who only took two steps to the wicket,
     had a low, slinging delivery, while Cumberbatch (thought the better of the two by
     Warner) was medium pace 'with a little work both ways.' (Warner, *Cricket in Many
     Climes*, 21–27.)

35   David Frith, *The Fast Men: A 200-Year Cavalcade of Speed Bowlers* (London: Corgi,
     1984 edn), 110. But Constantine's descriptions of George John before 1914 cast
     some doubt on how far this convention was honoured (see fn 56).

36   An intriguing piece in the *Sunday Dispatch,* reporting the arrival of the West Indies
     touring party to England in 1939, notes that the paper's racing correspondent,
     'Keystone', 'can recall as if it were yesterday' Constantine ('the black streak') playing
     as a boy for the 5th Battalion British West Indies Regiment in Egypt during the
     1914–18 War (*Sunday Dispatch*, 7 May 1939). I can find no other reference to
     this in any other account of Constantine's life. He would have been no more than
     seventeen at the time.

37   James, *Beyond a Boundary*, ch. 7; Simon Featherstone, 'Late Cuts: C. L. R. James,
     Cricket and Postcolonial England', *Sport in History*, vol. 31, 1 (2011): 49–61.

38   L. N. Constantine, *Cricket and I* (London: Philip Allan, 1933), 19; James, *Beyond a
     Boundary*, 60–64.

39   *Wisden Cricketers' Almanack*, 1929, www.espncricinfo.com/wisdenalmanack/
     content/story/151885.html. (Accessed 24 November 2014).

40   Rhodes was not in practice an all-rounder; he played (for Yorkshire and for
     England) as *either* a specialist batsman *or* a bowler, never both. Jessop is the closest
     to Constantine in the explosive manner of his play (see Gerald Brodribb, *The
     Croucher: the Biography of Gilbert Jessop* [London: Constable, n.d., c. 1985]).

41   *The Australian Cricketer*, 22 December 1930, 5.

42   See, for example, Learie Constantine, *The Coloured Catapult* (London: Pathe
     Super Gazette, b/w, 1928, 2 mins); R. C. Robertson Glasgow, *Cricket Prints: Some
     Batsmen and Bowlers, 1920–1940* (London: T. Werner Laurie, 1943), 123–24;
     Michael Manley, *A History of West Indies Cricket* (London: Pan Books, 1990 edn),
     27–28, 50–52.

43   NALIS, Constantine Collection (CC), unattributed press cutting, 6 August 1971,
     Box 19300/19387, JLB.

44 R. C. Robertson-Glasgow, *Cricket Prints*, 123.

45 Before the First World War one black player, C. A. Ollivierre, had emigrated to England and played county cricket with Derbyshire. (See Simon Lister, *Fire in Babylon: How the West Indies Cricket Team Brought a People to Its Feet*, London: Yellow Jersey Press, 2015, 85–89). S. G. Smith, a white man, had played for Northants. (See James, *Beyond a Boundary*, 96.)

46 Constantine, *Cricket and I*, 78.

47 'Bodyline' was a press term for the hostile, short-pitched fast bowling of this period. Many cricketers, especially those who practised it, preferred the more anodyne term 'fast leg theory'.

48 Patrick F. McDevitt, 'Bodyline, Jardine and Masculinity', in Bateman and Hill (eds), *Cambridge Companion to Cricket*, 73.

49 Constantine's assertion that George John had bowled bodyline to five men on the leg side in the islands before the War was queried by Arthur Somerset, the author of the chapter on the West Indies in Pelham Warner's *Imperial Cricket*, in a letter to Constantine: 'I have no recollection of it … according to my recollection he always bowled to slips.' (CC, 1500/1583, Somerset to Constantine, 23 July 1934). Somerset remarked that Learie would only have been a small boy at the time. In *Cricket and I* Constantine said that he heard it from 'my father and other cricketers'. (*Cricket and I*, 181.)

50 *Cricket and I*, 181, 183–88; Undine Giuseppe, *A Look at Learie Constantine* (London: Thomas Nelson, 1974), 56–58. Constantine admitted to a long-standing feud between himself and Hammond, beginning in 1925 and not patched up until 1933. It was partly to do with Constantine's fast bowling, which Hammond felt was too hostile, but seems also to have been sparked off (according to Constantine) by an air of racial superiority on Hammond's part. (Learie Constantine, *Cricketers' Carnival*, London: Stanley Paul, n.d., c. 1950, 37–38.)

51 David Foot, *Wally Hammond: the Reasons Why* (London: Robson Books, 1998 edn), 115.

52 'Notes by the Editor', *Wisden Cricketers' Almanack*, 1929, www.espncricinfo.com/wisdenalmanack/content/story/151774.html (Accessed 25 November 2014).

53 Constantine, *Cricket and I*, 184.

54 Ibid., 193.

55 Ibid.,197.

56 Jack Williams, *Cricket and Race* (Oxford: Berg, 2001), ch. 5; Simon Lister, *Fire in Babylon*, pp. 93–97; Chambers, *Roots and Culture*, ch. 8.

57 CC, 1900/1962, script for BBC Northern Programme talk on 'Cricket', with L. N. Constantine and H. D. Davies. Constantine's interviewer was 'Donny' Davies, later of the *Manchester Guardian* newspaper, who was killed in the Munich air disaster of 1958.

4 Nelson

1 *Nelson Leader*, 7 August, 9 October 1914.

2 Jeffrey Hill, *Nelson: Politics, Economy, Community* (Edinburgh: Keele University Press, 1997), ch. 2.

3 Hill, *Nelson*, 117–19.

4 *Nelson Leader*, 23 July 1937.

5 *Athletic News*, 27 March 1922.

6 *Nelson Leader*, 17 March 1922.

7 Neville Cardus, *The Summer Game: A Cricketer's Journal* (London: Rupert Hart-Davis, 1949), 183.

8 *Nelson Leader*, 13 April 1922.

9 Nelson Cricket Club, *Treasurer's Annual Accounts*, 1922–24 (Nelson Cricket Club); *Cricketer Annual* (London: The Cricketer, 1922–3), 95.

10 Nelson Cricket Club, *Balance Sheet for Season 1924* (Nelson CC). In 1928 Nelson Cricket Club was some £3000 in debt, part of which was underwritten by local manufacturers as a form of welfare provision. Committee members of the club had nonetheless to pledge themselves to repay the bank if club funds were insufficient. The arrival of Constantine ensured that this situation did not arise. See *Nelson Leader*, 13 September 1929; *The Cricketer Annual* (London: The Cricketer, 1929–30), 66. Also interview with K. Hartley, 20 September 2000.

11 *Nelson Leader*, 13 July 1928.

12 Ibid., 8 August 1919.

13 Many are related to reactions from children: e.g. they expect the black to come off when he shakes their hand; 'Uncle Learie – nobody ever told me you were a black man'; "'As ta bin down t'coal 'ole, Mister?'"

14 *Lancashire Evening Telegraph*, 13 June 1989.

15 For a suggestion that racial taunts on sports grounds were to be heard long before the era of black footballers see *Nelson Gazette*, 30 August 1938. Also *Lancashire Evening Telegraph*, 13 June, 11 July 1989; Don Howarth, *Figures in a Landscape: a Lancashire Childhood* (London: Methuen, 1987), 28–30. I am grateful to Jack Williams for some of these references. Alan Tomlinson has recorded a former Colne player as saying: 'a black chap, it didn't matter … 'e were an attraction as a cricketer if 'e were a good 'un.' Alan Tomlinson, 'Good Times, Bad Times, and the Politics of Leisure: Working-Class Culture in the 1930s in a Small Northern England Working-Class Community', in R. S. Gruneau (ed.), *Leisure, Sport and Working-Class Cultures: Theory and Practice*. Working Papers in the Sociological Study of Sports and Leisure Studies (Kingston, Ontario: Queen's University, 1984), 78.

16 A club that for many years employed only white professionals.

17 *Lancashire Evening Telegraph*, 11 July 1989.

18 Brian Bearshaw, *From the Stretford End: the Official History Lancashire County Cricket Club* (London: Partridge Press, 1990), 271; *Manchester Evening News*, interview with Len Hopwood, 9 July 1975.

19 See *Nelson Gazette*, 7 September 1943. Driver material made available courtesy of Nelson Public Library.

20 BBC Written Archives Centre (BBCWAC), 'Tonight's Talk', BBC Home Service, 3 September 1943, microfilm T. 89.

21 Ibid.

22 *Nelson Leader*, 6 July 1928, 12 April 1929.

23 Learie Constantine, *Cricket in the Sun* (London: Stanley Paul, n.d.), 11.

24 *Nelson Leader*, 13 September 1929.

25 Ibid., 20 September 1929.

26 It was the club's best ever season in financial terms. Over £2,300 was taken in home gate receipts, and £2,600 on the grounds of opposing clubs. (Ibid., 13 September 1929.)

27 See Gerald Howat, Learie Constantine (London: George Allen and Unwin, 1975), 75–80.

28 Richard Hoggart, *The Uses of Literacy: Aspects of Working-Class Life with Special Reference to Publications and Entertainments* (London: Pelican, 1958 edn), 80–83, 178, 294–97.

29 Hill, *Nelson*, 96.

30 C. L. R. James, *Beyond a Boundary* (London: Stanley Paul, 1969 edn), 127. See also *Nelson Leader*, 27 May 1932.

31 I am grateful to Malcolm MacLean for offering this reading of the anecdote.

32 *Nelson Leader*, 23 April 1937.

33 Ibid., 10 September 1937.

34 BBCWAC, 'Fields of Work and Play', North of England Home Service, 17 March 1946, m/f T89. Also script for 'Tonight's Talk', 3 September 1943. Constantine admitted to feeling 'at home' in Nelson, which he did not want to leave for Liverpool, where his wartime job was based.

35 *Nelson Leader*, 15 February 1963.

36 *Trinidad Guardian*, 6 January 1942.

37 Elias played as an amateur for Rochdale in 1937. On occasions a brilliant bat (a century in less than an hour against Crompton, for example, included eight sixes and seven fours) but he was inconsistent. (*Rochdale Observer*, 11 September 1937.)

38 Gloria Valere (GV) meeting, Port of Spain, 23 September 2016.

39 See Chapter 5.

40 BBCWAC, Norma Constantine, 'I Married a Cricketer', Light Programme, 20 November 1950.

41 GV meeting.

42 See *Trinidad Guardian*, 5 September 1971.

43 *Nelson Leader*, 4 June 1937.

44 Ibid., 27 August 1937.

45 *Blackburn Times*, 6 August 1937.

46 *Nelson Leader*, 20 August 1937.

47 NALIS, Constantine Collection (CC), 1300, Morgan to Constantine, 6 September, 1937.

48 *Nelson Leader*, 10 September 1937.

49 In 1938 he wrote for both the *Manchester Evening Chronicle* and the *Yorkshire Evening News* (Leeds), receiving as much as four guineas for 600 words.

50 The large crowds that could be expected at League grounds ensured a profitable collection for a player who scored 50 or took five wickets (and in some cases three catches). Buckets were taken around the ground for spectators to throw in whatever loose change they could afford. Professionals were often expected to take the proceeds home in the actual coinage donated.

51 Information partly based on an interview with Mr Ken Hartley, Nelson, 20 September 2000.

52 Lord Constantine, 'To the Lords … via Coconut Bat and Secondhand Car', in Ian Wooldridge (ed.), *The International Cavaliers' Cricket Book* (London: Purnell, 1969), 65. I am grateful to Dr Neil Carter for drawing my attention to this piece.

53 *The Cricketer Spring Annual* (London: The Cricketer, 1937), 105.

54 G. A. Brooking, 'Northern Notes', *The Cricketer Winter Annual* (London: The Cricketer, 1921–22), 124; *The Cricketer*, 19 May, 2 June 1934; *Nelson Leader*, 17 March 1922.

55 *Nelson Leader*, 14 May 1937. Two years earlier the President of the League had pointed out that matches involving Nelson had raised almost half of the total gate receipts in all matches in the 1933 season. (*Nelson Leader*, 2 February 1934.)

56 Tony Mason, *Association Football and English Society, 1863–1915* (Brighton: Harvester, 1981), 111–15; Ross McKibbin, *Classes and Cultures: England 1918–1951* (Oxford: Oxford University Press, 1998), 335–39.

57 Constantine, *Cricket and I*, 139.

58 CC, 1625, report of an interview given by Constantine to the *Lancashire Daily Post* (n.d. 1934) saying that he had not decided to join either Rochdale or Blackpool.

59 Ibid., 16251, 16367, 16541 – scrapbook 'Newspaper Cuttings 1933'– the date is approximate; Rochdale offered £800 for a season (CC, 1900/1911, Fred Berry to Constantine, 14 June 1937; Berry to T. A. Higson, 16 June 1937; C.C. 1900/1924, Berry to Constantine, 19 June 1937 – 'When you interviewed my Committee the verbal agreement between the Club and yourself was so amicably arranged that it is now difficult to understand the present position.'

60 Ibid., 1300/1313–32.

61 Ibid., 1300/1328, Constantine to George Close, 14 June 1937.

62   He later admitted that he had not been very happy at Rochdale (BBCWAC, 'Fields of Work and Play', North of England Home Service, 17 March 1946 (m/f T89).

63   CC, 1335, Constantine to Mintoft, 11 July 1938.

64   Ibid., 1347, Constantine to A. L. Taylor, 17 September 1938.

65   Chris Harte, *A History of Australian Cricket* (London: Andre Deutsch, 1993), 328–9.

66   Marylebone Cricket Club (MCC) Archives, Lord's Cricket Ground, London, West Indies Tour of the British Isles, 1939 (MCC/CRI/5/2/18): Constantine to Mallett, 6 April 1938.

67   Mallett had been anxious to keep the arrangement with Constantine confidential lest it 'embarrass the WI Board in their negotiations with other players'. (MCC/CRI/5/2/18): Mallett to John Dare, 16 December 1937; Martindale to Dare, 24 June 1938; Mallett to Dare, 30 August 1938). See also Richard Bentley, *Nightwatchman*, 7 (Autumn 2014): 36–41.

68   Higson to Mallett, 1 December 1937 (MCC/CRI/5/2/18.)

69   CC, 145000, in a BBC radio broadcast 'Frankly Speaking'.

70   Ibid., 2200/2201, Constantine to Mallett, 14 February 1939; 2300/2389, Constantine to Martindale, 17 October 1938; 2394, Martindale to Constantine, 18 October 1938; 2395, Constantine to Martindale, 21 October 1938; 2396, Martindale to Constantine, 23 October 1938; 2397, Constantine to Martindale, 26 October 1938.

71   Ibid., 2300/2396, Martindale to Constantine, 23 October 1938; 2300/2397, Constantine to Martindale, 26 October 1938.

72   *The Times*, 23 August 1939.

73   *Sunday Times*, 20 August 1939.

5   Writer

1   Richard Holt has pointed out that, while cricket had a 'large and literate upper and middle class following', professional football was watched largely by working-class men who did not, publishers assumed, buy books. Hence the relative paucity of professional footballers' autobiographies until the second half of the twentieth century. (Richard Holt, 'The Legend of Jackie Milburn and the Life of Godfrey Brown', in John Bale, Mette K. Christensen and Gertrud Pfister (eds), *Writing Lives in Sport: Biographies, Life Histories and Methods* (Aarhus: Aarhus University Press, 2004), 157–70.)

2   See Chapters 7 and 8 for a discussion of these titles.

3   In an interview in the 1960s, Constantine described himself as having been 'a terrific reader of cricket history'. ('Calypso for Constantine': Sir Learie Constantine MBE talks with Lewis Nkosi', directed by Malcolm Brown, BBC 1 Television, 1966.)

4   Chris Searle 'Race Before Wicket: Cricket, Empire and the White Rose', in Chris
     Searle, *Pitch of Life: Writings on Cricket* (Manchester: Parrs Wood Press, 2001), 1–22.

5   Hilary McD. Beckles, 'The Political Ideology of West Indies Cricket', in Hilary
     McD. Beckles and Brian Stoddart, *Liberation Cricket: West Indies Cricket Culture*
     (Manchester: Manchester University Press, 1995), 148–61.

6   'The Ideology of West Indies Cricket', paper presented to Caribbean Studies
     Association conference, Port of Spain, Trinidad, May, 1990, 14 http://ufdc.ufl.edu//
     CA00400070/00001 (Accessed 14 April 2014).

7   Everton Weekes, *Mastering the Craft: Ten Years of Weekes 1948–1958*
     (Jamaica: Universities of the Caribbean Press, 2007), 85.

8   C. L. R. James, *Beyond a Boundary* (London: Stanley Paul 1969 edn), 112.

9   L. N. Constantine, *Cricket and I* (London: Philip Allan, 1933).

10 Few books had done this. P. F. Warner's *Imperial Cricket* (London: London and
     Counties Press Association, 1912) and his autobiographical *Cricket in Many Climes*
     (London: William Heinemann, 1900) were probably the best.

11 NALIS, Constantine Collection (CC), boxes 17391, 17453, 17468, 17472, 17473.

12 Beckles, 'Political Ideology', 152.

13 See Chapter 3.

14 Simon Featherstone, *Postcolonial Cultures* (Edinburgh: Edinburgh University Press,
     2005), 84.

15 Gerald Howat, *Learie Constantine* (London: George Allen and Unwin, 1975), 79.

16 Jeffrey Hill, *Nelson: Politics, Economy, Community* (Edinburgh: Keele University
     Press, 1997), chs. 4 and 6.

17 Howat, *Learie Constantine*, 79.

18 CC, box 14500, BBC radio broadcast with Rex Alston, 29 June 1967.

19 Hill, *Nelson*, 123–24; Jeffrey Hill, 'League Cricket in the North and Midlands',
     in Richard Holt (ed.) *Sport and the Working Class in Modern Britain*
     (Manchester: Manchester University Press, 1990), 121–41.

20 *The Keys,* vol. 1, 1 (July 1933): 1

21 Christian John Hogsbjerg, 'C. L. R. James in Imperial Britain, 1932–38'
     (unpublished PhD thesis, University of York, 2009), 158–61.

22 Howat, *Learie Constantine*, 77–78.

23 *The Keys,* vol. 1, 1 (July 1933): 9.

24 *The Keys,* vol. 5, 1 (July–September 1937): 2, 5; vol. 5, 2 (October–December
     1937): 32, 60.

25 *The Keys,* vol. 5, 4 (April–June 1938): 80–82.

26 Constantine, *Cricket and I*, Author's Foreword.

27 James, *Beyond a Boundary*, 114.

28 Kent Worcester, *C. L. R. James: A Political Biography* (Albany, NY: SUNY Press,
     1996), 15.

29 C. L. R. James, 'The Bloomsbury Atmosphere', in Nicholas Laughlin (ed.), *Letters from London: Seven Essays by C. L. R. James* (Oxford: Signal Books, 2003), 19–34.

30 Frank Rosengarten, *Urbane Revolutionary: C. L. R. James and the Struggle for a New Society* (Jackson, MS: University of Mississippi Press, 2008), ch. 2.

31 James, *Beyond a Boundary*, 105.

32 Ibid., 108.

33 Ibid., 117–19.

34 Anthony Bateman, *Cricket, Literature and Culture: Symbolising the Nation, Destabilising Empire* (Farnham: Ashgate, 2009), 289.

35 Bridget Brereton, 'Introduction', in C. L. R. James (ed.), *The Life of Captain Cipriani: An Account of British Government in the West Indies* (Durham: Duke University Press, 2014), 1.

36 James, *Beyond a Boundary*, 115–17.

37 Ibid., 114, 119.

38 His personal library collection does include Trotsky's 'Revolution Betrayed' and a work on communism by Walter Kolartz. As against these there are many more books on religious themes (CC, 18000, 19000 series).

39 James did acknowledge, in pieces sent to the *Port of Spain Gazette*, the militant spirit of Nelson people, shown in a well-supported boycott of cinema attendance against the attempt to reduce the wages of cinema staff. (James, 'The Nucleus of a Great Civilisation' *Letters From London*, 123–25.)

40 Hogsbjerg, 'C. L. R. James in Imperial Britain', 86–88.

41 Learie Constantine, *Cricket in the Sun* (London: Stanley Paul, n.d., c. 1946).

42 Norman Baker, 'A More Even Playing Field? Sport During and After the War', in Nick Hayes and Jeff Hill (eds), *'Millions Like Us?: British Culture in the Second World War'* (Liverpool: Liverpool University Press, 1999), 125–55.

43 Constantine, *Cricket in the Sun*, 36–38.

44 Tony Collins, *Rugby's Great Split: Class, Culture and the Origins of Rugby League Football* (London: Routledge, 1998).

45 See Jeffrey Hill, ' "First-Class" Cricket and the Leagues: some notes on the development of English cricket, 1900–1940', *International Journal of the History of Sport*, vol. 4, 1 (1987): 68–81.

46 It is often claimed that Constantine's test career was affected by playing in Lancashire between 1929 and 1938. He appeared in eighteen tests altogether, only three fewer than George Headley, who had the most appearances for the West Indies before the 1939–45 War. Fifteen of Constantine's test matches took place after he had gone to play in the northern leagues. He had also played in several international matches in the 1920s that did not have 'test' status.

47 Constantine, *Cricket in the Sun*, 62. Similar comments were repeated in Learie Constantine, *Cricket Crackers* (London: Stanley Paul, n.d., c. 1949), 170–74, where he added observations on religious discrimination in Indian cricket.

48 Ibid., 63.

49 Stuart's headed notepaper proclaimed him as 'Freelance Contributor to the Press of the British Empire and the United States' (CC, 2865).

50 Ibid.

51 Ibid., 2897, Frank Stuart to Constantine, 3 March 1947.

52 Ibid., 2840, Stuart to Constantine, 23 March 1947.

53 Richard Holt, *Sport and the British: A Modern History* (Oxford: Clarendon Press, 1992 edn), 286–87.

54 Jack Williams, *Cricket and England: A Cultural and Social History of the Inter-war Years* (London: Frank Cass, 1999), 161.

55 Derek Birley, *A Social History of English Cricket* (London: Aurum Press, 2003 edn), 269.

56 The Edgbaston test match of 1957 was a case in point, famous for the record-breaking stand of 411 by the English players May and Cowdrey, employing pad play to counteract the bowling of Ramadhin and Valentine. See Clyde Walcott's observations in Clyde Walcott with Brian Scovell, *Sixty Years on the Back Foot: the Cricketing Life of Sir Clyde Walcott* (London: Orion Books, 2000 edn), 78–80.

57 Central Council of Physical Recreation (CCPR), *Sport and the Community* (London: CCPR, 1960).

58 Learie Constantine, *Cricketers' Cricket* (London: Eyre and Spottiswoode, 1949), 223.

59 Learie Constantine, *Cricketers' Carnival* (London: Stanley Paul, n.d., c. 1949–50).

60 CC, 2600.

61 Helen Tiffin, 'Cricket, Literature and the Politics of De-colonisation: The case of C. L. R. James', in Beckles and Stoddart, *Liberation Cricket*, 364.

62 Frank Birbalsingh, 'Learie Constantine: The Writer', *Caribbean Quarterly*, vol. 30, 2 (June 1984): 60–75.

63 Learie Constantine, *Cricketers' Cricket*, 81–82.

64 Constantine, *How to Play Cricket* 158.

65 Learie N. Constantine, *How to Play Cricket* (London: Eyre and Spottiswoode, 1951), 21.

66 Ibid., 37.

67 Ibid., 90.

68 Learie Constantine, *The Young Cricketer's Companion* (London: Souvenir Press, 1964), 202–3.

69 Constantine, *Cricketers' Cricket*, 262.

70 Constantine, *Young Cricketer's Companion*, 203.

71 Foreword to John Clarke and Brian Scovell, *Everything that's cricket; the West Indies tour 1966* (London: Stanley Paul, 1966), 11. 'The West Indies were zestful; England were lethargic by comparison' (12).

72 Learie Constantine, 'Cricket in the Sun', in Learie Constantine and Denzil Batchelor (eds), *The Changing Face of Cricket* (London: Eyre and Spottiswoode, 1966), 71–140.

73 Ibid., 68.

74 Ibid., 'Cricket in the Sun', 125.

75 Peter Mason, *Learie Constantine* (Oxford: Signal Books, 2008), viii.

76 Birbalsingh, 'Constantine: the Writer', 61–62.

77 Ibid., 70.

78 Constantine, *How to Play*, 146, 154.

79 Stephen Greenblatt, *Renaissance Self-Fashioning: From More to Shakespeare* (London: University of Chicago Press, 1984 edn), 1.

6 Race Relations

1 John Denvir, *The Irish in Britain: From the Earliest Times to the Fall and Death of Parnell* (London: Kegan, Paul, Trench, Trubner, 1992), 119.

2 Ray Costello, *Black Liverpool: The Early History of Britain's Oldest Black Community 1730–1918* (Liverpool: Picton Press, 2001), ch. 1.

3 John Belchem, *Before the Windrush: Race Relations in Twentieth-Century Liverpool* (Liverpool: Liverpool University Press, 2014), 43.

4 Learie Constantine, *Colour Bar* (London: Stanley Paul, 1954), 147. The general development of racial problems in Liverpool in the first half of the twentieth century is best covered in Andrea Murphy, *From the Empire to the Rialto: Racism and Reaction in Liverpool 1918–1948* (Birkenhead: Liver Press, 1995).

5 See British Pathe, *Our Jamaican Problem*, film, 1955.

6 Anthony H. Richmond, *Colour Prejudice in Britain: A Study of West Indian Workers in Liverpool, 1941–1951* (London: Routledge and Kegan Paul, 1954), 101.

7 See, for example, Grace Wilkie in Stephen Bourne, *Mother Country: Britain's Black Community on the Home Front 1939–45* (Stroud: The History Press, 2010), 42–43.

8 At the beginning of the war, Elder Dempster sought to reduce labour costs by setting its wage rates at the lower levels then applying in Lagos. Protests by the seamen were answered by dismissal, and in some cases led to imprisonment under wartime legislation. (Belchem, *Before the Windrush*, 81; Murphy, *Empire to Rialto*, 92–95, 109–10.)

9 Arnold Watson, *West Indian Workers in Great Britain* (London: Hodder and Stoughton, 1942), 15–20.

10 *Liverpool Daily Post*, 23 October 1943. The Colonial Office gave £3000 for the purchase of the site, and the Board of Education 'agreed to make grants for educational work.' (The National Archives (TNA), Colonial Office (CO), 876/17, Advisory Committee on the Welfare of Colonial People in the United Kingdom (ACWUK), No. 53a, 7 October 1943).

11 Quoted in Belchem, *Before the Windrush*, 159, fn. 68. Constantine made a similar point about the suitability of the location of Stanley House in a letter to Harold Moody of the League of Coloured Peoples (NALIS, Constantine Collection (CC), 7546, Constantine to Moody, 9 September 1944).

12 An exact date is difficult to trace. Peter Mason gives October 1941, Gerald Howat says 'early 1942'. I have been unable to find any references to his date of appointment in either the Colonial Office or Ministry of Labour files. There is no doubt about the date of the termination of his contract – 31 July 1946. Work in his department had 'fallen off considerably' and it was no longer possible to continue employing him. (CC, Grey Box, folder 31, R. M. Rice to Constantine, 5 June 1946.) Shortly afterwards, Constantine joined the Colonial Office Advisory Welfare Committee.

13 See Richmond, *Colour Prejudice*, 27 for the most complete description of technician occupations.

14 In fact, from the outset of the scheme there had been doubts about the qualifications of some workers. In a report compiled in 1942, Major-General Orde Brown noted: 'One speedily notices the lack of selection among the Jamaicans … there are some whose claims to be qualified mechanics must have been passed with only a cursory verification.' (TNA, CO, 876/17, ACWUK, No. 32, 'Memorandum of a Visit Paid to West Indian Artificers in Manchester and Liverpool, 22–25 September, 1942, by Major G. St. J. Orde Browne', 9 October 1942, 2.)

15 *Learie Constantine: Welfare Worker and Cricketer* (London: Colonial Office/ Ministry of Information film, n.d., c. 1944–45). It was a silent film made for showing in places – probably chiefly the Caribbean – where sound systems were unavailable. The film is in black and white and less than ten minutes in length.

16 Watson, *West Indian Workers*, 13.

17 Ibid., 15; Richmond, *Colour Prejudice*, 37–38.

18 Richmond, *Colour Prejudice*, 39–41.

19 Watson, *West Indian Workers*, 24.

20 Ibid., 17.

21 Ibid., 23.

22 TNA, CO 876/17, 'Report on Social Conditions of Liverpool's Coloured Population by Our Travelling Secretary Mr John Carter, League of Coloured Peoples', January 1943.

23 Some were sent home: 'the removal of certain of the men was essential to the well-being of West Indies House as well as to the reputation of Colonial war workers in this country.' (TNA, CO, 876/17, ACWUK, No. 48, 6 April 1943.)

24 Watson, *West Indian Workers*, 73.

25 Richmond, *Colour Prejudice*, chs. 6 and 7.

26 Watson, *West Indian Workers*, 77–83.

27 *Liverpool Daily Post*, 19 November 1945. The US Army would not permit black soldiers to marry local white women, and thus a long-term problem of single mothers needing housing, employment and care was created.

28 The Constantines had temporarily lodged two such children at their Meredith Street home in Nelson and discovered that the children had stolen a watch and a diamond ring. Both items were later returned. (CC, Big Grey Box, folder 31.)

29 Constantine had raised £110 by late 1944. On Ekarte, see Bourne, *Mother Country*, 28–29.

30 See Constantine, *Colour Bar*, 146–48.

31 TNA, Ministry of Labour and National Service (LAB) 26/54, Watson, 18 December 1943.

32 LAB 26/54. Laing's reference to 'Negroes' was primarily directed at black US troops, though clearly covered all men of colour.

33 Ibid., 26/54, Constantine to Watson, 8 May 1944.

34 Ibid., 26/54, Leggett to Gater, 7 March 1944 (emphasis added).

35 Ibid., Gater to Leggett, 29 March 1944.

36 Ibid., Watson to J. J. Taylor, 10 May 1944.

37 Ibid., Leggett to Gater, 13 June 1944.

38 Ibid., Gater to Leggett, 23 June 1944; see also Gater to Leggett, 18 July 1944: Gater suggested the setting up, with financial help from the Colonial Office, of a non-segregated social centre in Liverpool; this idea, already being progressed in the form of Stanley House, was strongly commended by Lord Leverhulme, President of MHC, which would have a role to play in its running.

39 Belchem, *Before the Windrush*, 122. See also Eleanne Devlin, a welfare officer for coloured people in Liverpool, on aspects of race prejudice immediately after the War (*Daily Mirror*, 12 October 1945).

40 Belchem, *Before the Windrush*, 123–25, 139–41; David Olusoga, *Black and British: A Forgotten History* (London: Macmillan, 2016), 496–97.

41 Constantine, *Colour Bar*, 148.

42 TNA, CO, 137/866/9/3, 3, Governor of Jamaica to Secretary of State Colonies, June 1946; administrative arrangements for re-settlement are outlined in the pamphlet 'Measures for the Establishment in Civil Life of Ex-service Men and Women and Munition Workers' (Kingston: 1946). The Colonial Office placed the responsibility for dealing with the problems on the local authorities (TNA, CO, 137/866/6/8, 27 June 1946).

43 See, for example, Peter Fryer, *Staying Power: The History of Black People in Britain* (London: Pluto Press, 2010 edn), 364–7; Olusoga, *Black and British*, 487–8; Anne Spry Rush, 'Imperial Identity in Coloured Minds: Harold Moody and the League of Coloured Peoples, 1931–50', *Twentieth Century British History*, vol. 13, 4 (2002): 356–83.

44 It is not clear who this was: Arnold Watson, according to Howat, *Constantine,* 136, 'probably Sam Morris', according to Mason, *Constantine*, 96. It was most likely the former.

45 Constantine, *Colour Bar*, 137.

46 *Nelson Leader*, 10 September 1943.

47 *Liverpool Echo*, 2 September 1943.

48 TNA, LAB 26/54, Watson, 'West Indian Trainees and Technicians: Discrimination', 24 July 1944.

49 *Daily Mirror*, 4 September 1943.

50 *Manchester Guardian*, 4 September 1943.

51 *Evening Standard*, 3 September 1943.

52 Interestingly, in the light of Constantine's experience, the LCP, which had previously favoured an educational process to combat racial discrimination, now called for government action to introduce a law against it. (LCP, *Newsletter*, 48, vol. 8, September 1943.)

53 H. Montgomery Hyde, *Norman Birkett: The Life of Lord Birkett of Ulverston* (London: Reprint Society, 1964), 487.

54 Spry Rush, 'Imperial Identity': 380. A rare note of criticism of Constantine's action was voiced by C. O'Conner, Director of Overseas Programme Services at the BBC. He felt the case had been a mistake, with Constantine awarded minimal damages but faced with legal costs. It would have been better, thought O'Conner, to have left it for protest through the press and Parliament to work its effects. He added: 'Were the Colonial Office behind the case, I wonder? It would be a nice gesture if they paid the heavy bill.' (BBC Written Archives Centre (BBCWAC), Radio Talks Scripts 1, O'Conner to A/AC (OS), 12 August 1944).

55 Constantine, *Colour Bar*, 138.

56 Peter Mason, *Learie Constantine* (Oxford: Signal Books, 2008), 97–98.

57 See Michael and Ann Dummett, 'The Role of Government in Britain's Racial Crisis', in Charles Husband (ed.), *Race in Britain: Continuity and Change* (London: Hutchinson, 1982, 97–127). Several attempts in the 1950s by the Labour MP Fenner Brockway had been rejected (113).

58 Mike Phillips and Trevor Phillips, *Windrush: The Irresistible Rise of Multi-Racial Britain* (London: Harper Collins, 1999 edn), 89–92; discrimination in housing and employment was not covered by legislation until the 1968 Race Relations Act.

59 Spry Rush, 'Imperial Identity': 379.

7 Colour Bar

1 See Stephen Bourne, *Mother Country: Britain's Black Community on the Home Front 1939–45* (Stroud: The History Press, 2010), 101.

2   Alice Bloch, Sarah Neal and John Solomos, *Race, Multiculture and Social Policy* (Basingstoke: Palgrave Macmillan, 2013), 56. The number rose to 42,650 the following year – 27,500 from the West Indies, plus 6,750 from India and Pakistan and 9,350 'others'. By 1961, the total net immigration from the New Commonwealth was 136,400.

3   See Stephen Tuck, *The Night Malcolm X Spoke at the Oxford Union: A Transatlantic Story of Antiracist Protest* (Oakland, CA: University of California Press, 2014), ch. 2. Also Marika Sherwood, 'White Myths, Black Omissions: the historical development of racism in Britain', *International Journal of Historical Teaching, Learning and Research*, vol. 3, 1 (January 2003).

4   Peter Fryer, *Staying Power: The History of Black People in Britain* (London: Pluto Press, 2010 edn), ch. 11.

5   Paul Foot, *Immigration and Race in British Politics* (Harmondsworth: Penguin, 1965), chs. 3 and 4; K. O. Morgan, *The People's Peace: British History 1945–1990* (Oxford: Oxford University Press, 1992 edn), 204; Arthur Marwick, *British Society Since 1945* (Harmondsworth: Pelican, 1996 edn), 163–65.

6   Peter Mason, *Learie Constantine* (Oxford: Signal Books, 2008), 118–26.

7   Ibid., 122.

8   Learie Constantine, *Colour Bar* (London: Stanley Paul, 1954), xvii.

9   Eric Posner, 'The Case Against Human Rights', *Guardian*, 4 December 2014, 39–41.

10 Constantine, Colour Bar, 67.

11 Ibid., 54.

12 Ibid., 190.

13 Ibid., 68.

14 Ibid.

15 Ibid., 108.

16 Ibid.

17 H. M. Champness, *Spectator*, 26 August 1954, 25.

18 Frank Birbalsingh, 'Learie Constantine: the Writer', *Caribbean Quarterly*, vol. 30, 2 (June 1984): 60–75.

19 Constantine, *Colour Bar*, 52–53.

20 Ibid., 61.

21 Ibid.

22 Ibid., 62.

23 'J. J. P.', *Irish Independent*, 21 August 1954.

24 *Daily Telegraph*, undated, from NALIS online newspaper collection.

25 *Catholic Herald*, 10 September 1954.

26 'J. H.', *The Friend*, 17 September 1954; J. P. Morpurgo, *Birmingham Post*, 19 August 1954.

27 *Liverpool Daily Post* and *Manchester Evening News*, 17 August 1954.

28 *Sheffield Telegraph*, 13 August 1954.

29 *Birmingham Post*, 10 August 1954.

30 *Birmingham Gazette*, 12 August 1954.

31 See Robert Miles, 'Racism and Nationalism in Britain', in Charles Husband (ed.), *'Race' in Britain: Continuity and Change* (London, Hutchinson, 1982), ch. 16.

32 Constantine, *Colour Bar*, 185.

33 NALIS, Constantine Collection (CC), 14400/14452, Fenner Brockway to Constantine, 8 April 1953.

34 Constantine, *Colour Bar*, 185. See also Susan Williams, *Colour Bar: The Triumph of Seretse Khama and His Nation* (London: Penguin Books, 2007).

35 *Nation*, 9 December 1960.

36 Ibid., 7 October 1960.

37 Quoted in Hilary McD. Beckles, *The Development of West Indies Cricket*, vol. 1 'The Age of Nationalism' (London: Pluto Press, 1998), 78.

38 See Derek Birley, *A Social History of English Cricket* (London: Aurum Press, 2003 edn), 286–87.

39 *Wisden Cricketers' Almanack* 1955 (London: Sporting Handbooks, 1955), 778.

40 See also Clyde Walcott (with Brian Scovell), *Sixty Years on the Back Foot: The Cricketing Life of Sir Clyde Walcott* (London: Victor Gollancz, 1999), 52.

41 The National Archives (TNA), Colonial Office (CO)1031/3718/10 (Beetham to Macleod, 17 March 1960).

42 C. L. R. James, *Beyond a Boundary* (London: Stanley Paul, 1969 edn), 220.

43 The naval base at Chaguaramas had been leased to the United States during the War as part of the Lease-Lend deal with Britain. By the late 1950s Eric Williams was campaigning strongly for Chaguaramas to be returned to Trinidad. See Colin A Palmer, *Eric Williams and the Making of the Modern Caribbean* (Chapel Hill: University of North Carolina Press, 2006), ch. 3; Maurice St Pierre, *Eric Williams and the Anti-Colonial Tradition* (Charlottesville, VA: University of Virginia Press, 2015), ch. 7.

44 *Nation*, 12 February 1960. James's letter is printed in full in James, *Beyond a Boundary*, 233–40. Emphasis added.

45 Nation, 4 March 1960.

46 Ibid., 16 March 1960.

47 Winston Mahabir, *In and Out of Politics: Tales of the Government of Dr Eric Williams, From the Notebooks of a Former Minister* (Port of Spain, Trinidad: Imprint Caribbean, 1978), 47.

48 *Nation,* 24 February 1961.

49 Ibid., 16 March 1960.

50 Ibid., 24 February 1961.

51 Ibid., 3 February 1961.

52   Ernest Eytle, *Frank Worrell* (London: Hodder and Stoughton, 1963), 31, 53.

53   See Canon L. John Collins, *Faith Under Fire* (London: Leslie Frewin, 1966),
     ch. 8. Collins had been on the same committee as Constantine campaigning for
     Seretse Khama in the early 1950s.

54   Church of England Archives, Canon L. John Collins Papers, Collins to Constantine,
     11 March 1958, MS 3299, ff. 212–25.

55   James, *Beyond a Boundary*, 229.

56   *Nation*, 20 February 1959.

57   See Denis Brutis, 'Memoir: Isolating Apartheid – South Africa and International
     Sports', in Lee Sustan and Aisha Karim (eds), *Poetry and Protest: A Dennis Brutus
     Reader* (Chicago, IL: Haymarket Books, 2006), 132.

58   Gerald Howat, *Learie Constantine* (London: George Allen and Unwin,
     1975), 201–2.

59   See Peter Oborne, *Basil D'Oliveira. Cricket and Conspiracy: The Untold Story*
     (London: Little, Brown, 2004).

60   *Daily Sketch*, 30 August 1968.

61   Ibid., 30 August 1968. See also Oborne, *Basil D'Oliveira*, 213–14.

62   A member of the original party withdrew through injury and D'Oliveira was added
     to the team in his place. The South African government then objected that anti-
     apartheid pressure had forced the change on the MCC and cancelled the tour.

8   Race Politics

1   Church of England Archive (CEA), Lambeth Palace Library, John Collins Papers,
    MS 3299, ff. 212, Constantine to Collins, 13 December 1954.

2   In August 1959, James wrote to Williams about Federation, asking the prime
    minister to settle concerns that he was planning to overthrow the Federal
    government, hold fresh elections, and oust Grantley Adams as Federation
    Prime Minister. (Institute of Commonwealth Studies, C. L. R. James Papers, 40,
    A/3/20: James to Williams 27 August 1959.) On the American military presence in
    Trinidad James had admired Williams's early determination to remove the US naval
    base at Chaguaramas but despaired when Williams later backed down. (*Nation*, 9
    February, 17 February 1961; Colin A. Palmer, *Eric Williams and the Making of the
    Modern Caribbean* (Chapel Hill, NC: University of North Carolina Press, 2006,
    137, ch. 3.)

3   Meeting with Mrs Gloria Valere (G. V.), Port of Spain, 23 September 2016.

4   Winston Mahabir, *In and Out of Politics: Tales of the Government of Dr Eric
    Williams from the Notebooks of a Former Minister* (Trinidad: Imprint Caribbean
    Ltd, 1978), 47.

5   Gerald Howat, *Learie Constantine* (London: George Allen and Unwin, 1975), 177.

6   Constantine began his new job on 31 August 1962, in the High Commission office in South Audley Street, Mayfair, with a salary of £3000 per annum plus allowances. This was less by £250 than that paid to Sir Edward Beetham, former Governor of Trinidad, as Consultant. (NALIS, Constantine Collection (CC), un-numbered file 'Learie Constantine', big grey box.)

7   CC 1416, esp. Constantine to Robert Lusty, 17 June 1967.

8   A great many of the documents in the Constantine Collection covering these years are letters to and from a host of societies and clubs throughout the United Kingdom inviting Constantine to speak.

9   Stuart Hall (with Bill Schwarz), *Familiar Stranger: A Life Between Two Islands* (London: Allen Lane, 2017), 190.

10 BBC Written Archives Centre (BBCWAC), Radio Talks Scripts (pre-1970), T 89, 'No Stranger Here', transmitted 24 December 1963.

11 Learie Constantine, *Colour Bar* (London: Stanley Paul, 1954), 147–48.

12 *Advocate* (Barbados), 7 January 1965.

13 BBCWAC, 'No Stranger Here', 24 December 1963.

14 Ibid.

15 *Trinidad Guardian*, 12 June 1964.

16 *West Indian Gazette and Afro-Asian Caribbean News* (WIG), October 1963, 4, 12.

17 *Sunday Times*, 28 September 1963. Also *Daily Express*, 28 September 1963; *Northampton Evening Telegraph*, 28 September 1963. 'Rather than put up with the Tory team's restrictions on West Indian immigrants, Sir Learie took one last swipe and started back for the pavilion.' (*Sunday Citizen*, 28 September 1963). Constantine denied that the British government had complained about his behaviour (*Times*, 30 September 1963).

18 It seems that only Williams stood between Constantine and a peerage in 1964. The proposal had the support of both main political parties in Britain, but needed Williams's agreement, which was not forthcoming. It was claimed that he even said he would resign from the Privy Council if Constantine were made a peer (*Sunday Times*, 17 May 1964).

19 Madge Dresser, *Black and White on the Buses: the 1963 Colour Bar Dispute in Bristol* (Bristol: Bristol Broadsides, 1986).

20 Dresser, *Black and White*, 11.

21 Stephen Tuck, *The Night Malcolm X Spoke at the Oxford Union: A Transatlantic Story of Antiracist Protest* (Oakland, CA: University of California Press, 2014), 182. Tuck's information about a direct American contact is based on his interview with Stephenson. Stephenson's recollection of the boycott in Mike and Trevor Phillips's *Windrush* does not mention a visit to America (*Windrush: the Irresistible Rise of Multi-Racial Britain*, London: Harper Collins, 1999 edn, 226–29).

22 The involvement of both men was resented by local trade unionists, who attributed the whole problem to 'troublemakers' among the West Indian community. Stephenson in particular was regarded as a communist by both trade unionists and the Bishop of Bristol. (Tony Benn, *Out of the Wilderness: Diaries 1963–67*, Random House Books, Kindle edn (Arrow Books, 1988), entries for 3 and 5 May 1963.)

23 Mike and Trevor Phillips, *Windrush*, 229.

24 See Jenny Bourne, 'Editorial', *Race and Class: the Colour of Struggle 1950s – 1980s*, vol. 58, 1 (July–September, 2016): 3–5. The emphasis in most writings has tended to be on London.

25 Harry Goulbourne, *Race Relations in Britain Since 1945* (Basingstoke: Macmillan, 1998), 72.

26 Mike and Trevor Phillips, *Windrush*, 199.

27 *Guardian*, 4 December 1967; *Observer*, 3 March 1968.

28 Tuck, *Malcolm X at Oxford Union*, 173–74. There is a detailed account of black activist groups at this time in Robin Bunce and Paul Field, *Darcus Howe: A Political Biography* (London: Bloomsbury Academic, 2014).

29 See R. E. R. Bunce and Paul Field, 'Obi B. Egbuna, C. L. R. James and the Birth of Black Power in Britain', *Twentieth Century British History*, vol. 22, 3 (2011): 391–414.

30 Mike and Trevor Phillips, *Windrush*, 223ff.

31 Among his papers in the Constantine Collection are several files of material on Ethiopia and Tanganyika, collected during his time as High Commissioner. The young Polly Toynbee, later a leading British journalist and social commentator, assisted Constantine on his Nigerian visit to investigate the plight of political prisoners following the 1966 coup there: she remembered 'splendid old Learie winkling information out of fellow lawyers.' (*Guardian*, 5 January 1981.)

32 See *Evening Standard*, 25 March 1969. It is interesting to note and to speculate on a comment made by the secretary of the BBC Director General a few months after Constantine had been appointed to the Board of Governors in 1968: 'Lord C gets a fair amount of abusive post and I'm heading it off while he is ill.' (BBC Written Archives Centre (BBCWAC), Board of Governors' Minutes, R78/1756, 'Monica' to 'Tony', n.d.). Could she have been referring to such a one as this anonymous letter from the NALIS Constantine Collection? 'Newquay, Cornwall (n.d.) I was absolutely horrified to see on TV that a memorial Service was held in London for a Black Cricket Player. This sort of thing will have to stop and all niggers must go back to their bananas and cocoanuts, including yourself, and leave your Knighthood behind.' The reference to the memorial service is surely that held for Frank Worrell in 1967.

33 *Express*, 11 March 1971; *Trinidad Guardian*, 11 March 1971.

34 *Evening Standard*, 25 March 1969.

35 *Express*, 12 March 1971.

36 Kwesi Owusu, 'The struggle for a radical Black political culture: an interview with A. Sivanandan', *Race and Class*, 58, July–September, 2016: 11. (The interview was originally carried out in March 1998.)

37 'Pendennis' in the *Observer Review*, 3 March 1968.

38 *Jewish Chronicle*, 25 February 1966.

39 See Harold Wilson, *The Labour Government 1964–70: A Personal Record* (Harmondsworth, Penguin Books, 1974 edn), 569, 665–67, 663–69.

40 The National Archives (TNA), Race Relations Board, Minutes of Board Meetings (RRB, Board), CK 2/9, 1 June, 13 July 1966.

41 Ibid., 11 May, 29 June, 27 July, 28 September 1967.

42 RRB, *Report of the Race Relations Board for 1967–68* (London: HMSO, 1968). (TNA, CK/1/2, pp. 7, 12–14.) See also *Sunday Times*, 8 January 1967; leading trade unionists had been approached for their views.

43 RRB, Board, CK 2/10, 25 January 1968.

44 CC, 1457.

45 CC, 4635, 4639.

46 Geoffrey Bindman, 'Evolution of Immigration', *New Law Journal*, vol. 157, 285 (August 2007): 10.

47 The phrase is Goulbourne's, *Race Relations in Britain Since 1945*, 53.

48 RRB, *Report 67–68*, 11.

49 Correspondence between Bonham Carter and Constantine in November 1968 refers to all three of the original members having written to the Home Secretary offering their resignation from the Board. Learie had sent Bonham Carter a cable to this effect. In the event only Langton left. (CC, 19640, Bonham Carter to Constantine, 18 November 1968.)

50 RRB, Board, CK 2/68, 13 March 1969.

51 Ibid., 12 February 1969.

52 Ibid., 17 July 1969.

53 Ibid.

54 Ibid., 25 April 1968, 16 January 1969.

55 This is not to suggest that there was personal enmity between the two. Indeed, on Constantine's death Wilson, by now Chairman of the Board, sent a most gracious letter to Norma, describing Learie as 'one of the great men of our time'. (CC, 14064, 1 July 1971.)

56 RRB, Board, CK 2/10, 7 September 1967. Constantine was absent throughout the autumn and winter, returning to the Board in late April 1968. He then was absent because of illness for a whole run of meetings from July 1968 to March 1969, resuming for the meeting of 13 March. From that point he also missed Board meetings in June and July, October to December 1969, and January and February

1970. Returning in March 1970 he was a regular attender, though absent again in November and December of that year.

57 James, *Beyond a Boundary*, 129.

58 See Bill Schwarz, 'Claudia Jones and the *West Indian Gazette*', *Twentieth- Century British History*, 14, 3 (2003): 264–85.

59 *Daily Mirror* (Trinidad), 9 January 1965.

60 Ibid.

61 The paper ceased publication in 1966, shortly after Jones's death.

62 Jones had initiated a Caribbean Carnival in 1959, a forerunner of the later and more celebrated Notting Hill Carnival.

63 Based on material from *West Indian Gazette* (WIG), 1958–64 (Accessed by kind permission of Lambeth Archives).

64 He was visiting Glasgow for the launching of one of the two ferry boats that had been commissioned by his ministry for the Tobago service.

65 'Meet Learie Constantine – At Heart a Cricketer', WIG, October 1959, 5.

66 Ibid., September 1963.

67 CC, Box 15121, James to Constantine, 28 October 1964.

68 Ibid., James to Constantine, 28 October 1964; Box 150100/15184, James to Constantine, 18 January 1965; Box 19185, Virtue to Constantine, 20 May 1966; Box 19195/AM, Virtue to S. Dunnett (Bagenal Harvey organization) – 'I am really rather depressed by the lack of MSS'; Virtue to Constantine, 21 April 1967 (13000 Series, Oversize items, Box 2, 13958).

69 Lord Constantine (ed.), *Living in Britain* (London: Virtue, 1970).

70 Columbia University NY, Rare Books and Manuscripts Library, C. L. R. James Papers, Box 1, Folder 5, Series 1, C. L. R. James to Constantine, 9 January 1969.

9 The BBC

1 He received four guineas for a series of talks in company with other speakers totalling 40-minutes airtime (BBC Written Archives Centre (BBCWAC), Talks R Cont 1, Constantine, Sir Learie, File 1, 1939–62 (hereafter Talks 1), 20 July 1939).

2 Ibid.

3 See, for example, Sian Nicholas, *The Echo of War: Home Front Propaganda and the B.B.C. 1939–45* (Manchester: Manchester University Press, 1996).

4 Asa Briggs, *The History of Broadcasting in the United Kingdom: vol. 1 The Birth of British Broadcasting* (London: Oxford University Press, 1961), pp. 164–83; P. Scannel and D. Cardiff, *A Social History of British Broadcasting: vol. 1 1922–1939, Serving the Nation* (Oxford: Basil Blackwell, 1991), ch. 1.

5 John Batten, *Manchester Evening News*, 21 July 1943.

6   Colonial Office, *Annual Report on Trinidad and Tobago for the Year 1946* (London: HMSO, 1948), 7–8.

7   Howard Johnson, 'The British Caribbean from Demobilization to Constitutional Decolonization', in Judith M. Brown and Wm. Roger Louis (eds), *The Oxford History of the British Empire, vol. 4 The Twentieth Century* (Oxford: Oxford University Press, 1999), 611–13.

8   See Anne Spry Rush, *Bonds of Empire: West Indians and Britishness from Victoria to Decolonisation* (Oxford: Oxford University Press, 2011), 148, 152, 160–61. Also John M. McKenzie, ' "In Touch With the Infinite": the BBC and the Empire 1923–53', in John M. McKenzie (ed.), *Imperialism and Popular Culture* (Manchester: Manchester University Press, 1986), ch. 8. Also Charlotte Higgins, *This New Noise: The Extraordinary Birth and Troubled Life of the BBC* (London: Guardian Books, 2015), 188.

9   For the background to these programmes see Glyne Griffith, ' "This Is London Calling the West Indies": the B.B.C.'s *Caribbean Voices*', in Bill Schwarz (ed.), *West Indian Intellectuals in Britain* (Manchester: Manchester University Press, 2003), 196–208; E. Robertson, ' "I Get a Real Kick out of Big Ben": BBC Versions of Britishness on the Empire and General Overseas Service, 1932–1948', *Historical Journal of Film, Radio and Television*, vol. 28, 4 (2008): 459–73.

10 BBCWAC, Talks 1, G.R. Barnes to Margaret Bucknall, 6 July 1943.

11 Ibid., Director of Talks to Miss Bucknall, 8 July 1943.

12 Ibid., Radio Talks Scripts (pre 1970), Cons-Coo, T 89 (hereafter T 89), 'Tonight's Talk', Home Service, 9.20–9.35 pm, 3 September 1943.

13 NALIS, Constantine Collection (CC), 2600/2677, Margaret Bucknall to Constantine, 21 September 1943, citing the letter from Forster.

14 BBCWAC, Talks 1, Arnold Watson to Margaret Bucknall, 18 April 1944.

15 Ibid., letter from a listener in Southampton, 30 June 1950.

16 Ibid., Marson to Empire Programme Executive, 29 December 1941; 22 September 1942; Peter Bax to Constantine, 17 February, 27 April, 28 April 1944. See also Stephen Bourne, *Mother Country: Britain's Black Community on the Home Front 1939–45* (Stroud: The History Press, 2010), 99–103.

17 Paul Rotha Productions/Ministry of Information, 'West Indies Calling', d. John Page (London, 1943), b/w, 14 minutes. A slightly longer version (23 minutes) using much of the same footage, entitled 'Hello! West Indies', was also produced.

18 See James A. Bough, 'The Caribbean Commission', *The IO Foundation*, vol. 3, 4 (November 1949), 643–55 (published online 1 May 2009), https://doi.org/10.1017/A0020818300014922. Charlie Whitham, *Bitter Rehearsal: British and American Planning for a Post-war West Indies* (Westport, CT: Praeger, 2002); Mary Chamberlain, *Empire and Nation Building in the Caribbean: Barbados, 1937–66* (Manchester: Manchester University Press, 2010).

19 BBCWAC, 'The World Goes By', 8 April 1944, Home Service/Forces Programme, 6.30 p.m–7 p.m. (T 89).

20 Bough, 'Caribbean Commission', 647.

21 CC, 15700/MFN 15713/JLB; *Daily Worker*, 21 March 1950.

22 CC, 14400, Lotbiniere to Constantine, 1 July 1950. Constantine was generous in his reply, acknowledging the help he had received from commentator Rex Alston (Constantine to Lotbiniere, 12 July 1950).

23 BBCWAC, Talks 1, Arnold Watson to Margaret Bucknall, 18 April 1944: Watson, an official of the Ministry of Labour in Manchester, commented on Constantine's 'pleasant and distinctive voice at the microphone'. Some years later a Light Programme producer noted 'We think him an excellent b[road]caster'. (Ibid., H.R. Pelletier to D. F. Boyd, 7 August 1953.)

24 Ibid., Prudence Smith to Constantine, 5, 15, 16 May 1950; 'Why Are There Colour Bars Today?', Third Programme, 9 June 1950 (T89).

25 Ibid., Talks 1, Scott to Constantine, 14 November; Constantine to Scott, 18 November 1952.

26 'Return to Trinidad', Light Programme, 29 March 1954 (T 89).

27 As a Governor he received no fees for broadcasts.

28 The appointment was in the gift of the prime minister.

29 It is difficult to ascertain the depth of Constantine's involvement with the Sports Council since its papers for this period reveal little about his activities.

30 Quoted in Asa Briggs, *Governing the BBC* (London: British Broadcasting Corporation, 1979), 17–18.

31 Lord Hill of Luton, *Behind the Screen: the Broadcasting Memoirs of Lord Hill of Luton* (London: Sidgwick and Jackson, 1974), 213–16.

32 Charlotte Higgins, *This New Noise: The Extraordinary Birth and Troubled Life of the BBC* (London: Guardian Books, 2015), 117.

33 Jeffrey Hill, *Sport, Leisure and Culture in Twentieth-Century Britain* (Basingstoke: Palgrave Macmillan, 2002), 105–6.

34 BBCWAC, Board of Governors Minutes (B of G Mins), 26 February, 1970

35 BBCWAC, Lord Constantine, Governors' Correspondence [LCGC], R78/1756; Constantine to Lord Hill, 21 November 1968; Hill to Constantine, 3 December 1968; Constantine to Charles Curran, 29 March 1969; B of G Mins, 3 October 1968. Absence without consent for a continuous period of three months was cause for the termination of a Governor's appointment (Briggs, *Governing the BBC*, 23).

36 BBCWAC, LCGC, R78/1756, Constantine to Hugh Carleton Greene, 24 July 1968.

37 See Robin Bunce and Paul Field, *Darcus Howe: A Political Biography* (London: Bloomsbury Academic, 2014), 51–57.

38 BBCWAC, B of G Mins, R1/36/2, 31 July 1968.

39 Bunce and Field, *Darcus Howe*, 54.

40 Ibid., 56–57.

41 Ray Costello, *Black Liverpool: The Early History of Britain's Oldest Black Community 1730–1918* (Liverpool: Picton Press, 2001), 52–54.

42 On the terms 'coloured' and 'black' Constantine maintained that black people preferred to be called "black" – as did Pakistanis. In their view, white people were also coloured– see BBCWAC, B of G Mins, R1/38/2 23 April 1970.

43 BBCWAC, LCGC, R78/1756, Bader to Constantine, 1 March 1969; Constantine to Bader, 10 April 1970.

44 The best known of all the cricket commentators, John Arlott, had publicly declined the BBC's invitation for him to broadcast on the matches. (David Rayvern Allen, *Arlott: the Authorised Biography* (London: HarperCollins, 1994), 277.)

45 BBCWAC, B of G Mins, R1/38/2, 23 April, 7 May 1970.

46 BBC TV, 'Panorama', 27 April 1970.

47 *Times*, 26 April 2004.

48 Hill, *Behind the Screen*, 119, 165.

10 Black Englishman

1 NALIS, Constantine Collection (CC), boxes 14100, 14200.

2 For a discussion of another kind of 'good immigrant' see Afua Hirsch's description of her grandfather, a German Jewish refugee who escaped Nazi Germany and arrived in Britain in 1938. (Afua Hirsch, *Brit(ish): On Race, Identity and Belonging* (London: Jonathan Cape, 2018), 255–57.)

3 'Calypso for Constantine: Sir Learie Constantine MBE talks with Lewis Nkosi', BBC 1 television film, d. Malcolm Brown (London,1966).

4 Lynsey Hanley, *Respectable: The Experience of Class* (London, Allen Lane, 2016.)

5 BBCWAC, 'Return to Trinidad', Light Programme, 29 March 1954.

6 *Times*, 10 June 1971.

7 See en.wikipedia.org/wiki/Talk%3APrivate_Eye%2FArchive_1?oldformat=true Sindie (Accessed 1 February 2017).

8 Stuart Hall, with Bill Schwarz, *Familiar Stranger: A Life Between Two Islands* (London: Allen Lane 2017), 15.

9 Joseph O'Neill, *Netherland* (London: Fourth Estate, 2008).

10 See Gideon Haigh, *Uncertain Corridors: Writings on Modern Cricket*, 'Gayle's World' (London: Simon and Schuster, 2014 edn), 300–3.

11 Colin Holmes, *John Bull's Island: Immigration and British Society, 1871–1971* (London: Macmillan, 1988), 153. Also Peter Fryer, *Staying Power: The History of Black People in Britain* (London, Pluto Press,1984), 364–66.

12 Written about by Roth in his novel *American Pastoral*.

13   Robin Bunce and Paul Field, *Darcus Howe: A Political Biography* (London: Bloomsbury Academic, 2015 edn), chs. 7–10; Sarah Callaway, 'Taking Inspiration From the Mangrove Nine', *Morning Star*, 16 December 2016, 9.

14   David Remnick, *King of the World: Muhammad Ali and the Rise of an American Hero* (New York: Random House, 1998), 291. See also 'The Double War', BBC Radio 4, bbc.co.uk/radio4, 15 September 2016 (Accessed 17 September 2016).

15   For example, Colin A. Palmer, *Eric Williams and the Making of the Modern Caribbean* (Chapel Hill, NC: University of North Carolina Press, 2006); Kent Worcester, *C. L. R. James: A Political Biography* (Albany, New York: State University of New York Press, 1996); slightly more is included in Maurice St. Pierre, *Eric Williams and the Anticolonial Tradition: The Making of a Diasporan Intellectual* (Charlottesville, VA: University of Virginia Press, 2015).

16   Sam Morris, 'Tribute to Learie Constantine', *Journal of Ethnic and Migration Studies,* vol. 1, 1 (1971): 68.

17   David Olusoga, 'Black and British; A Forgotten History', *The Observer*, 30 October 2016, 35–37.

18   *Guardian*, 18 August 2016.

19   Learie Constantine, *Colour Bar* (London: Stanley Paul, 1954), 27. Constantine frequently recalled that, when he was very young, his mother would warn him against playing in the street when horses were approaching: 'the white man will pass on you' (i.e. run you over). There was, he said, fear in her voice.

20   Harry Goulbourne, *Race Relations in Britain Since 1945* (Basingstoke: Macmillan, 1998), 20–21.

21   David Olusoga, *Black and British: A Forgotten History* (London: Macmillan, 2016), 487–88.

22   See Robert Young and Jean Khalfa (eds), *Frantz Fanon: Ecrits sur l'Alienation et la Liberte* (Paris: La Decouverte, 2015).

23   See J. D. Macauley, *The Life of Una Marson 1905–65* (Manchester: Manchester University Press, 1998).

24   See Bennetta Jules-Rosette, *Josephine Baker in Art and Life: the Icon and the Image* (Urbana/Chicago: University of Illinois Press, 2007); Ean Wood, *The Josephine Baker Story* (London: Sanctuary Press, 2000).

25   Martin Duberman, *Paul Robeson: A Biography* (New York: Open Road Media – Kindle edn, 2014).

26   Jeffrey Hill, *Nelson: Politics, Economy, Community* (Edinburgh: Keele University Press, 1997), 140. I once asked a former administrator of Nelson Cricket Club whether the Pakistan test cricketer Saeed Ahmed had been engaged by the club as professional in 1965 because of the increasing presence in the town of immigrants from South Asia. I had imagined it might have been a move to make contact with a new group of cricket fans. His answer was unambiguously 'No'. It was simply that

Saeed was a good player. Asian people were entitled to join the club but there was no specific plan to recruit them.

27 *Nelson Leader*, 21 June 1968; *Guardian*, 26, 27, 29 June 1968.

28 'Three pounds in my pocket', BBC Radio 4, excerpt on 'Pick of the Week', 9 August 2015, 6.15 pm, bbc.co.uk/radio 4 (Accessed 9 August 2015).

29 'Calypso for Constantine': Sir Learie Constantine MBE talks with Lewis Nkosi', directed by Malcolm Brown, BBC 1 television, 1966.

Bibliography

Archival Sources

British Broadcasting Corporation Written Archives Centre (BBC/WAC), Caversham Park, Reading

Constantine File: Talks 1 (1939–62), Talks II (1962–68), Talks III (1968–71)
Radio Talks Scripts (pre-1970) Cons – Coo, T 89
Board of Governors' Minutes 1968–71 (R1/36/2; R1/37/1–2; R1/38/1–3; R1/39/1)
Lord Constantine, Governor's Correspondence, 1968–71 (R78/1756)

Church of England Archives, Lambeth Palace Library, London

John Collins Papers, MS 3299, ff. 212–25.

Columbia University, New York

C. L. R. James papers, Rare Books and Manuscripts Library, MS 1529, series 1, folders 1–7, correspondence 1952–90.

Institute of Commonwealth Studies, Special Collections, Senate House Library, London

C. L. R. James papers, ICS40, A/3/1–97; ICS40/F/1/2–19; P/1/2; K/3

London Borough of Lambeth Archives

Various publications, including copies of the West Indian Gazette, 1959–73

Marylebone Cricket Club (MCC) Archive, Lord's Cricket Ground, London

West Indies Tour of British Isles 1939, MCC/CRI 5/2/18

National Library and Information System Authority (NALIS), Port of Spain, Trinidad and Tobago

Lord Learie Constantine Collection (CC)

Personal papers: personal and business correspondence, photographs, manuscripts, handwritten notes of meetings and events, typescripts of speeches, interviews, transcripts of broadcasts and other miscellaneous material. Filed in boxes. Material consulted on theme/topic basis and referenced as: 056, 175, 1300, 1335, 1500, 1522, 1988, 2200, 2248, 2582, 2600, 2865, 2897, 3074, 3075, 3181, 3198, 3562, 3806, 4051, 4281, 4635, 5430, 6059, 6120, 6131, 6161, 7546, 8036, 8243, 11586, 11624, 11933, 12234, 13701, 14237, 14500, 15015, 15493, 15801, 16028, 16064, 16049, 16145, 16220, 16227, 16242, 16251, 16327, 16367, 16399, 16439, 16541, 16798, 16961, 16981, 17085, 17118, 17131, 17195, 17249, 17277, 17391, 17416, 17453, 17468, 18014, 18093, 18959, 19300. See chapter footnotes for description of individual items.

Photographs: 1000C, 9300, 9500, 10100, 10200, 10300, 10600, 1900

National Archives, Kew, London

Colonial Office (CO), 876/17, 137/866, 1031/3718, 3720, 1071/393 (material relating mainly to West Indian technicians working in the north west of England; relations with US army authorities; and resettlement of technicians after the war; c. 1941–46; also political developments in Trinidad c. 1958–62).

Ministry of Labour and National Service (LAB), 26/54 (West Indian technicians in north west of England)

Race Relations Board (RRB), Minutes of Board Meetings 1966–71, CK 1/2, 2/9, 2/10, 2/67, 2/68, 2/69

Newspapers and periodicals

Advocate (Barbados)
Athletic News
Birmingham Gazette
Birmingham Post
Blackburn Times
Catholic Herald
Daily Mirror (London)
Daily Mirror (Trinidad)
Daily Sketch
Daily Telegraph

Daily Worker
Evening Standard
Express (Trinidad)
Friend
Guardian (and Manchester Guardian)
Irish Independent
The Keys
Lancashire Telegraph
Lancashire Evening Telegraph
Liverpool Daily Post
Liverpool Echo
Manchester Evening News
Morning Star
Nation
Nelson Gazette
Nelson Leader
New York Review of Books
Northampton Evening Telegraph
Observer
Port of Spain Gazette
Sheffield Telegraph
Sunday Citizen
Sunday Times
Times
Trinidad Guardian
West Indian Gazette and Afro-Asian Caribbean News

Secondary sources

Appiah, Kwame Anthony, *Lines of Descent: W. E. B. Du Bois and the Emergence of Identity* (Boston, MA: Harvard University Press, 2014).

Arlott, John, 'Lord Learie Constantine: The Spontaneous Cricketer', *Wisden Cricketers' Almanack* (London: Sporting Handbooks, 1972), 125–29.

Baker, Norman, 'A More Even Playing Field? Sport During and After the War', in Nick Hayes and Jeff Hill (eds), *'Millions Like Us?: British Culture in the Second World War'* (Liverpool: Liverpool University Press, 1999), 125–55.

Bateman, Anthony and Jeffrey Hill (eds), *The Cambridge Companion to Cricket* (Cambridge: Cambridge University Press, 2011).

Bateman, Anthony, *Cricket, Literature and Culture: Symbolising the Nation, Destabilising Empire* (Farnham: Ashgate, 2009).

BBC Radio 4, 'Great Lives', 7 April 2015.

Bearshaw, Brian, *From the Stretford End: the Official History of Lancashire County Cricket Club* (London: Partridge Press, 1990).

Beckles, Hilary McD. and Brian Stoddart, *Liberation Cricket: West Indies Cricket Culture* (Manchester: Manchester University Press, 1995)

Beckles, Hilary McD. and Harclyde Walcott, 'Redemption Sounds: Music, Literature and Popular Ideology of West Indian Cricket Crowds', in Hilary McD. Beckles and Brian Stoddart (eds), *Liberation Cricket: West Indies Cricket Culture* (Manchester: Manchester University Press, 1995), 370–83.

Beckles, Hilary McD., 'The Political Ideology of West Indies Cricket Culture', in Hilary McD. Beckles and Brian Stoddart (eds), *Liberation Cricket: West Indies Cricket Culture* (Manchester: Manchester University Press, 1995), 148–161.

Bekele, Frances L., 'The History of Cocoa Production in Trinidad and Tobago', in L. A. Wilson (ed.), *Re-vitalisation of the Trinidad and Tobago Cocoa Industry* (Proceedings of the APAST Seminar-Exhibition, St Augustine, Trinidad, September 2003).

Belchem, John, *Before the Windrush: Race Relations in Twentieth Century Liverpool* (Liverpool: Liverpool University Press, 2014).

Benn, Tony, *Out of the Wilderness: Diaries 1963–67*, Random House Books, Kindle edn (London: Arrow Books, 1988).

Bindman, Geoffrey, 'Evolution of Immigration', *New Law Journal*, vol. 157, 7285 (10 August 2007).

Birbalsingh, Frank, 'Learie Constantine: the Writer', *Caribbean Quarterly*, vol. 30, 2 (June 1984): 60–75.

Birley, Derek, *A Social History of English Cricket* (London: Aurum Press, 2003 edn).

Bloch, Alice, Sarah Neal and John Solomos, *Race, Multiculture and Social Policy* (Basingstoke: Palgrave Macmillan, 2013).

Bolland, O. Nigel, *On the March: Labour Rebellions in the Caribbean, 1934–39* (Kingston: Ian Randle, 2001).

Bough, James A., 'The Caribbean Commission', *The IO Foundation*, vol. 3, 4 (November 1949): 643–55.

Bourne, Jenny, 'Editorial', *Race and Class: the Colour of Struggle 1950s–1980s*, vol. 58, 1 (July–September, 2016): 3–5.

Bourne, Stephen, *Mother Country: Britain's Black Community on the Home Front 1939–45* (Stroud: The History Press, 2010).

Brereton, Bridget, 'Introduction', in C. L. R. James, *The Life of Captain Cipriani: An Account of British Government in the West Indies* (London: Duke University Press, 2014).

Brereton, Bridget, *A History of Modern Trinidad 1783–1962* (London: Heinemann, 1981).

Brereton, Bridget, *Race Relations in Colonial Trinidad* (Cambridge: Cambridge University Press, 1979).

Briggs, Asa, *Governing the BBC* (London: British Broadcasting Corporation, 1979).

British Pathe, *Our Jamaican Problem*, film, 1955.

Brodribb, Gerald, *The Croucher: the Biography of Gilbert Jessop* (London: Constable, n.d.).

Bulmer-Thomas, Victor, *The Economic History of the Caribbean Since the Napoleonic Wars* (Cambridge: Cambridge University Press, 2012).

Bunce, R. E. R. and Paul Field, 'Obi B. Egbuna, C. L. R. James and the Birth of Black Power in Britain', *Twentieth Century British History*, vol. 22, 3 (2011): 391–414.

Bunce, Robin and Paul Field, *Darcus Howe: A Political Biography* (London: Bloomsbury Academic, 2014).

Burton, Richard D. E. 'Cricket, Carnival and Street Culture', in Hilary McD. Beckles and Brian Stoddart (eds), *Liberation Cricket: West Indies Cricket Culture* (Manchester: Manchester University Press, 1995), 89–106.

Calder Marshall, Arthur, *Glory Dead* (London: Michael Joseph, 1939).

Callaway, Sarah, 'Taking Inspiration from the Mangrove Nine', *Morning Star*, 16 December 2016, 9.

Cardus, Neville, *Autobiography* (London: Readers' Union, 1949).

Cardus, Neville, *Good Days* (London: Rupert Hart-Davis, 1948 edn).

Cardus, Neville, *The Summer Game: A Cricketer's Journal* (London: Rupert Hart-Davis, 1949).

Cashmore, Ernest, *Black Sportsmen* (London: Routledge and Kegan Paul, 1982).

Central Council of Physical Recreation, *Sport and the Community* (London: CCPR, 1960).

Chamberlain, Mary, *Empire and Nation Building in the Caribbean: Barbados, 1937–66* (Manchester: Manchester University Press, 2010).

Chambers, Eddie, *Roots Culture: Cultural Politics in the Making of Black Britain* (London: I.B. Tauris, 2017).

Chater, Kathleen, 'Black British History', *Making History: the Changing Face of the Profession in Britain* (The Institute of Historical Research, 2008) www.history.ac.uk/makinghistory/resources/articles/black_history.html (Accessed 23 June 2017).

Clarke, John and Brian Scovell, *Everything that's Cricket; the West Indies Tour 1966* (London: Stanley Paul, 1966).

Coates, Ta-Nehisi, 'We Should Have Seen Trump Coming', *Guardian*, 30 September 2017, 37–39.

Collins, Canon L. John, *Faith Under Fire* (London: Leslie Frewin, 1966).

Collins, Tony, *Rugby's Great Split: Class, Culture and the Origins of Rugby League Football* (London: Routledge, 1998).

Colonial Office, *Annual Report on Trinidad and Tobago for the Year 1946* (London: HMSO, 1948).

Colonial Office/Ministry of Information, *Learie Constantine: Welfare Worker and Cricketer* (film, Colonial Office: London, nd, c. 1944–45).

Constantine, Learie, *Colour Bar* (London: Stanley Paul, 1954).

Constantine, Learie, *Cricket and I* (London: Philip Allan, 1933)

Constantine, Learie, *Cricket in the Sun* (London: Stanley Paul, n.d., c. 1946).

Constantine, Learie N., *How to Play Cricket* (London: Eyre and Spottiswoode, 1951).

Constantine, Learie, 'Backwoodsmen on Tour', in A. A. Thomas (ed.), *Daily Worker Cricket Handbook 1950* (London: People's Printing Society Ltd), 9–14.

Constantine, Learie, 'Cricket in the Sun', in Learie Constantine and Denzil Batchelor (eds), *The Changing Face of Cricket* (London: Eyre and Spottiswoode, 1966), 71–140.

Constantine, Learie, *Cricketers' Carnival* (London: Stanley Paul, n.d., c. 1950).

Constantine, Learie, *The Young Cricketer's Companion* (London: Souvenir Press, 1964).

Constantine, Lord (ed.), *Living in Britain* (London: Virtue and Co. Ltd, 1970).

Constantine, Lord, 'To the Lords … via Coconut Bat and Secondhand Car', in Ian Wooldridge (ed.), *The International Cavaliers' Cricket Book* (London: Purnell, 1969), 60–65.

Costello, Ray, *Black Liverpool: The Early History of Britain's Oldest Black Community 1730–1918* (Liverpool: Picton Press, 2001).

Crick, Bernard, 'Throw the R-word Away: We Should Attack Racism by Ceasing to Use the Word "Race"', *New Statesman*, 18 October 1996.

Cummings, Christine, 'The Ideology of West Indies Cricket', paper presented to Caribbean Studies Association conference, Port of Spain, Trinidad, May, 1990, http://ufdc.ufl.edu//CA00400070/00001 (Accessed 14 April 2014).

Denvir, John, *The Irish in Britain, from the earliest times to the fall and death of Parnell* (London: Kegan, Paul, Trench, Trubner and Co., 1892).

Dingle, Ceri and Rob Harris, *Every Cook Can Govern: The Life, Impact and Works of C. L. R. James* (film, Worldwide: London, 2016).

Downes, Aviston D., ' "Flannelled Fools"? Cricket and the Political Economy of the British West Indies c. 1895–1906', *International Journal of the History of Sport*, vol. 17, 4 (2000): 59–80.

Dresser, Madge, *Black and White on the Buses: the 1963 Colour Bar Dispute in Bristol* (Bristol: Bristol Broadsides, 1986).

Duberman, Martin, *Paul Robeson: A Biography* (New York, NY: Open Road Media – Kindle edn, 2014).

Dummett, Michael and Ann Dummett, 'The Role of Government in Britain's Racial Crisis', in Charles Husband (ed.), *Race in Britain: Continuity and Change* (London: Hutchinson, 1982).

Eytle, Ernest, *Frank Worrell: The Career of a Great Cricketer* (London: Hodder and Stoughton, 1963).

Featherstone, Simon, 'Late Cuts: C. L. R. James, Cricket and Postcolonial England', *Sport in History*, vol. 31, 1 (2011): 49–61.

Featherstone, Simon, *Postcolonial Cultures* (Edinburgh: Edinburgh University Press, 2005).

Foot, David, *Wally Hammond: the Reasons Why* (London: Robson Books, 1998 edn).

Foot, Paul, *Immigration and Race in British Politics* (Harmondsworth: Penguin, 1965).

Frith, David, *The Fast Men: A 200-year Cavalcade of Speed Bowlers* (London: Corgi, 1984 edn).

Fryer, Peter, *Staying Power: The History of Black People in Britain* (London: Pluto Press, 2010 edn).

Garrett, Bryan A. and Isabelle Rispler, 'Introduction: Mirrored Sea – Reflective Glance', *Traversea*, vol. 3 (2013): 1–3.

Gilroy, Paul, *Against Race: Imagining Political Culture beyond the Colour Line* (Cambridge, MA: Harvard University Press, 2000).

Gilroy, Paul, *The Black Atlantic: Modernity and Double Consciousness* (Cambridge, MA: Harvard University Press, 1992/London: Verso, 1993).

Giuseppi, Undine, *A Look at Learie Constantine* (London: Thomas Nelson, 1974).

Glass, Ruth, *London's Newcomers: The West Indian Migrants* (London: Centre for Urban Studies/George Allen and Unwin, 1960).

Goulbourne, Harry, *Race Relations in Britain Since 1945* (Basingstoke: Macmillan, 1998).

Green, Benny (ed.), *The Wisden Book of Cricketers' Lives* (London: MacDonald Queen Anne Press, 1986).

Greenblatt, Stephen, *Renaissance Self-Fashioning: From More to Shakespeare* (London: University of Chicago Press, 1984 edn).

Griffith, Glyne, ' "This Is London Calling the West Indies": the B.B.C's *Caribbean Voices*', in Bill Schwarz (ed.), *West Indian Intellectuals in Britain* (Manchester: Manchester University Press, 2003), 196–208.

Hall, Stuart (with Bill Schwarz), *Familiar Stranger: A Life Between Two Islands* (London: Allen Lane, 2017).

Hall, Stuart, *The Fateful Triangle: Race, Ethnicity, Nation*, ed. Kobena Mercer (Cambridge, MA: Harvard University Press, 2017).

Hall, Stuart, 'The Spectacle of the "Other" ', in S. Hall (ed.), *Representation: Cultural Representations and Signifying Practices* (London: Sage Publications, 1997), 223–290.

Hanley, Lynsey, *Respectable: The Experience of Class* (London: Allen Lane, 2016).

Harte, Chris, *A History of Australian Cricket* (London: Andre Deutsch, 1993).

Hayes, Nick and Jeff Hill, *'Millions Like Us?' British Culture in the Second World War* (Liverpool: Liverpool University Press, 1999).

Higgins, Charlotte, *This New Noise: The Extraordinary Birth and Troubled Life of the BBC* (London: Guardian Books, 2015).

Hill, Charles (Lord Hill of Luton), *Behind the Screen: the Broadcasting Memoirs of Lord Hill of Luton* (London: Sidgwick and Jackson, 1974).

Hill, Jeffrey, ' "First-Class Cricket and the Leagues: Some Notes on the Development of English cricket, 1900–1940', *International Journal of the History of Sport*, vol. 4, 1 (1987): 68–81.

Hill, Jeffrey, 'League Cricket in the North and Midlands', in Richard Holt (ed.), *Sport and the Working Class in Modern Britain* (Manchester: Manchester University Press, 1990), 121–41.

Hill, Jeffrey, 'War, Remembrance and Sport: "Abide With Me" and the FA Cup Final in the 1920s', in Anthony Bateman and John Bale (eds), *Sporting Sounds: Relationships Between Sport and Music* (London: Routledge, 2009).

Hill, Jeffrey, *Nelson: Politics, Economy, Community* (Edinburgh: Keele University Press, 1997).

Hill, Jeffrey, *Sport Leisure and Culture in Twentieth Century Britain* (Basingstoke: Palgave Macmillan, 2002).

Hirsch, Afua, *Brit(ish): On Race, Identity and Belonging* (London: Jonathan Cape, 2017).

Hoggart, Richard, *The Uses of Literacy: Aspects of Working-Class Life With Special Reference to Publications and Entertainments* (London: Pelican, 1958 edn).

Hogsbjerg, Christian John, 'C. L. R. James in Imperial Britain, 1932–38' (PhD thesis, University of York, 2009).

Holmes, Colin, *John Bull's Island: Immigration and British Society, 1871–1971* (Basingstoke: Macmillan, 1988).

Holt, Richard, *Sport and the British: A Modern History* (Oxford: Clarendon Press, 1992 edn).

Holt, Richard, 'The Legend of Jackie Milburn and the Life of Godfrey Brown', in John Bale, Mette K. Christensen and Gertrud Pfister (eds), *Writing Lives in Sport: Biographies, Life Histories and Methods* (Aarhus: Aarhus University Press, 2004), 157–70.

Howarth, Don, *Figures in a Landscape: a Lancashire Childhood* (London: Methuen, 1987).

Howat, Gerald M. D., 'Constantine, Learie Nicholas, Baron Constantine (1901–1971)' *Oxford Dictionary of National Biography* (Oxford: Oxford University Press, 2004); online edn, Jan. 2011, http://dx.doi.org/10.1093/ref:odnb/30961 (Accessed 9 June 2014).

Howat, Gerald, *Learie Constantine* (London: George Allen and Unwin, 1975).

Howe, Stephen, 'Cyril Leonard Robert James (1901–1989)', *Oxford Dictionary of National Biography* (Oxford: Oxford University Press, 2004) online edn, Jan 2011 http://www.oxforddnb.com/view/article/59637 (Accessed 9 June 2014).

Hyde, H. Montgomery, *Norman Birkett: The Life of Lord Birkett of Ulverston* (London: Reprint Society, 1964).

Ignatiev, Noel, *How the Irish Became White* (London: Routledge, 2008).

James, C. L. R., *Beyond a Boundary* (London: Stanley Paul, 1969 edn).

James, C. L. R. 'The Bloomsbury Atmosphere' and 'The Nucleus of a Great Civilisation', in Nicholas Laughlin (ed.), *Letters from London: Seven Essays by C. L. R. James* (Oxford: Signal Books, 2003), 19–34, 123–5.

James, C. L. R., *The Life of Captain Cipriani: An Account of British Government in the West Indies* (Durham, NC: Duke University Press, 2014).

Johnson, Howard, 'The British Caribbean from Demobilization to Constitutional Decolonization', in Judith M. Brown and Wm. Roger Louis (eds), *The Oxford History of the British Empire, volume IV, The Twentieth Century* (Oxford: Oxford University Press, 1999).

Judt, Tony, *Ill Fares the Land: A Treatise On Our Present Discontents* (London: Allen Lane, 2010).

Jules-Rosette, Bennetta, *Josephine Baker in Art and Life: the Icon and the Image* (Urbana/ Chicago, IL: University of Illinois Press, 2007).

Little, K. L., *Negroes in Britain: A Study of Racial Relations in English Society* (London: Kegan Paul, Trench and Trubner, 1947).

Killingray, David, 'Learie Constantine', in David Dabydeen, John Gilmore and Cecily Jones (eds), *The Oxford Companion to Black British History* (Oxford: Oxford University Press, 2007), 114–16.

Kolchin, Peter, 'Whiteness Studies: The New History of Race in America', *Journal of American History*, vol. 89, 1 (June, 2002): 154–73.

Lawrence, Bridgette, *Masterclass: the Biography of George Headley* (Leicester: Polar Press, 1995).

Lehmann, Nicholas, 'Who Was W. E. B. Dubois?' (review of Kwame Anthony Appiah, *Lines of Descent: W. E. B. Du Bois and the Emergence of Identity*, Cambridge, MA: Harvard University Press, 2014) in *New York Review of Books*, September 25, 2014.

Levett, Geoffrey, ' "Englishmen Who Happen to Reside in the West Indies": Early West Indian Cricket Tours and Imperial Identity', paper delivered to British Society of Sport History seminar, Senate House, London, 27 January 2014.

Lister, Simon, *Fire in Babylon: How the West Indies Cricket Team Brought a People to its Feet* (London: Yellow Jersey Press, 2015).

Macauley, J. D., *The Life of Una Marson 1905–65* (Manchester: Manchester University Press, 1998).

Mahabir, Wilfred, *In and Out of Politics: Tales of the Government of Dr Eric Williams, From the Notebooks of a Former Minister* (Port of Spain, Trinidad: Imprint Caribbean, 1978).

Manley, Michael, *A History of West Indies Cricket* (London: Pan Books, 1990 edn).

Marshall, Roy, *Test Outcast* (London: Pelham Books, 1970).

Marwick, Arthur, *British Society Since 1945* (Harmondsworth: Pelican, 1996 edn).

Mason, Peter, *Learie Constantine* (Oxford: Signal Books, 2008).

Mason, Tony, *Association Football and English Society, 1863–1915* (Brighton: Harvester, 1981).

McCourt, Ian, 'Albert Johannson: First Black Footballer to Play in the FA Cup Final', www.theguardian.com., 28 May 2015. (Accessed 12 April 2016).

McDevitt, Patrick F., 'Bodyline, Jardine and Masculinity', in Anthony Bateman and Jeffrey Hill (eds), *The Cambridge Companion to Cricket* (Cambridge: Cambridge University Press, 2011), ch. 5.

McKenzie, John M., ' "In Touch With the Infinite": the BBC and the Empire 1923–53', in John M. McKenzie (ed.), *Imperialism and Popular Culture* (Manchester: Manchester University Press, 1986), ch. 8.

McRae, Donald, *Black and White: The Untold Story of Joe Louis and Jesse Owens* (London: Simon and Schuster, 2014 edn).

Miles, Robert, 'Racism and Nationalism in Britain', in Charles Husband (ed.), *'Race' in Britain: Continuity and Change* (London, Hutchinson, 1982), ch. 16.

Morgan, K. O., *The People's Peace: British History 1945–1990* (Oxford: Oxford University Press, 1992 edn).

Morris, Sam, 'Tribute to Learie Constantine', *Journal of Ethnic and Migration Studies*, vol. 1, 1 (1971): 68–70.

Murphy, Andrea, *From the EMPIRE to the RIALTO: Racism and Reaction in Liverpool 1918–1948* (Birkenhead: Liver Press, 1995).

Nicholas, Sian, *The Echo of War: Home Front Propaganda and the BBC 1939–45* (Manchester: Manchester University Press, 1996).

O'Connor, P. E. T., *Some Trinidad Yesterdays* (Trinidad: Imprint Caribbean Ltd, 1975).

O'Neill, Joseph, *Netherland* (London: Fourth Estate, 2008).

Oborne, Peter, *Basil D'Oliveira. Cricket and Conspiracy: The Untold Story* (London: Little, Brown, 2004).

Olusoga, David, *Black and British: A Forgotten History* (London: Macmillan, 2016).

Olusoga, David, 'Black and British; A Forgotten History', *The Observer*, 30 October 2016, 35–7.

Owusu, Kwesi, 'The Struggle for a Black Political Culture: An Interview with A. Sivanandan', *Race and Class*, vol. 58, 1 (July–September 2016): 6–16.

Palmer, Colin A., *Eric Williams and the Making of the Modern Caribbean* (Chapel Hill, NC: University of North Carolina Press, 2006.)

Pathe Super Gazette, *The Coloured Catapult* (film, London, 1928).

Patterson, Sheila, *Dark Strangers: A Sociological Study of the Absorption of a Recent West Indian Migrant Group in Brixton, South London* (London: Tavistock Publications, 1963).

Paul Rotha Productions/Ministry of Information, 'West Indies Calling' (film, d. John Page, London, 1943).

Posner, Eric, 'The Case Against Human Rights', *Guardian*, 4 December 2014, 39–41.

Putnam, Lara, 'The Panama Cannonball's Transnational Ties: Migrants, Sport, and Belonging in the Interwar Greater Caribbean', *Journal of Sport History*, vol. 41, 3 (Fall 2014): 401–24.

Race Relations Board, *Report of the Race Relations Board for 1967–68* (London: HMSO, 1968).

Rayvern Allen, David, *Arlott: the Authorised Biography* (London: HarperCollins, 1994).

Remnick, David, *King of the World: Muhammad Ali and the Rise of an American Hero* (New York, NY: Random House, 1998).

Rich, Paul B., *Race and Empire in British Politics* (Cambridge: Cambridge University Press, 1986).

Richmond, Anthony H., *Colour Prejudice in Britain: A Study of West Indian Workers in Liverpool, 1941–1951* (London: Routledge and Kegan Paul, 1954).

Robertson Glasgow, R. C., *Cricket Prints: Some Batsmen and Bowlers, 1920–1940* (London: T. Werner Laurie, 1943).

Robertson, E., ' "I Get a Real Kick out of Big Ben": BBC Versions of Britishness on the Empire and General Overseas Service, 1932–1948', *Historical Journal of Film, Radio and Television*, vol. 28, 4 (2008): 459–73.

Roediger, David R., *The Wages of Whiteness: Race and the Making of the American Working Class* (London: Verso, 2007 edn).

Rosengarten, Frank, *Urbane Revolutionary: C. L. R. James and the Struggle for a New Society* (Jackson, MS: University of Mississippi Press, 2008).

Sandiford, Keith A. P. and Brian Stoddart, 'The Elite Schools and Cricket in Barbados: A Study in Colonial Continuity', in Hilary McD. Beckles and Brian Stoddart (eds), *Liberation Cricket: West Indies Cricket Culture* (Manchester: Manchester University Press, 1995), 44–60.

Schwarz, Bill, 'Claudia Jones and the *West Indian Gazette*', *Twentieth Century British History*, vol. 14, 3 (2003): 264–85.

Searle, Chris, 'Race before Wicket: Cricket, Empire and the White Rose', in Chris Searle (ed.), *Pitch of Life: Writings on Cricket* (Manchester: Parrs Wood Press, 2001), 1–22.

Sherwood, Marika, 'White Myths, Black Omissions: the Historical Development of Racism in Britain', *International Journal of Historical Teaching, Learning and Research*, vol. 3, 1 (January 2003).

Spracklen, Karl, *Whiteness and Leisure: Leisure Studies in a Global Era* (Basingstoke: Palgrave Macmillan, 2013).

Spry Rush, Anne, 'Imperial Identity in Colonial Minds: Harold Moody and the League of Coloured Peoples', *Twentieth-Century British History*, vol. 13, 4 (2002): 356–83.

Spry Rush, Anne, *Bonds of Empire: West Indians and Britishness from Victoria to Decolonisation* (Oxford: Oxford University Press, 2011).

St Pierre, Maurice, *Eric Williams and the Anti-Colonial Tradition* (Charlottesville, VA: University of Virginia Press, 2015).

Stoddart, Brian, 'Cricket and Colonialism in the English-speaking Caribbean to 1914: Towards a Cultural Analysis', in Hilary McD. Beckles and Brian Stoddart (eds), *Liberation Cricket: West Indies Cricket Culture* (Manchester: Manchester University Press, 1995), 9–32.

Stollmeyer, Jeff, *Everything Under the Sun: My Life in West Indies Cricket* (London: Stanley Paul, 1983).

Sustan, Lee and Aisha Karim (eds), *Poetry and Protest: A Dennis Brutus Reader* (Chicago, IL: Haymarket Books, 2006).

The Cricketer Annual (London: The Cricketer, 1929–30).

The Cricketer Spring Annual (London: The Cricketer, 1937)

Tiffin, Helen, 'Cricket, Literature and the Politics of Decolonisation: The case of C.L.R. James', in Hilary McD. Beckles and Brian Stoddart (eds), *Liberation Cricket: West Indies Cricket Culture* (Manchester: Manchester University Press, 1995), 356–69.

Tomlinson, Alan, 'Good Times, Bad Times, and the Politics of Leisure: Working-Class Culture in the 1930s in a Small Northern England Working-Class Community', in R. S. Gruneau (ed.), *Leisure, Sport and Working-Class Cultures: Theory and Practice*. Working Papers in the Sociological Study of Sports and Leisure Studies (Kingston, Ontario: Queen's University, 1984).

Tuck, Stephen, *The Night Malcolm X Spoke at the Oxford Union: A Transatlantic Story of Antiracist Protest* (Oakland, CA: University of California Press, 2014).

Tyler, Katharine, *Whiteness, Class and the Legacies of Empire: On Home Ground* (Basingstoke: Palgrave Macmillan, 2012).

Vasili, Phil, *The First Black Footballer: Arthur Wharton 1865–1930: An Absence of Memory* (London: Frank Cass, 1998).

Walcott, Clyde, with Brian Scovell, *Sixty Years on the Back Foot: the Cricketing Life of Sir Clyde Walcott* (London: Orion Books, 2000 edn).

Walvin, James, *Making the Black Atlantic: Britain and the African Diaspora* (London: Cassell, 2000).

Warner, P. F., *Cricket in Many Climes* (London: William Heinemann, 1900).

Warner, P. F., *Imperial Cricket* (London: London and Counties Press Association, 1912).

Waters, Chris, '"Dark Strangers" in Our Midst: Discourses of Race and Nation in Britain, 1947–1963', *Journal of British Studies*, vol. 6, 2 (April 1997): 207–38.

Watson, Arnold, *West Indian Workers in Great Britain* (London: Hodder and Stoughton, 1942).

Weekes, Everton, *Mastering the Craft: Ten Years of Weekes 1948–1958* (Jamaica: Universities of the Caribbean Press, 2007), 85.

Whitham, Charlie. *Bitter Rehearsal: British and American Planning for a Post-war West Indies* (Westport, CT: Praeger, 2002).

Williams, Eric, *History of the People of Trinidad and Tobago* (Buffalo, NY: EWord Inc. 1962).

Williams, Jack, *Cricket and Broadcasting* (Manchester: Manchester University Press, 2011).

Williams, Jack, *Cricket and England: A Cultural and Social History of the Inter-war Years* (London: Frank Cass, 1999).

Williams, Jack, *Cricket and Race* (Oxford: Berg, 2001).

Williams, Susan, *Colour Bar: The Triumph of Seretse Khama and His Nation* (London: Penguin Books, 2007).

Wills, Clair, *Lovers and Strangers: An Immigrant History of Postwar Britain* (London: Allen Lane, 2017).

Wilson, Harold, *The Labour Government 1964–70: A Personal Record* (Harmondsworth, Penguin Books, 1974 edn).

Wint, Valerie, *The Longer Run: A Daughter's Memoir of Arthur Wint* (Kingston Jamaica: Ian Randle Publishing, 2011).

Wisden Cricketer's Almanack (London, 1940), www.espncricinfo.com/wisdenalmanack/content/story/154641.html (Accessed 24 November 2014).

Wisden Cricketers' Almanack (London, 1929), www.espncricinfo.com/wisdenalmanack/
content/story/151774.html (Accessed 25 November 2014).

Wood, Ean, *The Josephine Baker Story* (London: Sanctuary Press, 2000).

Worcester, Kent, *C.L.R. James: A Political Biography* (Albany, NY: SUNY Press, 1996).

Young, Robert and Jean Khalfa eds, *Frantz Fanon: Ecrits sur l'Alienation et la Liberte*
(Paris: La Decouverte, 2015).

Index

Lightning Source UK Ltd.
Milton Keynes UK
UKHW022350170123
415540UK00006B/129

9 781350 168749